Task Sequencing and Instructed Second Language Learning

Edited by Melissa Baralt, Roger Gilabert and
Peter Robinson

Advances in Instructed Second Language Acquisition Research

Bloomsbury Academic
An imprint of Bloomsbury Publishing Plc

B L O O M S B U R Y
LONDON · OXFORD · NEW YORK · NEW DELHI · SYDNEY

Bloomsbury Academic

An imprint of Bloomsbury Publishing Plc

50 Bedford Square　　　　1385 Broadway
London　　　　　　　　　New York
WC1B 3DP　　　　　　　　NY 10018
UK　　　　　　　　　　　　USA

www.bloomsbury.com

BLOOMSBURY and the Diana logo are trademarks of Bloomsbury Publishing Plc

First published 2014
Paperback edition first published 2016

© Melissa Baralt, Roger Gilabert, Peter Robinson and Contributors 2014

Melissa Baralt, Roger Gilabert and Peter Robinson have asserted their right under the
Copyright, Designs and Patents Act, 1988, to be identified as the Editors of this work.

British Library Cataloguing-in-Publication Data
A catalogue record for this book is available from the British Library.

ISBN: HB: 978-1-6235-6276-2
PB: 978-1-4742-7407-4
ePDF: 978-1-6235-6408-7
ePub: 978-1-4725-7025-3

Library of Congress Cataloging-in-Publication Data
Task sequencing and instructed second language learning / Edited by Melissa Baralt,
Roger Gilabert, Peter Robinson.
pages cm.
ISBN 978-1-62356-276-2 (hardback) — ISBN 978-1-62356-408-7 (edf) —
ISBN 978-1-4725-7025-3 (epub) 1. Second language acquisition. 2. Language and
languages--Study and teaching. I. Baralt, Melissa, editor of compilation. II. Gilabert,
Roger, editor of compilation. III. Robinson, Peter Jake editor of compilation.
P118.2.T37 2014
401'.93–dc23
2014002156

Series: Advances in Instructed Second Language Acquisition Research

Typeset by RefineCatch Limited, Bungay, Suffolk

Contents

Contributors

Melissa Baralt is Assistant Professor of Spanish Applied Linguistics at Florida International University in Miami, Florida, USA. She teaches courses on task-based language teaching, foreign and heritage language teaching methodologies, and linguistics. Her research areas include bilingualism, bilingual education, task-based language teaching and learning, cognitive variables that mediate language learning, and computer-assisted language teaching. She also does work on teacher training, teacher cognition, and task-based language teaching in Western compared to Eastern contexts.

Roger Gilabert is a lecturer and researcher at the University of Barcelona, Spain, where he is a member of the GRAL group (Language Acquisition Research Group). He has worked and published extensively in the areas of task design and SLA, with a focus on the manipulation of the cognitive complexity of tasks and their effects on complexity, accuracy, and fluency (CAF), interaction, and development. His research and interests also include individual differences (attention and working memory capacity) and their role in second language performance and acquisition. His most recent work focuses on the independent measurement of task complexity by means of time estimation, affective variable questionnaires, dual task methodology and eye-tracking.

Simone Harmath-de Lemos has a BS in Computer Engineering from PUC-PR, Brazil, and an MA in Linguistics from Florida International University. She is currently pursuing her PhD in Computational Linguistics at Cornell University. Her research interests are language processing in the brain, mathematical modelling of language, heritage languages, perception vs. production, prosody, and parsers for more than one language, encompassing Romance languages as well as languages from the low-Amazon basin.

YouJin Kim is Assistant Professor in the Department of Applied Linguistics and ESL at Georgia State University, USA. Her primary research interests include the role of interaction and individual differences in second language acquisition, task-based language teaching, and syntactic priming focusing both on adolescent and adult language learning. Her research articles can be found in journals such as *Studies in Second Language Acquisition, Language Learning, Modern Language Journal, Applied Linguistics, TESOL Quarterly, Language Teaching Research* and *System* among others.

Craig Lambert is Associate Professor in the English Department at the University of Kitakyushu in Japan. He works in the English teacher training program and leads practical seminars on designing task-based language instruction as well as courses required for secondary school English teacher certification. He has published research on task-based needs analysis, materials design, motivational intensity, and the effects of interactive factors in task design on L2 production. He is currently doing research on the effects of referent similarity, discourse demands, and task repetition on L2 production as well as classroom-based longitudinal research on the development of L2 fluency.

Mayya Levkina is a lecturer at the Department of English and German Philology, University of Barcelona, Spain, where she also works as a researcher in the GRAL group, headed by Dr Carmen Muñoz. Her research interests are in task complexity, task sequencing in laboratory and classroom contexts; individual differences, aptitude, working memory capacity, phonological short-term memory and attention control. Her most recent publication is: 'The effect of cognitive task complexity on L2 oral production' (2012), co-authored by R. Gilabert, in Housen, A., Kuiken, F., and Vedder, I. (eds), *Dimension of L2 Performance and Proficiency: Complexity, Accuracy and Fluency in SLA.* Amsterdam/Philadelphia: John Benjamins Publishing Co.

Aleksandra Malicka is a PhD candidate at the University of Barcelona, Spain. She obtained her Bachelor's degree in Ethnolinguistics from Adam Mickiewicz University in Poznań, Poland. She then completed a Master's degree in Applied Linguistics and Language Acquisition at the University of Barcelona. She is currently working on her PhD dissertation on task complexity, task sequencing and language performance. She works as a research assistant at the University of Barcelona and as an English teacher at University College of Tourism CETA in Barcelona. Her research interests include task-based teaching, bilingual teaching, and language policy and planning.

Caroline Payant is an Assistant Professor in the MA TESL program at the University of Idaho. Her areas of interests include cognitive and sociocultural aspects of language acquisition as well as second language teacher education. Her recent work has examined the impact of pedagogical tasks on learner-learner interaction and language development. Her work can be found in the *TESL Canada Journal* and the *International Review of Applied Linguistics*.

Peter Robinson is Professor of Second Language Acquisition in the Department of English, Aoyama Gakuin University, Shibuya, Japan. His research interests include attention, awareness and learning under implicit, incidental, enhanced and explicit conditions; the structure of aptitude complexes for instructed language learning; and task complexity and instructed language learning. His recent publications include *Second Language Task Complexity: Researching the Cognition Hypothesis of Language Learning and Performance* (2011), John Benjamins; and *The Routledge Encyclopedia of Second Language Acquisition* (2013), Routledge.

Colin Thompson is a PhD student at the University of Central Lancashire, UK, and a part-time English lecturer at Shimonoseki City University, Japan. He is the editor of the Japan Association for Language Teaching *Task-based Learning SIG Journal*. His main research interests are task-based learning and cognitive development.

Sawsan Werfelli is currently the representative of AMIDEAST, which is a US, non-profit organization, engaging in training, education and administering exchange programs, and is also a content developer to teach Libyan Arabic for the National Foreign Language Center at the University of Maryland. Sawsan received her Master's Degree in Linguistics from Florida International University after being awarded a Fulbright scholarship to study linguistics. Her research areas include the study of syntax and semantics, especially that of Arabic, and the social- and cultural aspects of language learning. She is currently working on a project that investigates subject positioning in spoken Saudi Arabic, and hopes to implement task-based approaches to EFL teaching in Libya.

Acknowledgements

This book developed out of a symposium on task sequencing and task-based language learning at the 4th Task-Based Language Teaching (TBLT) conference, held at the University of Auckland, in November 2011. Versions of some of the studies reported in this book were also presented at the 5th Task-Based Language Teaching (TBLT) conference, hosted by the University of Alberta, in Banff, Canada, in October 2013, and the AILA World Congress of Applied Linguistics (AILA), in Brisbane, Australia, in August 2014. We thank the organizers of those conferences for the opportunity to present papers, and the audiences for their feedback. We are also very grateful to our external reviewers of chapters: Marta González-Lloret, University of Hawai'i at Manoa; Laura Gurzynski-Weiss, Indiana University; Tomohito Ishikawa, Soka Women's College; Folkert Kuiken, University of Amsterdam; Kim McDonough, Concordia University; Jonathan Newton, Victoria University of Wellington; Andrea Révész, University of London Institute of Education; Virginia Samuda, Lancaster University; and Ali Shehadeh, United Arab Emirates University. Their prompt, helpful and timely comments have been much appreciated, and have considerably helped improve the presentation of ideas and findings in this book.

An Introduction to Theory and Research in Task Sequencing and Instructed Second Language Learning

Melissa Baralt
Florida International University

Roger Gilabert
University of Barcelona

Peter Robinson
Aoyama Gakuin University

Introduction

This book is about task sequencing in second language (L2) teaching, and how task sequencing options can be implemented over various instructional time-spans, as well as the consequences of task sequencing decisions for L2 learning and success in using the L2 to achieve desired task outcomes. For years, L2 tasks have provided the context where research and pedagogy come together: researchers use tasks to test theoretical claims, and teachers use tasks to promote L2 use and acquisition among their students. A growing body of empirical research exists on task design features and their effects on language production, interaction, uptake of information provided during task performance, and learning (e.g., Bygate, Skehan and Swain, 2001; Crookes and Gass, 1993; Ellis, 2003; García Mayo, 2007; Robinson, 1996a, 2011a, 2011b; Robinson and Gilabert, 2007a; Samuda and Bygate, 2008; Shehadeh and Coombe, 2012; Skehan, 1998; Thomas and Reinders, 2010; Van den Branden, 2006; also see work generated by the biennial Task-Based Language Teaching [TBLT] conference, started in 2005). To date, however, there is still no widely agreed-upon set of criteria that can be used to grade and sequence tasks (although some have been proposed, and are the subject of current research, as we describe later in this chapter). This is essential to address because at the level of curriculum or lesson plan, tasks do not exist in a vacuum. On the one hand, in the classroom, tasks are planned and sequenced alongside other curricular or classroom activities, and a shared set of guidelines and criteria for *articulating* how to manage such sequencing is important. In a broader sense, such criteria and guidelines are important not only to articulating the progression of tasks and other activities in a single classroom, across a week, or semester, but also in general to articulating and *coordinating* task-based education across a wide range of institutional settings that seek to compare findings for the effects of task-based instruction (see Shehadeh and Coombe, 2012; Van den Branden, 2006). We agree with the statement by Long and Crookes: "Identification of valid, user-friendly sequencing criteria remains one of the oldest unsolved problems in language teaching of all kinds" (Long and Crookes, 1992, p. 46). But in the years since Long and Crookes made this observation, there have been considerable conceptual and empirical advances in our understanding of the effects of task design on language learning, and some promising evidence-based proposals for how to optimally sequence tasks in L2 programs. The purpose of this book is to contribute further to that understanding, and the evidence-base for it, and specifically, to add to what we know about sequencing tasks in order to maximize second language learning in both the short and the longer term.

Task sequencing

Designing a syllabus inherently implies sequencing content with the goal of maximizing language learning. Today, it is still largely the case that syllabus content is sequenced based on some notion of linguistic complexity, as this is assumed to affect the ease with which structures can be learned (more complex structures being optimally learned only after simpler structures have been mastered, in this account). Long (2007, pp. 126–7) has argued that this is problematic and ineffective. The claim that one grammatical form (e.g., relative clauses) is more complex than another (e.g., conditionals) is often based on intuition rather than any empirical evidence of the supposed difference in learnability of the two structures. And given that time periods of instructional exposure are usually limited (sometimes extremely so), there is no clear rationale for why some aspects of language and not others should be chosen for presentation and practice in classrooms. These, and other long-acknowledged problems with the 'structural' linguistic syllabus, have recently been summarized by Robinson (2009) and Ellis and Shintani (2013) and we refer readers to these sources for further discussion.

It is worth pointing out that apart from proposals for structural syllabus design, there have been many other rationalizations for second language syllabus design, including Notional Functional syllabuses (Wilkins, 1976), Communicative syllabuses (Yalden, 1983) and Lexical syllabuses (Willis, 1990), but none of these proposals have been supported by empirical research that provides an evidentiary basis for judging whether or not these proposals have effects on learning and performance in L2 programs, when implemented in the short and longer terms. As Bygate, Norris and Van den Branden (2009) note:

> The communicative movement itself was also heavily dependent on theoretical reflection. For example, key publications in the 1970s .... were almost entirely grounded in the authors' various first-hand experiences of learning and teaching, and were principally elaborated via theoretical examination – generally informed by linguistic theory – of the nature of language and language learning.
>
> (Bygate et al., 2009, pp. 495–6)

In contrast, the growing and cumulative research into the effects of task complexity, within the framework for task design provided by the Triadic Componential Framework (Robinson, 2001b, 2005, 2007a; Robinson and Gilabert, 2007b), as guided by the Cognition Hypothesis (Robinson, 2001b, 2003a, 2011a), and its stated implications for syllabus design (which we describe later in this chapter), aims to provide an evidentiary, empirical research basis for task sequencing decisions, to which it is the purpose of this book to contribute.

As an alternative to using language items as units of analysis for syllabus design, task-based approaches to instruction use tasks. Pedagogic tasks are sequenced from simple to complex for learners, following theoretical rationales for the effects of these sequencing decisions on learning, and L2 development. One such claim, for example, has been that simple versions of tasks (as operationalized in the empirical studies which follow this introductory chapter) which are cognitively and conceptually undemanding elicit what Givon (1985) called the pragmatic mode of communication, resulting in a basic variety of interlanguage, characterized by little use of morphology, avoidance of subordination and complex syntax, etc. (see Klein and Perdue, 1993; Robinson, 1995, 2005; Sato, 1990). As learners attempt more progressively complex and conceptually demanding versions of tasks, they are prompted to use and develop the linguistic resources needed to meet these more complex demands, such as subordination and use of psychological state terms necessary for intentional reasoning and for explaining why people behaved in a certain way (*she thought that he ... he wondered whether it ...* etc). (See Chapter 5, by Colin Thompson, and Chapter 8, by Craig Lambert and Peter Robinson.)

There have, of course, been a number of rationales offered for how tasks should be presented to learners, and in this introductory chapter, we begin by providing a critical survey of previous proposals for task sequencing in second language instruction. These include Candlin's (1984) suggestion that pre-determined syllabuses and sequencing are ineffective and that students determine their own learning content; Prabhu's (1987) concept of the 'reasonable challenge'; Long and Crookes' (1992) argument for needs analyses to determine target tasks, and that pedagogic tasks be sequenced in increased complexity to approximate target tasks; and Skehan's (1996, 1998, 2003) organizational framework to ensure a balance between the three goals of complexity, accuracy and fluency. We also review Ellis' more recent (2003) proposal for four criteria to be used in grading tasks: (1) task input, (2) task conditions, (3) learning processes, and (4) outcomes. We then discuss the Cognition Hypothesis and SSARC (simplify-stabilize, automatize, restructure-complexify) model for the sequencing of tasks (Robinson, 2001b, 2010). To follow, we make the case for theoretical perspectives on instructional design and task sequencing, and describe the collection of chapters in this volume.

Early proposals for task design and sequencing decisions in second language instruction

In 1984, Candlin argued that task sequencing decisions should be taken out of the teacher's control entirely, and that curriculum be negotiated between the teacher and the learners.[1] Candlin wrote that it is impossible for scholars to identify learning items and the optimum sequence in which they should be presented to learners. In fact, he argued, it would be a 'travesty' to assume that all learners value the same language forms and in the same sequence (Candlin, 1984, p. 38). Candlin made the case for considering the classroom as a 'society' (1984, p. 36), and felt that imposing a prospective syllabus on learners is equivalent to imposing an ideology or a set of values. Instead of pushing learners to 'conform to values and principles transmitted through teaching', Candlin argued that a more effective syllabus would encourage learners to challenge the world and their own ways of interpreting knowledge (1984, p. 36). A syllabus, according to Candlin, should be interactive and serve as the synergistic point between curriculum guidelines and classroom action. All of this should be done via problem-solving tasks in the classroom. Predictive sequencing, i.e., not placing the content decisions in the learners' hands, is ineffective: 'Given that we do not know how best to sequence content and experience to optimize learning there is a certain futility in attempting to impose such a sequence' (Candlin, 1984, p. 35).

At the same time, Candlin recognized that institutions require planning in order to meet objectives, and proposed that this be done by (1) citing guidelines to determine learning (taking into account ideological, social and psychological influences), (2) creating 'banks of items and accounts of procedures', and (3) allowing the teacher and learners to negotiate the selection of these items, so that the syllabus is jointly constructed between them. In this way, 'tactical sequencing of action and activity' would be realized in the classroom (Candlin, 1984, p. 36). In essence, Candlin argued that researchers do not know how best to sequence tasks to maximize language learning, and in fact, attempting to do so would be equivalent to imposing a philosophy onto students. Instead, all tasks, and their sequenced order, should be negotiated as based on learners' own interpretations of how they are relevant to society, through the language.

Influenced by Krashen (1982), Candlin's paper presented a very strong interpretation of focusing on the learner in the second language classroom, where language forms are not the primary object of study. His writing seemingly implies that he views theoretical work aimed at informing sequencing decisions as impracticable: '[past] arguments against any principled sequencing on grounds of frequency and difficulty being unoperationalizable in practice are cogent ...' (Candlin, 1984, pp. 40–41). Implementational problems with Candlin's proposal are obvious, especially the idea that teachers should not have a syllabus or that learning should be decided entirely by learners. This would require a redefinition of power roles in the classroom that are not plausible in many cultures. It also requires learners to have very high competence in the language in order to be able to negotiate the tasks and task sequences themselves. And while he seems to discuss means by which tasks can be sequenced, Candlin's suggestion that 'banks of items' be chosen so that students can negotiate and realize their sequencing in the classroom is arguably not feasible in practice in many instructional contexts.

N. S. Prabhu (1987) was one of the first to make recommendations for sequencing criteria when he published a description of how he implemented the Communicational Teaching Project, also known as the Bangalore Project. This project resulted out of dissatisfaction with the structural method (Structural-Oral-Situational, known as S-O-S) pedagogy previously implemented by Bangalore's Regional Institute of English. In all, 390 boys and girls, ages eight to eleven and from seven different schools, participated in the project. Prabhu argued for tasks to be sequenced by increasing complexity, which he conceptualized as a 'reasonable challenge' (Prabhu, 1987, p. 55). Inspired by Vygotsky's concept of 'zone of proximal development',[2] he explained that a task's posed 'challenge' should not be too easy for students and they should be able to meet the task with some effort. Thus, task sequencing increased in complexity when 'the demand on thinking made by the activity was just above the level which learners could meet without help' (Prabhu, 1987, pp. 23–4). Methodologically speaking, the way in which a teacher worked a 'reasonable challenge' into a sequence, whether in a lesson plan or a unit, was essentially determined by the teacher's 'commonsense judgment':

> ...tasks within a given sequence ... were ordered by a commonsense judgment of increasing complexity, the later tasks being either inclusive of the earlier ones or involving a larger amount of information, or an extension of the kind of reasoning done earlier.
>
> (Prabhu, 1987, p. 39)

A reasonable challenge, according to Prabhu, was thus based on (1) teachers' assessment of learners' task performance and abilities (often determined in the task feedback stage, based on homework grading after class), and on (2) learners' perceptions of the task (determined during class time, requiring teacher online-decision-making about what to include or not include in a task). The working criterion that teachers used to assess a task's reasonable challenge was based on performance: half of the learners needed to be successful on half of the task, shown by their markings on their work (Prabhu, 1987, p. 56). Prabhu claimed that this was an adequate means to measure students' progress, and also served as a guide to the design of sequences, i.e., how many tasks of the same type should be increased in complexity until students begin to get fatigued or bored, etc.

A major limitation with this approach to task complexity is the reliance on teachers' real-time judgments, combined with their having to confirm how 'approximately half the learners in the class' appear to be doing on 'approximately half the task' during class time (Prabhu, 1987, p. 56). This procedure for assessing task complexity to inform task sequencing is vague (what does 'approximately' half the class mean?) and certainly not a methodologically feasible criterion that teachers can use in a consistent way. Prabhu's operationalization of a task's 'reasonable challenge' also does not explicitly state what makes one task easier than another, leaving it unclear on what basis teachers can make the decision to present learners with more complex task versions.

In 1992, Long and Crookes published a seminal paper in which they advocated the use of a pre-determined syllabus with task as its organizational unit. Long and Crookes pointed out that both Prabhu and Candlin's suggestions for tasks were not based on any needs identification, and highlighted how and why a needs analysis is psycholinguistically justified based on what was known about how second language acquisition works. First, they argued – following what was current accepted practice in most instructional design models of the time (e.g., Gagne, 1985; Popham and Baker, 1970), as it still is today (e.g., Dick, Carey and Carey, 2005; Jonassen, Tessmer and Hannum, 1999) – a needs analysis should be conducted to determine target tasks that the learners will need to be able to do in the real world. Target tasks should then be classified into task types, and from these, pedagogical tasks can be derived. Pedagogic tasks are subsequently sequenced to form a task-based syllabus, and these are the tasks that teachers and students work on together in the classroom (Long and Crookes, 1992, p. 44). In addressing sequencing criteria, Long and Crookes wrote that pedagogic tasks should be sequenced by 'complexity', so that the tasks increasingly 'approximate' the target tasks that merited their inclusion in the syllabus in the first place. While Long and Crookes did not explain or operationalize the construct of complexity, they did suggest what it could imply:

> The number of steps involved, the number of solutions to a problem, the number of parties involved and the saliency of their distinguishing features, the location (or not) of the task in displaced time and space, the amount and kind of language required, the number of sources competing for attention, and other aspects of the intellectual challenge a pedagogic task poses ...
>
> (Long and Crookes, 1992, p. 44)

Long and Crookes went on to say that sequencing decisions can also be a 'function of which various pedagogic options are selected to accompany their use', such as (1) how interactionally modified input affects student comprehension, (2) whole-class versus small-group interaction, and how that might affect a task, and (3) the interaction between task types (e.g., open versus closed, or planned versus unplanned) and the way they mediate language production (Long and Crookes, 1992, p. 45). They conclude by arguing for the compatibility between second language acquisition research and task-based language teaching (TBLT), and highlight that sequencing criteria is still a problem to be addressed in TBLT research. In sum, their paper was influential in terms of how to determine which tasks to give learners in a task-based syllabus (starting with a needs analysis), and they put forward an argument for sequencing pedagogic tasks in more and more complex versions so that they approximate real-world target tasks. The researchers do not, however, provide specific suggestions about how to implement sequencing based on the complexity level of a task.

Skehan (1996, 1998, 2002, 2003; Skehan and Foster, 2001) agreed largely with many of the proposals made by Long and Crookes, but argued that researchers and practitioners must take care in putting too much emphasis on meaning instead of form in language teaching. For example, learners can rely on communication strategies and succeed in conveying meaning while bypassing attention to correct form; if this strategy use is proceduralized, it will prevent interlanguage growth and change (Skehan, 1996, p. 41). Like Long and Crookes, Skehan eschewed the 'interesting possibility' that students should be involved in negotiating which tasks to use, and how they will be sequenced in a subsequent syllabus, as advocated by Candlin (Skehan, 1996, p. 39). Looking at language learning from an information-processing perspective, Skehan pointed out the utility of examining language learning as a three-pronged goal: accuracy, complexity and fluency. Given that language learners have limited attentional-capacity, they cannot dedicate their attentional resources to all three of these goals at the same time. Skehan argued that task-based instruction must find a way to balance attention allocation (Skehan, 1996, p. 51) so that fluency (proceduralized accessibility to a lexicalized competence) is not promoted at the expense of accuracy and complexity-restructuring.

Skehan has proposed an organizational framework to accomplish the goals of promoting (1) restructuring, accuracy, and complexity, and (2) iterative cycles of analysis and synthesis. He argues that this can be achieved by the way that tasks are sequenced (syllabus), and by teaching methodology (implementation). Skehan does not propose a set of criteria for how tasks might be sequenced, but does say that 'it is imperative that … tasks are sequenceable on some principled criterion, since the basis on which tasks are ordered will be a reflection of what attentional resources they require' (Skehan, 1996, p. 52). He points out that while it is impossible to provide a universally valid comprehensive sequence of tasks, what educators can do is employ methods for analysing tasks 'both for difficulty and type' with the end goal of establishing syllabus units in a principled way. Skehan then proposes the schema illustrated in Table 1.1 for establishing the level of difficulty of a task.

Skehan argues that 'this scheme allows tasks to be analyzed, compared, and best of all, sequenced according to some principled basis' (1996, p. 52). If one chooses tasks well, the result will lead to (1) a balance between accomplishing fluency and accuracy and (2) restructuring opportunities.

Table 1.1 Skehan's criteria for establishing task difficulty

code complexity	(syntactic and lexical difficulty)
cognitive complexity	(content of what is said, i.e., Levelt's conceptualization stage)
cognitive processing	(amount of on-line computation required while doing task)
cognitive familiarity	(does task rely on ready-made or pre-packaged solutions?)
communicative stress	(how quickly task has to be done)
time pressure	(speaking vs. writing, listening vs. reading)
modality	(# of participants, # of relationships involved)
scale	(how important it is to do the task? Any real consequence?)
stakes	(can participants exert an influence on how a task is done?)
control	(can they negotiate task goals, request a clarification?)

The task itself must be chosen carefully and must be of the appropriate difficulty level:

> Tasks ... should not be so difficult that excessive mental processing is required simply to communicate any sort of meaning. ... Nor should tasks be so easy that learners are bored ...
>
> (Skehan 1996, p. 55)

Alongside his schema for analysing and comparing tasks, Skehan drives home the importance of methodology in order to successfully implement task-based instruction and argues for the three phases of *pre-task, task,* and *post-task activities* (following Willis, 1996).

To date, Skehan's proposal is one of the most detailed and includes many classroom implementation considerations. His model does not appear to propose a principled set of criteria for sequencing, but rather, a means to confirm that a *balanced* selection of tasks is used in order to promote development in the three areas of complexity, accuracy and fluency (to be done in tandem with a task-based methodology, which he describes in thoroughly). Skehan's work on the cognitive perspective for language learning alongside task-based methodology considerations has impacted the field greatly.

In Table 1.2 we provide the reader with a visual synopsis of the different ways in which the above-described proposals have conceptualized sequencing tasks so that they increase in complexity, with the goal of providing learners with more and more complex tasks.

Table 1.2 Early proposals for task sequencing in second language instruction

Candlin (1984)	**No predetermined sequencing.** A syllabus, its content, and the way that content is sequenced should be jointly-constructed and negotiated between the teacher and the learners. Pre-selecting tasks and the order in which they are sequenced would be a 'travesty' (p. 38) and an imposition of ideologies.	'Given that we do not know how best to sequence content and experience to optimize learning there is a certain futility in attempting to impose such a sequence' (p. 35).
Prabhu (1987)	**Sequencing should be determined by task's level of 'reasonable challenge'.**	'The concept of reasonable challenge implies that learners should not be able to meet the challenge too easily but *should* be able to meet it with some effort' (p. 55).
Long and Crookes (1992)	**After establishing task types from a needs analysis, pedagogic tasks should be designed and then sequenced in 'increasingly complex approximations to the target tasks'.**	'[By increasingly complex approximations we mean] some aspect of the tasks themselves. [This might include] the number of steps involved . . . the amount and kind of language required, the number and sources for competing attention, and other aspects of the intellectual challenge a pedagogic task poses . . .' (p. 44).
Skehan (1996, 1998)	**Tasks must be of the 'appropriate difficulty' level and should be sequenced based on their code complexity, cognitive complexity, and communicative stress criteria in order to achieve a balance between the three goals of accuracy, complexity, and fluency. Tasks should also be implemented via the three task phases of pre-task, task, and post-task (e.g., Willis, 1996).**	"'Appropriate difficulty' means not too easy but not too difficult. "Tasks . . . should not be so difficult that excessive mental processing is required simply to communicate any sort of meaning . . . Nor should tasks be so easy that learners are bored . . . with the result that no gain is made in terms of stretching interlanguage or developing greater automaticity'" (1996, p. 55).

Ellis' proposals for grading and sequencing tasks

In his (2003) book on task-based language teaching, Ellis highlights the fact that we do not have much research on how to best sequence tasks, but points out that sequencing tasks so that they are suited to learners' developmental levels, and subsequently allow learners to choose their resources to arrive at a task outcome, is essential for syllabus design (Ellis, 2003, p. 220). Ellis then briefly reviews past proposals for what he calls the *grading* of tasks. By synthesizing past typological work in the areas of rhetoric, cognition, and psycholinguistics, Ellis proposes four criteria that account for task complexity ('the ease with which learners are able to perform different tasks'; Ellis, 2003, p. 220). These are: (1) input, (2) conditions, (3) processes, and (4) outcomes. His suggested criteria are provided in Table 1.3.

Table 1.3 Summary of Ellis' criteria for grading tasks (Ellis, 2003, pp. 217–28)

Criterion	Easy	Difficult
A. *Input* (i.e., nature of the input provided in the task)		
1. Medium	pictorial → written	→ oral
2. Code complexity	high frequency vocabulary; short and simple sentences	low frequency vocabulary; complex sentence structure
3. Cognitive complexity		
a. information type	static → dynamic	→ abstract
b. amount of information	few elements/ relationships	many elements/ relationships
c. degree of structure	well-defined structure	little structure
d. context dependency	here-and-now	there-and-then
4. Familiarity of information	familiar	unfamiliar
B. *Conditions* (i.e., way in which the information is presented to learners and the way in which it is to be used)		
1. Interactant relationship (negotiation of meaning)	two-way	one-way
2. Task demands	single task	dual task
3. Discourse mode in which learners must perform the task	dialogic	monologic

(continued)

Table 1.3 continued

Criterion	Easy	Difficult
C. *Processes* (i.e., the nature of the cognitive operations and discourse that the task requires)	⟶	
1. Cognitive operations:		
a. type	exchanging information reasoning	⟶ exchanging opinions
b. reasoning need	few steps involved	many steps involved
D. *Outcomes* (i.e., the nature of the product that results from performing the task)	⟶	
1. Medium	pictorial	⟶ written ⟶ oral
2. Scope	closed (?)	open (?)
3. Discourse mode of task outcome	lists, descriptions, narratives, classifications	⟶ instructions, arguments

Ellis also cites Robinson's (2001a, 2001b) proposals for task complexity (detailed below) and, like Skehan (1998), argues that task complexity can also be modulated by the methodological procedures that teachers can use to teach a task (e.g., the provision of planning time or pre-teaching vocabulary in the pre-task stage). Ellis essentially makes one sole argument for how to sequence tasks. First, determine an individual task's level of cognitive complexity and then use the criteria he provides to evaluate the reliability of its assessment. He conceptualizes sequencing in terms of 'easy ⟶ difficult', and suggests that this 'grading' can eventually inform how tasks are sequenced into a lesson and a syllabus. While he does not provide a guide for how to sequence tasks, Ellis's grading concept essentially appears to be an attempt to confirm cognitive complexity increases in individual tasks.

The Triadic Componential Framework for task design and classification

Work by Robinson (1995, 1996a, 1996b, 2001a, 2001b, 2003a, 2005, 2007a, 2010, 2011a, 2011c; Robinson and Gilabert, 2007b; Robinson, Ting and Urwin, 1995) has sought to provide a universal set of parameters for manipulating the complexity level of a task in order to inform task sequencing. Robinson (2001a) operationalized cognitive complexity (what others have referred to as 'difficulty' or 'reasonable challenge') as:

> ... the result of the attentional, memory, reasoning, and other information processing demands imposed by the structure of the task on the language learner. These differences in information processing demands, resulting from design characteristics, are relatively fixed and invariant.
>
> (Robinson, 2001a, p. 29)

In order for task cognitive complexity to be the basis on which task-based syllabuses are designed, Robinson has argued that task designers need *invariant*, universal parameters to reference the way in which task features will affect a learner's attentional and memory capacities. In 2001, he published the first version of his Triadic Componential Framework (see also Robinson, 2007a; Robinson and Gilabert, 2007b). Three parameters serve as the basis of the framework: task complexity (the cognitive demand features that are proactively manipulable), task difficulty (learner-dependent factors, such as anxiety, working memory capacity) and task conditions (the interactive demands of a task, such as whether it is two-way or one-way, involves people with the same cultural knowledge or not, etc.). Thus, an important difference in terminology is highlighted with Robinson's model: task *complexity* refers to the differential ways a task modulates learners' attentional resources while they perform the task (task-dependent), while task *difficulty* is what the learner brings to the task (learner-dependent). Cognitive complexity is therefore the basis on which researchers and practitioners can grade and sequence tasks, with the goal of progressively increasing the cognitive demands of pedagogic tasks so that they approach the full complexity level of a target task.

This construct of cognitive complexity (e.g., Robinson, 2001a, 2001b, 2005, 2007a, 2010, 2011a, 2011c; Robinson, Cadierno and Shirai, 2009; Robinson and Gilabert 2007b) has two fundamental components. The first is resource-dispersing variables, such as +/- planning time, which allow for increased automatization of a learner's linguistic resources. Increasing a task's complexity along these lines will promote a learner's ability to perform the task, simulating the processing conditions that learners may encounter in the real world – but increasing complexity in this way does not direct learners' processing resources to any aspects of language that can help them resolve the more complex (unplanned) tasks' demands. The second is resource-directing variables, such as having to communicate in the +/- here and now, which can promote attention to form-function mappings in the L2, such as using past tense morphology to refer to the past in the more attentionally and memory demanding – here and now (or + there and then) condition. This is because the learner may recognize where he or she has linguistic deficiencies, in the sense of not having language available for use that can be used to code task-relevant communicative and conceptual demands (for example, tense and aspectual distinctions), and so will be more receptive to noticing and subsequently using feedback on their own production that provides such L2 information in order that he/she can perform the task successfully. Increases in cognitive complexity along these resource-directing dimensions are argued by Robinson to promote interlanguage development. Integrating both information-processing and interactionist accounts of L2 task effects (Long, 1996; Schmidt, 2001), Robinson predicts that increasing the cognitive demands of tasks will push learners to greater accuracy and complexity, and promote interaction and heightened attention to, uptake of and memory for input. Since publishing his Triadic Componential Framework, a sizeable research program has emerged that examines how differences in cognitive complexity (features from the Triadic Componential Framework) affect L2 production, features of interaction and language learning developmental outcomes (e.g., Albert, 2011; Baralt, 2013; Cadierno and Robinson, 2009; Collentine, 2010; Declerck and Kormos, 2012; Gilabert, 2007a, 2007b; Gilabert, Barón, and Levkina, 2011; Gilabert, Barón, and Llanes, 2009; Ishikawa, 2006, 2007, 2008a, 2008b, 2011; Iwashita, McNamara, and Elder, 2001; Kim, 2009, 2012; Kim and Tracy-Ventura, 2011; Kormos, 2011; Kormos and Trebits, 2011; Kuiken, Mos and Vedder, 2005; Kuiken and Vedder, 2007a, 2007b, 2008, 2011; Lee, 2002; Levkina and Gilabert, 2012; Malicka and Levkina, 2012; Michel, 2011a, 2011b, 2013; Michel, Kuiken and Vedder, 2007, 2012; Nuevo, 2006; Nuevo, Adama and Ross-Feldman, 2011; Rahimpour, 1997; Rahimpour and Hosseini, 2010; Révész, 2009, 2011; Révész and Han, 2006; Révész, Sachs and Mackey, 2011; Rezai and Kashani, 2011; Robinson, 1995, 2001a, 2007b; Robinson, Cadierno and Shirai, 2009; Robinson, Ting and Urwin, 1995; Sasayama and Izumi, 2012; Shiau and Adams, 2011; Shin, 2012; Salimi and Dadashpour, 2012a, 2012b; Shin, 2012; Steenkamp and Visser, 2011; Torres, 2013; Wu, Lowcyk, Sercu and Elen, 2013a, 2013b).

All of this research has *also* sought to empirically confirm the effects of cognitive complexity as an *independent* variable looking at task design features theorized to make a task cognitively simple versus features theorized (based on claims in the broader domains of cognitive and developmental psychology) to make a task cognitively complex (e.g., giving learners a task that does not require intentional reasoning (simple version) versus giving them a task that does (complex version)). As a result, a growing aim of this research program's agenda is to devise techniques – independent of linguistic production (the *dependent* variable in these studies) – that can be used to identify the extent to which task demand features increase a task's cognitive complexity (see Gilabert and Révész, 2013; Norris, 2013; Révész and Gilabert, 2013). To date, the most common method for independently confirming a hypothesized difference in the complexity of task demands has been to ask participants in studies to complete a post-task questionnaire (the Robinson TDQ: Robinson, 2001a), similar in design to the NASA Task Workload Index, in which they report their perceptions of how difficult the tasks were. The results have almost always shown that tasks hypothesized to be more cognitively complex are also rated as more *difficult* by learners, are rated as more *stressful*, and that learners have *less confidence* in being able to successfully complete them (e.g., Baralt, 2013; Gilabert, 2007a; Ishikawa, 2007, 2008a, 2008b, 2011; Robinson, 2001a, 2007b). Nonetheless, additional measures to task difficulty questionnaire (TDQ) responses are desirable as a means of having further confidence in the hypothesized and operationalized task complexity differential. Many of these measures have been adopted in the domains of ergonomics, educational, and cognitive psychology also concerned with the operationalization and construct validity of task complexity, and which have used various approaches to cognitive task analysis (see e.g., Jonassen, Tessmer and Hannum, 1999). As Robinson (2001b) noted in this respect:

> There are a number of general indices used by applied cognitive psychologists to assess the effects of task difficulty and mental workload on task performance ... that can be applied, with some modifications, to validating complexity dimensions of L2 tasks. Such measures include whether or not the task was completed, and if so the time taken to task completion, the learners' ratings of task difficulty, and the extent of interference and intrusion on the main task by secondary tasks. Complex tasks are less likely to be completed successfully; take longer than simple counterparts; are rated by learners as more difficult; have physiological consequences (e.g., pupillary dilation, increased heart rate); and are more susceptible to interference from competing tasks.
>
> (Robinson, 2001b, p. 306)

Notably, none of the studies so far addressing this issue have examined tasks in a sequence or the effects of cognitive complexity across a sequence. This is potentially important, since complex tasks occurring in sequences are likely to vary in their level of demand compared to when they are performed individually – such that performing prior versions of complex tasks in a sequence can structure and scaffold later attempts to perform them, reducing their overall level of demand.

The SSARC model of pedagogic task sequencing

In 2010, Robinson made explicit his SSARC model of pedagogic task sequencing, which had been implicit in his earlier work on the Cognition Hypothesis and syllabus design.[3] The fundamental pedagogic claim of the Cognition Hypothesis is that accommodating the temporal-cognitive dynamics of learning by distributing task-based L2 use and learning opportunities over time, i.e., task *sequencing*, is done by designing and having learners first perform tasks simple on all the relevant parameters of task demands, and then gradually increasing their cognitive complexity on subsequent versions. Such sequences allow for *cumulative* learning, since each task version differs in only small respects from the previous one, but also introduces an incremental *increase* in the *conceptual* and *communicative challenge* of the task which prompts learners to adjust and expand their interlanguage resources to meet it, thereby creating the conditions for L2 development. Operationalizing the claims of the Cognition Hypothesis, and drawing on the Triadic Componential Framework for task classification, the SSARC model describes two instructional-design *principles* for task sequencing, making this an operationally feasible proposal for task-based syllabus design. We describe these principles here, since many of the empirical studies which follow this introductory chapter operationalize the SSARC model in their empirical studies of the effects of task sequencing.

Task sequencing principle 1

Only the cognitive demands of tasks contributing to their intrinsic conceptual and cognitive processing complexity are sequenced. Following this principle, for example, tasks that do not require intentional reasoning are performed before those that require it. In contrast, the interactive demands of tasks (such as whether they require one-way or two-way information exchange) are replicated each time pedagogic task versions are performed so as to help ensure deep semantic processing (Craik and Lockhart, 1972; Healy and Kole, 2013; Hulstijn, 2001), rehearsal in memory (Robinson, 2003b) and elaboration and successful transfer of the particular 'schema' for interactive or monologic task performance to real-world contexts of use (Schank, 1999; Schank and Abelson, 1977). The theory is thus parsimonious, placing the sole emphasis for task sequencing on task complexity.

Task sequencing principle 2

Increase resource-dispersing dimensions of complexity first (e.g., from + to – planning time), and then increase resource-directing dimensions (e.g., from – to + intentional reasoning). The rationale for this can be described in the following way. First (*Step 1*), tasks simple on all dimensions are performed (e.g. + planning, – intentional reasoning). Task performance thus draws on the simple, stable (SS) '*attractor state*' of current interlanguage (cf. Larsen-Freeman, 2013; Larsen-Freeman and Cameron, 2007; van Geert, 2008). Next (*Step 2*), complexity on resource-dispersing dimensions is increased (e.g., – planning, – intentional reasoning). This promotes speedier access to, and so automatization (A) of, the current interlanguage system (Segalowitz, 2010, 2013). Finally (*Step 3*), complexity on both resource-dispersing and resource-directing dimensions is increased (e.g., – planning, + intentional reasoning). This promotes restructuring (R) of the current interlanguage system, and the development of new form-function/concept mappings along resource-directing dimensions of task demands (cf. Robinson and Ellis, 2008; von Stutterheim and Klein, 1987; Williams, 2013) and introduces maximum complexity (C) destabilizing the current interlanguage system. Increasing task complexity by sequencing shifts in task demands induces (in the theory proposed here) similar shifts in the structure of interlanguage resources used to accomplish them.

The SSARC model

The steps described above constitute the 'SSARC model' for increasing L2 pedagogic task complexity, and can be represented in the following way, where i = current interlanguage state; e = mental effort; 's' = simple task demands; 'c' = complex task demands; rdisp = resource dispersing dimensions of tasks; rdir = resource directing dimensions of tasks; and n = potential number of practice opportunities on tasks, which are determined *in situ* by teachers observing pedagogic task performance by individuals, dyads and groups:

Step 1. SS (stabilize, simplify) = $i \times e \ [('s'rdisp) + ('s'rdir)]^n$

Step 2. A (automatize) = $i \times e \ [('c'rdisp) + ('s'rdir)]^n$

Step 3. RC (restructure, complexify) = $i \times e \ [('c'rdisp) + ('c'rdir)]^n$

In summary, the fundamental claim of the Cognition Hypothesis is that tasks should be presented to learners that are cognitively simple first, and then gradually increase in cognitive complexity, so as to eventually approximate target tasks. *Ancillary theoretical claims* of the Cognition Hypothesis are that simpler tasks will lead to greater fluency of production, but more complex tasks will lead to greater accuracy, and complexity of production, and also more interaction, uptake of information provided during interaction and L2 development (see Robinson, 2001b, 2003a, 2005, 2011c). The task design features presented in the Triadic Componential Framework can be used to shape a task's level of cognitive complexity, and the SSARC model makes specific suggestions of how to sequence tasks in accordance with these features, in an order of increasing complexity, so as to promote these hypothesized beneficial effects for language learners in TBLT programs. Consequently, by investigating cognitive dimensions of tasks, and the ancillary theoretical claims of the Cognition Hypothesis mentioned above, we can understand the differences they help lead to in language learning and performance, and, critically, be able to make the most informed decisions on how to sequence tasks in a lesson or syllabus to generate maximal learning of form that is contextualized in meaning.

Evidence supporting the Cognition Hypothesis and the need for longer-term studies of task sequencing effects

It is worth adding, as we conclude this introductory overview of previous proposals for task sequencing and the effects of task complexity, that while it is true that most of the studies of task complexity, and its effects on spoken and written production, interaction and uptake and L2 development, have been short-term studies – to date – (see for example the studies on the effects of task complexity on learning and performance reported in Robinson, 2011a), this has been an important step towards studying *longer term* effects of task complexity over lengthy periods of time in actual instructional programs. Since longitudinal, classroom-based research is extremely time- and resource-consuming, we need to have some confidence that task complexity, manipulated in some of the ways described above, has positive short-term effects on learner language and task performance so that we can then go on to see the extent to which these effects (e.g., on speech production, writing, or L2 development) are also found, or multiplied, in the longer term.

To date, task complexity studies addressing the Cognition Hypothesis in the Triadic Componential Framework have found many of the predicted beneficial effects of manipulating and increasing task complexity, such as more spoken *fluency* on prior simple versions, followed by more *accuracy* on later complex versions (see the research synthesis and meta-analysis of the findings predicted by the Cognition Hypothesis for oral production on studies of monologic tasks in Jackson and Suethanapornkul, 2013). Recent studies also suggest that task complexity promotes, as the Cognition Hypothesis predicts, greater amounts of *interaction, uptake of corrective feedback,* and *L2 development* on complex versions of interactive tasks (see Baralt, 2013; Kim, 2009, 2012; Kim and Ventura, 2011; Révész, 2009; Révész, Sachs and Mackey, 2011).

Although the Cognition Hypothesis only predicts greater *complexity* of spoken production on monologic tasks (due to the fact that the greater amount of interaction that interactive complex tasks lead to will mitigate attempts at extended turns and complex language) combined average effect sizes used in the meta-analysis (albeit, of only nine studies) performed by Jackson and Suethanapornkul (2013) show little difference between the complexity of speech on monologic simple and complex tasks. However, a number of individual studies *do* show greater accuracy *and* complexity on complex versions of oral tasks, along with less fluency (e.g., Gilabert, 2007a; Ishikawa, 2008a, 2008b) thus confirming the predictions of the Cognition Hypothesis that increases in task complexity can promote *both* greater accuracy and complexity of production, in contrast to the claims of Skehan's (1998, 2009) Limited Capacity/Trade-off Hypothesis, which claims increasing task demands will promote only one, at the expense of the other.

So there is evidence from these, albeit few, individual studies that the claims of the Cognition Hypothesis concerning joint positive effects of task complexity on complexity and accuracy of production have been shown to be true, and this evidence stands in direct contrast to the rival and oppositional claims of Skehan's Limited Capacity/Trade-off Hypothesis. However, overall, evidence supporting the particular prediction for increased complexity of production on complex tasks made by the Cognition Hypothesis, though it has been found, is slim, at present. With this in mind, for written and for oral monologic tasks, it may well be that evidence in favour of this prediction will be found more consistently if performances on complex tasks in *sequences, spaced* over longer periods of time are studied (see Chapter 6 by YouJin Kim and Caroline Payant, this volume). That is, rather than performance on a single complex task, it may well be that repeated attempts to perform complex tasks will prompt the use of more complex language in such a way that the proposed effects of task complexity on 'pushing' the complexity of responses to task demands, and 'stretching interlanguage', are more obvious. This prospect, then, leads us in to the final section of this chapter, which introduces the studies reported in subsequent chapters of this book.

The chapters in this book

The following chapters in this book all address the issue of task sequencing by operationalizing task characteristics, and sequences of tasks drawing either on the Triadic Componential Framework and SSARC model described above, or by adopting other closely related rationales. They either test the effects of task sequencing on oral and written production and/or development by exploring a variety of task sequences, or give sequencing a crucial role in their designs, or examine how teachers understand and plan for task sequencing in their lessons. The studies report on a variety of L2 English, Spanish, and Italian language learning environments in labs, face-to-face interaction in classrooms, and computer-mediated communication, with learners ranging from early adolescents to young adults, and they all fill important gaps in the literature (and suggest other new gaps) in relation to issues of task sequencing. The chapters in the first section of the book report on studies of task sequencing effects under controlled laboratory conditions, while the chapters in the second section of the book study task sequencing effects in instructional programs, and over lengthy periods of exposure.

In Chapter 2 Levkina and Gilabert report on a study whose goal is to test the effects of different types of sequencing on the development of spatial relations by young adults who are native speakers of Catalan/Spanish learning English as a foreign language. By drawing on the Cognition Hypothesis, the Triadic Componential Framework and the SSARC model, the study enquires into both the immediate and delayed effects of three different types of sequences (i.e. simple-to-complex, complex-to-simple and randomized). Based on findings from the cognitive psychology literature, three levels of cognitive task complexity (i.e. simple, complex, +complex) are operationalized along +/- spatial reasoning in an oral, interactive room furnishing task ranging from a task version requiring the simple transmission of information about the distribution of objects in a room, to a task imposing spatial reasoning demands by making learners make decisions about object placement and the availability of space and by inducing perspective taking. The three-level operationalization of task complexity is confirmed by independently measuring task demands with an affective variable questionnaire. The experiment follows a pre-test, post-test and delayed post-test design and it measures the use and retention of spatial expressions (e.g. *at the back, on top*) immediately following a one-session treatment and two weeks later. A detailed description of procedures is provided in which both productive and receptive tests measuring development are used. Results suggest that while people in the complex-to-simple sequence seem to retain and use more spatial expressions right after the treatment, it is the learners in the simple-to-complex sequence that show higher and sustained learning gains both productively and receptively over time, thus confirming the predictions of the SSARC model for more effective scheduling of resources and higher retention of input under a simple-to-complex sequence.

In Chapter 3, Malicka describes an experiment exploring the effects of two task sequences on the complexity, accuracy and fluency of L1 Catalan/Spanish young adult learners of English as a foreign language. After contrasting the tenets of the Cognition Hypothesis proposed by Robinson and the Trade-off Hypothesis proposed by Skehan, Malicka asks how the manipulation of the number of elements and the amount of reasoning simultaneously affect performance and whether there exists an interaction between task complexity and sequencing. In a design where the operationalization along the number of elements and amount of reasoning dimensions of task complexity arises from carefully conducted needs analyses, learners carry out three monologic oral tasks with differing levels of complexity in the context of a hotel reception. As with Levkina and Gilabert, task complexity is independently confirmed by means of an affective variable questionnaire, and it ranges from a task version where learners are asked to simply describe a few characteristics of a hotel mini crisis to one where learners have to refer to a larger number of features at the same time that they justify their choices about how to solve the crisis. The outcome measures in the study tap into the constructs of lexical and structural complexity, accuracy and fluency (CAF). Malicka finds that while there is a clear effect for task complexity on performance, there is little or no effect for task sequencing. Hence, regardless of the sequence, when learners engage in a more complex task their fluency decreases significantly while both accuracy and lexical complexity increase, with little or no effect on structural complexity. However, Malicka observes that 'a closer look at the descriptive statistics reveals that even though statistical significance was not reached in the case of one structural complexity measure, the increase in structural complexity is proportional to that in cognitive complexity' and that these results are largely in line with the predictions of the Cognition Hypothesis. One important contribution of Malicka's study is that her results point at the dynamic, fluctuating nature of the effects of task complexity when measured across a longer sequence of tasks, as opposed to operationalizing task complexity as a dichotomous, simple–complex task variable.

Baralt addresses the issue of task complexity and task sequencing in both a face-to-face and a computer-mediated communication context with young adults learning Spanish as a foreign language in Chapter 4. Baralt's study aims to test the SSARC model and it starts with a complete and thorough contextualization which includes a detailed review of the benefits and drawbacks of online chat. Baralt asks whether different task sequences differentially impact language-related episodes in relation to the Spanish past subjunctive, and she compares the results of that question in both an oral face-to-face context and a computer-mediated communication, chat environment. Three narrative retelling tasks with two levels of cognitive task complexity (simple vs. complex) are presented to learners in four different sequences which contain either two simple versions of the tasks (e.g. simple-simple-complex) or two complex versions of the tasks (e.g. complex-complex-simple). The study uses a pre-test, post-test, delayed post-test design in which cognitive complexity, operationalized as more or less intentional reasoning, is low in the simple version where the intentions of characters are already provided, intentions which must be worked out by the task takers in the complex version of the task. As was the case in the study by Malicka, Baralt finds that it is task complexity that has an impact on her outcome measures (i.e. a higher number of Spanish subjunctive language-related episodes in more complex tasks) regardless of the sequence, and it raises the crucial issue of whether sequencing should be operationalized in a more U-shaped or discontinuous manner rather than in an ever increasing cognitive complexity organization. Another important finding in Baralt's study is that whatever happens in face-to-face interaction is not necessarily applicable to computer-mediated communication, where she does not find an effect for either cognitive complexity or sequencing.

In Chapter 5, Thompson explores the impact of a combined manipulation of a resource-directing variable (+/- intentional reasoning) and a resource-dispersing variable (+/- strategic planning) on the production of relative clauses by L1 Japanese learners of English as a foreign language. Thompson draws on Levelt's model of L2 production for both the contextualization and explanation of his findings. Five different oral narrative tasks are organized by increasing their intentional reasoning demands, and by simultaneously reducing the time allotted to pre-task planning thus creating five different levels of task complexity for the oral production of relative clauses. He applies a pre-test, post-test, delayed post-test design to examine within-learner performance, and compares groups who are either given guided planning throughout the whole sequence or guided planning only at the beginning of the sequence, which constitutes the between-learner variable. An affective variable questionnaire is also used to check learners' perception of task difficulty. Thompson's results show: 1) that task performance leads to increased use of relative clauses; 2) that guided and partially guided sequential treatments contribute equally to the improvement in the use of relative clauses; 3) that task difficulty perceptions coincide with his operationalization of cognitive task complexity.

In Chapter 6, Kim and Payant investigate the effects of task repetition and increasing task complexity on language-related episodes by Korean junior high students learning English as a foreign language. In the design of an oral, two-way information gap task, task repetition is operationalized as either the repetition of the exact same task (task repetition of a hosting-a-friend task) or of the same task procedure with different but comparable content (procedural repetition – hosting a friend, describing school events, discussing mayoral candidates). Task complexity, operationalized as more or less reasoning demands, has two levels where the simple task requires the simple exchange of information and the complex task requires L2 learners to make decisions while exchanging information. Both variables are combined into four different conditions and the effects on both grammatical and lexical language-related episodes (correctly resolved by learners or the teacher, incorrectly resolved and unresolved) are analyzed. The results of the study suggest that there are positive effects of procedural repetition (different versions of the same task) as compared to content/procedural repetition (the same task), whereby learners who engage in the repetition of the same procedure display a higher number of language-related episodes than those who merely repeated the exact same task. Kim and Payant do not find any effects for task complexity on the production of language-related episodes and suggest that task repetition may mediate the predictions for task complexity and task sequencing, and they suggest that it is important that task repetition should be included in any model predicting performance or development.

Baralt, Harmath-de Lemos and Werfelli in Chapter 7 report the first case study to look at how teachers interpret and apply the Cognition Hypothesis. They analyze perceptions of task complexity and task sequencing by two teachers teaching Spanish and Italian as foreign languages to young adult learners. After completing a workshop on the Cognition Hyphothesis and task sequencing, the teachers designed task-based materials on the basis of their own interpretation of the tenets and recommendations of the Cognition Hyposthesis and its associated Triadic Componential Framework. The research inquires into how sequencing tasks from simple to complex is done by teachers in their natural teaching environment, what their perception of task complexity is, and how (or whether) task-based principles covered in the workshop converge with their current pedagogy. Triangulation of methods is applied with interviews, teachers' own reflections, observations and thinking-aloud while lesson planning. The authors conclude that the principles of the Cognition Hypothesis are reinterpreted by teachers to match their syllabus mandate to include a specific grammar form in their design. Teachers also rely on pre-existing repertoire (e.g., Johnson, 2003) and apply the new 'theory' to what works already for them. The researchers conclude by calling for more research on teacher cognition in conjunction with task complexity sequencing for language learning.

In the final chapter, Chapter 8, Lambert and Robinson report on the only one-semester-long (15-week), longitudinal study in the book on the impact of task sequencing, as mediated by proficiency and working memory, on narrative summarization production in English by L1 Japanese university students. The study makes use of a quasi-experimental pre-test and post-test design where two groups, with comparable levels of proficiency, working memory capacity and motivational orientation, performed narratives based on comic strips throughout the whole semester. The experimental SSARC group performed written narrative tasks that followed a simple-to-complex sequence (where they first started with simple versions until they reached the full, complex versions of tasks), whereas the control group's task performance followed no particular principles for task sequencing. Task complexity is operationalized along both resource-directing variables (number of elements and intentional reasoning demands) and resource-dispersing variables (planning time, prior knowledge, number of steps and multi-tasking). Tasks written outcomes are analysed for syntactic complexity, the use of explicit intentional reasoning markers, grammatical accuracy and expert ratings of successful task performance. Lambert and Robinson find significant improvements for both groups in terms of syntactic complexity (both coordination and subordination), and the language used to express intentional reasoning (verbs of emotion, desire, cognition and intentionality) but with no differences in grammatical accuracy of production between the pre-test and the post-test. When comparing the two groups, no significant differences were found for either structural complexity, reasoning or accuracy between the two groups. The simple-to-complex group, however, showed a higher percentage of pre-post test gain over time (14 per cent control; 38 per cent SSARC) using the data provided by expert raters' judgements of pre and post-test task performance. Contrary to expectations, Lambert and Robinson also found that whereas proficiency positively influenced the development of language used for subordination across the groups studied, higher working memory capacity had a negative influence, such that earners with higher working memory scores used fewer cognitive mental state words (MSW) and made more grammatical errors than learners with lower scores.

All in all, the following seven chapters in this book describe carefully designed, well-researched studies that provide us with direct results about the application of sequencing theories to both experimentally controlled and classroom environments, in both the short and the longer term. The rationales offered for each study, their findings and the conclusions drawn from them will be important to accommodate in broad theories of instructed second language acquisition. Equally important, the studies that follow launch a new and fascinating research agenda for further empirically researching the design principles underlying practical decisions made by *teachers* in classrooms, as well as local, national and international educational *institutions and authorities* charged with coordinating the effective delivery of instruction across a variety of settings. As such they provide us with food for thought that should encourage further research – contributing, thereby, to the establishment of greater evidence-based confidence in the application of principles for task sequencing to effective language pedagogy.

Notes

1   For further discussion, see Breen (1987), Clarke (1991) and Rahimpour's (2010) brief review of the history of language teaching syllabus design, including the 'Lancaster School of Thought', which he argues was given early expression in Breen and Candlin (1980).

2   Vygotsky defines the zone of proximal development as '... the distance between the actual development stage as determined by independent problem solving and the level of potential development as determined through problem solving under adult guidance or in collaboration with more capable peers' (Vygotsky, 1978, p. 86; cited in Prabhu, 1987, p. 66).

3   The claims of the SSARC model are consistent with proposals for increasing task complexity, following the Cognition Hypothesis, made in all Robinson's previous work on syllabus design (e.g., Robinson 2001b, pp. 313–14; 2007a, pp. 22–3; 2009,

p. 305). But the need to formalize and further highlight these claims explicitly in the notational form of the SSARC model was prompted by our colleagues Folkert Kuiken and Ineke Vedder (2007b), who wrote of the Triadic Componential Framework, when describing factors listed there as contributing to Task Complexity, Task Conditions and Task Difficulty: 'One may wonder how all [the 36] variables [in the 2007 version of the model] can be operationalised and differentiated' (Kuiken and Vedder, 2007b, p. 265). The SSARC model makes it clear that for task sequencing purposes, only the subset of task design characteristics nominated in the TCF as contributing to Task Complexity are to be operationalized in sequencing pedagogic tasks, which are further selected depending only on whether those characteristics are appropriate to the demands of the target tasks they are intended to promote success on (see Robinson, 2011c, pp. 9–11, and pp. 14–18 for further discussion and examples).

References

Albert, A. (2011). When individual differences come into play: The effect of learner creativity on simple and complex task performance. In P. Robinson (ed.) *Second Language Task Complexity: Researching the Cognition Hypothesis of Language Learning and Performance* (pp. 239–64). Amsterdam: John Benjamins.

Baralt, M. (2013). The impact of cognitive complexity on feedback efficacy during online versus face-to-face interactive tasks. *Studies in Second Language Acquisition*, 36, 1–37.

Breen, M. (1987). Learner contributions to task design. In C. Candlin and D. Murphy (eds), *Language Learning Tasks* (pp. 23–46). London: Prentice Hall.

Breen, M. and Candlin, C. N. (1980). The essentials of a communicative curriculum in language teaching. *Applied Linguistics*, 1, 89–112.

Bygate, M., Norris, J. and Van den Branden, K. (2009). Understanding TBLT at the interface of research and pedagogy. In Van den Branden, K., Bygate, M. and Norris, J. (eds), *Task-based Language Teaching: A Reader* (pp. 495–500). Amsterdam: John Benjamins.

Bygate, M., Skehan, P. and Swain, M. (2001). *Researching Pedagogic Tasks: Second Language Learning, Teaching and Testing.* London: Longman.

Cadierno, T. and Robinson, P. (2009). Language typology, task complexity and the development of L2 lexicalization patterns for describing motion events. *Annual Review of Cognitive Linguistics*, 6, 245–76.

Candlin, C. N. (1984). Syllabus design as a critical process. In C. J. Brumfit (ed.), *General English Syllabus Design: Curriculum and Syllabus Design for the General English Classroom* (pp. 29–46). London: The British Council and Pergamon Press.

Clarke, D. (1991). The negotiated syllabus: What is it and is it likely to work? *Applied Linguistics*, 12, 13–28.

Collentine, K. (2010). Measuring complexity in task-based synchronous computer-mediated communication. In M. Thomas and H. Reinders (eds), *Task-based Language Learning and Teaching with Technology* (pp. 105–28). New York: Continuum.

Craik, F. and Lockhart, R. (1972). Levels of processing: A framework for memory research. *Journal of Verbal Learning and Verbal Behavior*, 11, 671–84.

Crookes, G. and Gass, S. (1993). *Tasks in a Pedagogical Context: Integrating Theory and Practice*. Clevedon: Multilingual Matters.

Declerck, M. and Kormos, J. (2012). The effects of dual task demands and proficiency on second language speech production. *Bilingualism: Language and Cognition*, 15, 782–96.

Dick, W., Carey, L. and Carey, J. (2005). *The Systematic Design of Instruction* (6th edn). Boston, MA: Allyn and Bacon.

Ellis, R. (2003). *Task-based Language Learning and Teaching*. Oxford: Oxford University Press.

Ellis, R. and Shintani, N. (2013). *Exploring Language Pedagogy Through Second Language Acquisition Research*. London: Routledge.

Gagne, R.M. (1985). *The Conditions of Learning* (4th edn). New York: Holt, Rinehart and Winston.

García Mayo, M. (2007). *Investigating Tasks in Formal Language Learning*. Clevedon: Multilingual Matters.

Gilabert, R. (2007a). The simultaneous manipulation of task complexity along planning time and [+/- here-and-now]: Effects on L2 oral production. In M. P. García Mayo (ed.), *Investigating Tasks in Formal Language Learning* (pp. 44–68). Clevedon, UK: Multilingual Matters.

—— (2007b). Effects of manipulating task complexity on self-repairs during L2 oral production. *International Review of Applied Linguistics in Language Teaching*, 45, 215–40.

Gilabert, R., Barón, J. and Levkina, M. (2011). Manipulating task complexity across task types and modes. In P. Robinson (ed.) *Second Language Task Complexity: Researching the Cognition Hypothesis of Language Learning and Performance* (pp. 105–38). Amsterdam: John Benjamins.

Gilabert, R., Barón, J., and Llanes, À. (2009). Manipulating cognitive complexity across task types and its impact on learners' interaction during oral performance. *International Review of Applied Linguistics in Language Teaching*, 47, 367–95.

Gilabert, R. and Révész, A. (2013). *Cognitive Approaches to Task-based Instruction*. Symposium convened at the 5th TBLT Conference, October, Banff, Canada.

Givon, T. (1985). Function, structure and language acquisition. In D. I. Slobin (ed.), *The Crosslinguistic Study of Language Acquisition*, Vol. 1, (pp. 1008–25). Hillsdale, NJ: Lawrence Erlbaum.

Healy, A. and Kole, J. (2013). Depth of processing. In P. Robinson (ed.), *The Routledge Encyclopedia of Second Language Acquisition* (pp. 164–5). New York: Routledge.

Hulstijn, J. (2001). Intentional and incidental second language vocabulary learning: A reappraisal of rehearsal, elaboration and automaticity. In P. Robinson (ed.), *Cognition and Second Language Instruction* (349–81). Cambridge: Cambridge University Press.

Ishikawa, T. (2006). The effects of task complexity and language proficiency on task-based language performance. *Journal of Asia TEFL*, 3, 193–225.

—— (2007). The effect of manipulating task complexity along the (+/- here-and- now) dimension on L2 written narrative discourse. In M. P. García Mayo (ed.), *Investigating Tasks in Formal Language Learning* (pp. 136–56). Clevedon, UK: Multilingual Matters.

—— (2008a). Investigating the effects of intentional reasoning demands on L2 speech production. Unpublished Ph.D dissertation, Aoyama Gakuin University, Tokyo, Japan.

—— (2008b). The effects of task demands of intentional reasoning on L2 speech performance. *Journal of Asia TEFL*, 5, 29–63.

—— (2011). Examining the effects of intentional reasoning demands on learner perceptions of task difficulty and L2 monologic speech. In P. Robinson (ed.) *Second Language Task Complexity: Researching the Cognition Hypothesis of Language Learning and Performance* (pp. 307–28). Amsterdam: John Benjamins.

Iwashita, N., McNamara, T. and Elder, C. (2001). Can we predict task difficulty in an oral proficiency test? Exploring the potential of an information-processing approach to task design. *Language Learning*, 51, 401–36.

Jackson, D. O. and Suethanapornkul, S. (2013). The Cognition Hypothesis: A synthesis and meta analysis of research on second language task complexity. *Language Learning*, 63 (2), 330–67.

Jonassen, D., Tessmer, M. and Hannum, W. (1999). *Task Analysis Methods for Instructional Design*. Mahwah, NJ: Erlbaum.

Kim, Y. (2009). The effects of task complexity on learner-learner interaction. *System*, 37, 254–68.

—— (2012). Task complexity, learning opportunities, and Korean EFL learners' question development. *Studies in Second Language Acquisition*, 34, 627–58.

Kim, Y. and Tracy-Ventura, N. (2011). Task complexity, language anxiety and the development of the simple past. In P. Robinson (ed.) *Second Language Task Complexity: Researching the Cognition Hypothesis of Language Learning and Performance* (pp. 287–306). Amsterdam: John Benjamins.

Klein, W. and Purdue, C. (1993). Utterance structure. In C. Purdue (ed.), *Adult Language Acquisition: Cross-linguistic Perspectives*, Vol. II: *The Results* (pp. 4–40). Cambridge: Cambridge University Press.

Kormos, J. (2011). Task complexity and linguistic and discourse features of narrative writing performance. *Journal of Second Language Writing*, 20, 148–61.

Kormos, J. and Trebits, A. (2011). Working memory capacity and narrative task performance. In P. Robinson (ed.) *Second Language Task Complexity: Researching the Cognition Hypothesis of Language Learning and Performance* (pp. 268–85). Amsterdam: John Benjamins.

Krashen, S. (1982). *Principles and Practice in Second Language Acquisition.* New York: Pergamon Press.

Kuiken, F., Mos, M. and Vedder, I. (2005). Cognitive task complexity and second language writing performance. In S. Foster-Cohen, M. García Mayo and J. Cenoz (eds), *Eurosla Yearbook,* 5 (pp. 195–222). Amsterdam: John Benjamins.

Kuiken, F., and Vedder, I. (2007a). Cognitive task complexity and linguistic performance in French L2 writing. In M. García Mayo (ed.), *Investigating Tasks in Formal Language Learning* (pp. 117–35). Clevedon, UK: Multilingual Matters.

—— (2007b). Task complexity and measures of linguistic performance in L2 writing. *International Review of Applied Linguistics,* 45, 261–84.

—— (2008). Cognitive task complexity and written output in Italian and French as a foreign language. *Journal of Second Language Writing,* 17, 48–60.

—— (2011). Task complexity and linguistic performance in L2 writing and speaking. In P. Robinson (ed.), *Second Language Task Complexity: Researching the Cognition Hypothesis of Language Learning and Performance* (pp. 91–104). Amsterdam: John Benjamins.

Larsen-Freeman, D. (2013). Complexity theory/Dynamic Systems Theory. In P. Robinson (ed.), *The Routledge Encyclopedia of Second Language Acquisition* (pp. 103–6). New York: Routledge.

Larsen-Freeman, D. and Cameron, L. (2007). *Complex Systems and Applied Linguistics.* Oxford: Oxford University Press.

Lee, Y. (2002). Effects of Task Complexity on the Complexity and Accuracy of Oral Production in L2 Korean. Unpublished doctoral dissertation, University of Hawai'i, Manoa.

Levkina, M. and Gilabert, R. (2012). The effects of cognitive task complexity on L2 oral production. In A. Housen, F. Kuiken, and I. Vedder (eds), *Dimensions of L2 Performance and Proficiency: Complexity, Accuracy and Fluency in SLA* (pp. 171–98). Amsterdam: John Benjamins.

Long, M. H. (1996). The linguistic environment for second language acquisition. In W. C. Ritchie and T.K. Bhatia (eds), *Handbook of Second Language Acquisition,* (pp. 413–68). San Diego, CA: Academic Press.

—— (2007). *Problems in SLA.* Mahwah, NJ: Lawrence Erlbaum.

Long, M. H. and Crookes, G. (1992). Three approaches to task-based syllabus design. *TESOL Quarterly,* 26, 27–55.

Malicka, A. and Levkina, M. (2012). Measuring task complexity: Does EFL proficiency matter? In A. Shehadeh and C. Coombe (eds), *Task-based Language Teaching in Foreign Language Contexts* (pp. 43–66). Amsterdam: John Benjamins.

Michel, M. C. (2011a). *Cognitive and Interactive Aspects of Task-based Performance in Dutch as a Second Language* (Ph.D. thesis, University of Amsterdam). Oisterwijk: BoxPress.

—— (2011b). Effects of task complexity and interaction on L2-performance. In P. Robinson (ed.), *Second Language Task Complexity: Researching the Cognition*

Hypothesis of Language Learning and Performance (pp. 141–74). Amsterdam: John Benjamins.

—— (2013). Effects of task complexity on the use of conjunctions in oral L2 task performance. *The Modern Language Journal*, 97, 178–95.

Michel, M. C., F. Kuiken, and I. Vedder (2007) Effects of task complexity and task condition on Dutch L2. *International Review of Applied Linguistics*, 45, 241–59.

—— (2012) Task complexity and interaction: (Combined) effects on task-based performance in Dutch as a second language. In L. Roberts, C. Lindqvist, C. Bardel and A. Abrahamsson (eds), *EUROSLA Yearbook 2012* (pp. 164–90).

Norris, J. M. (2013). *Measuring Task Complexity for Task-based Research*. Paper presented at the colloquium 'Methodological advances in TBLT research: measurement of task demands and processes', at the annual conference of the American Association of Applied Linguistics, Dallas, Texas (18 March 2013).

Nuevo, A. (2006). *Task Complexity and Interaction: L2 Learning Opportunities and Interaction.* Unpublished doctoral dissertation, Georgetown University, Washington, DC.

Nuevo, A., Adams, R. and Ross-Feldman, L. (2011). Task complexity, modified output, and L2 development in learner-learner interaction. In P. Robinson (ed.) *Second Language Task Complexity: Researching the Cognition Hypothesis of Language Learning and Performance* (pp. 175–201). Amsterdam: John Benjamins.

Popham, W. and Baker, E. L. (1970). *Establishing Instructional Goals.* Englewood Cliffs, NJ: Prentice Hall.

Prabhu, N. S. (1987). *Second Language Pedagogy.* Oxford: Oxford University Press.

Rahimpour, M. (1997). *Task Condition, Task Complexity, and Variation in L2 Discourse.* Unpublished doctoral dissertation, University of Queensland, Brisbane, Australia.

—— (2010). Current trends on syllabus design in foreign language instruction. *Procedia Social and Behavioral Sciences*, 2, 1660–4.

Rahimpour, M. and Hosseini, P. (2010). The impact of task complexity on L2 learners' written narratives. *English Language Teaching*, 3, 198–205.

Révész, A. (2009). Task complexity, focus on form, and second language development. *Studies in Second Language Acquisition*, 31, 437–70.

—— (2011). Task complexity, focus on L2 constructions, and individual differences: A classroom-based study. *The Modern Language Journal*, 95, 162–81.

Révész, A. and Gilabert, R. (2013). *Methodological Advances in TBLT Research: Measurement of Task Demands and Processes.* Symposium convened at the American Association of Applied Linguistics (AAAL) Annual Conference, March, Dallas, USA.

Révész, A. and Han, Z. (2006). Task content familiarity, task type and efficacy of recasts. *Language Awareness*, 15, 160–79.

Révész, A., Sachs, R., and Mackey, A. (2011). Task Complexity, Uptake of Recasts, and Second Language Development. In P. Robinson (ed.), *Second Language Task Complexity: Researching the Cognition Hypothesis of Language Learning and Performance* (pp. 203–35). Amsterdam: John Benjamins.

Rezai, S. and Kasani, A. F. (2011). *Task Complexity, Language Proficiency and Task-based Writing*. Saarbrucken; VDM Verlag Dr. Muller.

Robinson, P. (1995). Task complexity and second language narrative discourse. *Language Learning*, 45, 99–140.

—— (1996a). *Task Complexity and Second Language Syllabus Design: Data-based Studies and Speculations*. (Special issue) University of Queensland Working Papers on Language and Linguistics (Vol. 1). Brisbane: Center for Language Teaching and Research.

—— (1996b). Introduction: Connecting tasks, cognition and syllabus design. In P. Robinson (ed.), *Task Complexity and Second Language Syllabus Design: Data-based Studies and Speculations*. (Special issue) University of Queensland Working Papers on Language and Linguistics (Vol. 1) (pp. 1–14). Brisbane: Center for Language Teaching and Research.

—— (2001a). Task complexity, task difficulty, and task production: Exploring interactions in a componential framework. *Applied Linguistics*, 22, 27–57.

—— (2001b). Task complexity, cognitive resources, and syllabus design: A triadic framework for examining task influences on SLA. In P. Robinson (ed.), *Cognition and Second Language Instruction*. (pp. 287–318). Cambridge: Cambridge University Press.

—— (2003a). The Cognition Hypothesis, task design and adult task-based language learning. *Second Language Studies*, 21 (2), 45–107.

—— (2003b). Attention and memory during SLA. In C. Doughty and M. H. Long (eds), *Handbook of Second Language Acquisition* (pp. 631–78). Oxford: Blackwell.

—— (2005). Cognitive complexity and task sequencing: Studies in a componential framework for second language task design. *International Review of Applied Linguistics in Language Teaching*, 43 (1), 1–32.

—— (2007a). Criteria for classifying and sequencing pedagogic tasks. In M. P. García-Mayo (ed.), *Investigating Tasks in Formal Language Learning* (pp. 7–27). Clevedon: Multilingual Matters.

—— (2007b). Task complexity, theory of mind, and intentional reasoning: Effects on L2 speech production, interaction, and perceptions of task difficulty. *International Review of Applied Linguistics in Language Teaching*, 45, 191–213.

—— (2009). Syllabus design. In M. Long and C. Doughty (eds), *Handbook of Language Teaching* (pp. 294–310). Oxford: Blackwell.

—— (2010). Situating and distributing cognition across task demands: The SSARC model of pedagogic task sequencing. In M. Putz and L. Sicola (eds), *Cognitive processing in second language acquisition: Inside the learner's mind*. (pp. 243–68). Amsterdam/Philadelphia: John Benjamins.

—— (2011a). *Second Language Task Complexity: Researching the Cognition Hypothesis of Language Learning and Performance*. Amsterdam: John Benjamins.

—— (2011b). *Task-based Language Learning*. Malden, MA: Wiley-Blackwell.

—— (2011c). Second language task complexity, the Cognition Hypothesis, language learning, and performance. In P. Robinson (ed.), *Second Language Task Complexity: Researching the Cognition Hypothesis of Language Learning and Performance* (pp. 3–38). Amsterdam: John Benjamins.

Robinson, P., Cadierno, T. and Shirai, Y. (2009). Time and motion: Measuring the effects of the conceptual demands of tasks on second language speech production. *Applied Linguistics*, 38, 533–54.

Robinson, P. and Ellis, N. C. (2008). Conclusion: Cognitive Linguistics, Second Language Acquisition, and L2 instruction – Issues for research. In P. Robinson and N. C. Ellis (eds), *Handbook of Cognitive Linguistics and Second Language Acquisition* (pp. 489–566). New York: Routledge.

Robinson, P. and Gilabert, R. (eds) (2007a). Task Complexity, the Cognition Hypothesis and Second Language Instruction. *International Review of Applied Linguistics in Language Teaching* (Special Issue), 45 (3). Berlin/New York: Mouton de Gruyter.

Robinson, P. and Gilabert, R. (2007b). Task complexity, the Cognition Hypothesis and second language learning and performance. *International Review of Applied Linguistics in Language Teaching*, 45, 161–76.

Robinson, P., Ting, S., and Urwin, J. (1995). Investigating second language task complexity. *RELC Journal*, 26, 62–79.

Salimi, A. and Dadashour, S. (2012a). Task complexity and language production dilemmas (Robinson's Cognition Hypothesis vs. Skehan's Trade-off Model). *Procedia Social and Behavioural Sciences*, 46, 643–52.

—— (2012b). Task complexity and SL development: Does task complexity matter. *Procedia Social and Behavioural Sciences*, 46, 726–35.

Samuda, V. and Bygate, M. (2008). *Tasks in Second Language Learning*. Basingstoke: Palgrave Macmillan.

Sasayama, S. and Izumi, S. (2012). Effects of task complexity and pre-task planning on Japanese EFL learners' oral production. In A. Shehadeh and C. Coombe (eds), *Task-based Language Teaching in Foreign Language Contexts* (pp. 43–66). Amsterdam: John Benjamins.

Sato, C. (1990). *The Syntax of Conversation in Interlanguage Development*. Tübingen: Gunter Narr.

Schank, R. (1999). *Dynamic Memory Revisited*. New York: Cambridge University Press.

Schank, R. and Abelson, R. (1977). *Scripts, Plans, Goals and Understanding*. Hillsdale, NJ: Erlbaum.

Schmidt, R. (2001). Attention. In P. Robinson (ed.), *Cognition and Second Language Instruction* (pp. 3–32). Cambridge: Cambridge University Press.

Segalowitz, N. (2010). *Cognitive Bases of Second Language Fluency*. New York: Routledge.

—— (2013). Automaticity. In P. Robinson (ed.), *The Routledge Encyclopedia of Second Language Acquisition* (pp. 53–7). New York: Routledge.

Shehadeh, A., and Coombe, C. A. (2012). *Task-based Language Teaching in Foreign Language Contexts: Research and Implementation.* Philadelphia: John Benjamins.

Shiau, Y. S. and Adams, R. (2011). The effects of increasing reasoning demands on accuracy and complexity in oral L2 production. *University of Sydney Papers in TESOL,* 6, 121–46.

Shin, M. (2012). *Effects of Task Modality Sequenced by Task Complexity, Lexical Aspect and Verb Regularity on Korean Students' Learning of the English Past Tense.* Unpublished Ed.D. dissertation, Seoul National University, South Korea.

Skehan, P. (1996). A framework for the implementation of task-based instruction. *Applied Linguistics,* 17, 38–62.

—— (1998). *A Cognitive Approach to Language Learning.* Cambridge: Cambridge University Press.

—— (2002). A non-marginal role for tasks. *ELT Journal,* 56, 289–95.

—— (2003). Task-based instruction. *Language Teaching,* 36, 1–14.

—— (2009). Modelling second language performance: Integrating complexity, accuracy, fluency and lexis. *Applied Linguistics,* 28, 510–32.

Skehan, P. and Foster, P. (2001). Cognition and tasks. In P. Robinson (ed.), *Cognition and Second Language Instruction* (pp.183–205). Cambridge: Cambridge University Press.

Steenkamp, A. and Visser, M. (2011). Using cognitive complexity analysis for the grading and sequencing of Ixhosa tasks in the curriculum design of a communication course for education students. *Per Linguam,* 27 (1), 11–27.

Thomas, M., and Reinders, H. (2010). *Task-based Language Learning and Teaching with Technology.* London: Continuum.

Torres, J. (2013). *Heritage and Second Language Learners of Spanish: The Roles of Task Complexity and Inhibitory Control.* Unpublished doctoral dissertation, Georgetown University, Washington, DC.

Van den Branden, K. (2006). *Task-based Language Education: From Theory to Practice.* Cambridge: Cambridge University Press.

Van Geert, P. (2008). The Dynamic Systems approach in the study of L1 and L2 acquisition: An introduction. *Modern Language Journal,* 92, 179–99.

von Stutterheim, C. and Klein, W. (1987). A concept-oriented approach to second language studies. In C. Pfaff (ed.), *First and Second Language Acquisition Processes* (pp. 191–205). Rowley, MA: Newbury House.

Vygotsky, L. S. (1978). *Mind in Society: The Development of Higher Psychological Processes.* Cambridge, MA: Harvard University Press.

Wilkins, D. (1976). *Notional Syllabuses.* Oxford: Oxford University Press.

Williams, J. (2013). Form-meaning connection (FMC). In P. Robinson (ed.), *The Routledge Encyclopedia of Second Language Acquisition* (pp. 249–52). New York: Routledge.

Willis, D. (1990). *The Lexical Syllabus: A New Approach to Language Teaching.* London: Collins.

Willis, J. (1996). *A Framework for Task-based Learning.* London: Longman.

Wu, X., Lowyck, J., Sercu, L., and Elen, J. (2013a). Task complexity, student perceptions of vocabulary learning in EFL, and task performance. *British Journal of Educational Psychology*, 83 (1), 160–81.

—— (2013b). Vocabulary learning from reading: examining interactions between task and learner related variables. *European Journal of Psychology of Education*, 1–20.

Yalden, J. (1983). *The Communicative Syllabus: Evolution, Design and Implementation*. Oxford: Pergamon Press.

Section I

Experimental Studies of Task Sequencing

2

Task Sequencing in the L2 Development of Spatial Expressions

Mayya Levkina and Roger Gilabert
University of Barcelona

Introduction

In recent years, syllabus designers and teachers have shown a growing interest in implementing syllabi based on pedagogic tasks, especially because of the potential of pedagogic tasks to approximate L2 performance to real-life conditions. Through the use of tasks, learners get an opportunity to learn the L2 gradually by preparing themselves for real-life needs as users of a second or foreign language. In this context, it has been widely admitted that there exists a need to organize tasks in a well-reasoned way which will optimize opportunities for language learning. While some scholars have argued that difficulty of input or content should be the main criterion for sequencing, other scholars have already suggested models of task sequencing that organize pedagogic tasks from cognitively simple to cognitively complex. Cognitive complexity has been a well-established basis for task sequencing in other fields of science, such as mathematics, mechanics, engineering, informatics or physics among many others. In most of those areas scientists have had few problems identifying what constitutes a simple task (e.g. simple addition in mathematics) and what is complex (e.g. an algorithm). However, in the field of applied linguistics, there is not yet a general agreement as to which criteria should be used by designers and teachers to organize and sequence pedagogic tasks. The present study is based on the theoretically well-grounded and systematically organized proposal of task sequencing advanced by Robinson (2005, 2010), where he claims that tasks should be organized and sequenced by means of manipulating their cognitive complexity, that is, the conceptual, attention, memory and reasoning demands that the structure of tasks imposes on the learner's processing. Taking into account that task sequencing in SLA is still empirically under-researched, the goal of the present study is to test Robinson's (2010) SSARC[1] model in order to see whether sequencing tasks from simple to complex according to their cognitive complexity is more beneficial for L2 development than some other alternative ways of task sequencing, such as organizing tasks from complex to simple or in a randomized way. In this study we focus on the learning of language related to spatial relations and we explore whether different sequences of task practice have differential effects on the learning and retention of spatial expressions.

Task sequencing: early studies

Before Robinson forwarded his proposal on task sequencing which suggests that tasks should be graded according to their cognitive complexity, there had been previous proposals concerned with the issue of task sequencing. In what follows, a brief overview of some of the crucial moments in the evolution of this issue is provided.

The first early attempt at dealing with sequencing was presented and explicitly mentioned within the task-based language teaching project known as the Bangalore Project (Prahbu, 1987): a large-scale project carried out in different schools of Bangalore, the main goal of which was to teach the foreign language through the use of communicative tasks. In order to make task performance easier and more manageable for the students, it was decided that attempts at complex tasks should be preceded by demonstrations of simpler versions. After some experience with using tasks in the project, the basic criteria for task sequencing were elaborated: 'tasks within a given sequence (i.e. tasks of the same type forming the basis of several lessons) were ordered by a commonsense judgment of increasing complexity, the later tasks being either inclusive of the earlier ones or involving a larger amount of information, or an extension of the kind of reasoning done earlier' (Prahbu, 1987: 40). While the principle of sequencing tasks from simple to complex had appeared, no clear scheme of how to actually identify a task as more or less complex was given, as it was done solely intuitively and arbitrarily by teachers.

In the late 1980s, Nunan (1989) devoted a whole chapter to the grading and sequencing of tasks within syllabus design in his book on task-based learning. Apart from a general principle guiding sequencing from simple to complex, he distinguished between a number of factors according to which tasks could be graded. The first factor is input, where a task is considered more complex when the input to it is less elaborated (e.g. a text with no visual support, such as photographs, highlighted text, tables and so on) or does not contain contextual support. All this makes the task more complex to process and to carry out. The second factor is the learner, who will perceive a task as more or less difficult depending on factors such as his or her background knowledge. Also following Brindley (1987), he suggested a list of affective and cognitive variables that affect the grading of task complexity (i.e. motivation, confidence, prior learning experience, learning pace, observed ability in language skills, cultural knowledge or awareness, and linguistic knowledge). The final set of factors has to do with the task procedure, which is also likely to affect the cognitive complexity of the task. When it comes to this factor, task input should be stable and, by contrast, the procedure followed in order to achieve task completion should be modified in order to gradually increase the cognitive complexity of a task.

Long (1985, 2005) and Long and Crookes (1992) raised the problem of a lack of empirical studies on task sequencing. They noticed that task sequencing processes mostly 'appear to be arbitrary processes, left partly to real-time impressionistic judgments by the classroom teacher' (1992: 37). Moreover, they urged greater clarity in definitions of the operational terms used for task sequencing. Importantly, Long and Crookes suggested that pedagogic tasks to be graded and sequenced should be based on target tasks identified via needs analysis, and that pedagogic task grading should be based on communicative criteria rather than linguistic functions.

Finally, Skehan (1996, 1998) proposed a model of sequencing tasks in a logical way from simple to complex on the basis of the attentional resources that each task would require. Drawing on previous work by Candlin (1987) and Nunan (1989), he distinguished three sets of features to consider during task sequencing: code complexity, cognitive complexity and communicative stress. Code complexity is considered the formal factor related to lexical and syntactic difficulty, whereas cognitive complexity and communicative stress are seen as individual characteristics affecting task performance. Cognitive complexity is related to content concerning two areas: processing and familiarity. Finally, communicative stress is referred to as related factors of task difficulty, such as time pressure or task modality. Sequencing tasks with the proper selection of task features, according to Skehan, will lead to 'an affective balance between fluency and accuracy' and 'the opportunity for previous restructuring to be applied' (Skehan, 1996, p. 53).

To sum up, previous proposals related to task sequencing have all agreed on the idea that task sequencing should have L2 learners move from simple tasks to complex tasks. Also, it has been agreed that tasks should be graded following some kind of notion of cognitive complexity and not only a linguistic one as traditional syllabi have done. Up until the 21st century, however, no clear model of task grading according to its cognitive complexity has been elaborated. In this context, Robinson made an attempt to fill this gap by formalizing the SSARC (2010) model which, on the basis of the Cognition Hypothesis and in conjunction with the Triadic Componential Framework for task classification, he argues, is a theoretically motivated, feasible and researchable model for task sequencing.

The Cognition Hypothesis and task sequencing

In order to understand the SSARC model, we first need to understand the Cognition Hypothesis, which makes predictions regarding two aspects of second language acquisition: (1) it predicts the effects task complexity may have on L2 performance, which is typically measured in terms of fluency, linguistic complexity and accuracy; and (2) it predicts how task complexity may impact L2 development through tasks graded according to their cognitive demands.

Robinson makes an important distinction between two dimensions of task complexity: resource-directing variables, which direct learner's attention to particular linguistic features needed to meet the demands of the task at hand, and resource-dispersing variables, which deplete learner's attention by dispersing resources over various aspects of task performance. An example of a resource-directing dimension is reasoning demands, where tasks with no reasoning demands leading to only simple transmission of information may typically require simple linguistic devices (and, but), as opposed to tasks with some reasoning demands where, for example, subordination is likely to be needed to express cause–consequence relations (because, therefore). Similarly, in the case of map tasks, dealing with a well-organized map with all the landmarks in place is incomparably easier and does not require as much mental effort as dealing with a confusing, fuzzy map with no clear landmarks (Becker and Carroll, 1997). On the other hand, a clear example of a resource-depleting variable is access to planning time before or during task performance. Giving no planning time before task performance simply disperses attentional resources during performance. In spite of its apparently negative function for L2 performance and development, this dimension is also seen as important as it approximates performance to real-life conditions, so integrating this kind of variable 'could be argued to facilitate real-time access to an already established and developing repertoire of language' (Robinson, 2003, p. 59). In the SSARC model (2010), Robinson suggests that the cognitive demands of tasks (i.e. task complexity features) should be the sole basis for sequencing decisions, and that tasks should first be made more complex along resource-directing variables and only later along resource-dispersing ones. As for performance, Robinson predicts that increasing cognitive complexity along resource-directing variables will affect fluency negatively, but will promote accuracy and complexity.[2] With regard to development, the prediction is that higher task demands will cause more attention to and retention of input during task performance.

When grading tasks according to their cognitive demands, Robinson (2005) claims that it is important (where possible) to pursue a natural order for sequencing, e.g., from tasks that require spatial reasoning first based on simple topological relations to tasks that include axis-based relations (Taylor and Tversky, 1996), which is the sequence in which children learn to make reference to location (Becker and Carroll, 1997), or from tasks which do not require participants to establish casual relations to tasks which do (Berman and Slobin, 1994). L2 adult learners, Robinson claims, with their fully developed conceptual cognitive apparatus in place still retain the basic notion of cognitive complexity that guides child conceptual and linguistic development (see Robinson, 2005, pp. 4–7), and so organizing tasks from cognitively simple to cognitively complex in this natural order will help adult L2 learners in at least three ways: 1) to more efficiently allocate their attentional and memory resources; 2) to move from the use of simple linguistic devices to the use of complex ones and so help them through the process of development; 3) to play closer attention to input and achieve higher retention of that input.

One crucial aspect of the Cognition Hypothesis is the triadic componential framework which organizes variables that may affect task design into three dimensions: task complexity, task conditions and task difficulty. In what follows a schematic overview of the triadic componential framework (its first version and an updated version) will be presented (Robinson, 2001a, 2001b; Robinson and Gilabert, 2007).

Triadic Componential Framework for task classification and sequencing and L2 development of spatial expressions

The Triadic Componential Framework pursues two main objectives: to guide the decision of how to grade tasks within syllabus design on the basis of task complexity (1) and to help in making online decisions according to task conditions (2) and task difficulty (3). It is important to note that even though task complexity, task conditions and task difficulty interact during performance, they should be kept separate when making sequencing decisions since, for example, no information about either task conditions or task difficulty may be available prior to program design and implementation. In this chapter we focus on the task complexity dimension. As described above, task complexity contains two dimensions: (a) resource-directing and (b) resource-depleting. In the first version of the Triadic Componential Framework (2001a), Robinson distinguished three resource-directing variables (i.e. +/− few elements; +/− here-and-now; +/− no reasoning demands) and three resource-depleting variables (i.e. +/− planning time; +/− single task; +/− prior knowledge). All these variables are proposed as a guide for decisions in task design and as recommendations for sequencing criteria. The factors affecting task difficulty are divided into two categories: (a) affective variables that have the potential to be changed in a relatively short period of time (e.g. motivation, anxiety and confidence), and (b) relatively stable ability variables, which could even be measured beforehand (e.g. aptitude, proficiency and intelligence). Finally, task conditions are organized into participation (e.g. open vs. close task; one-way vs. two-way task; convergent vs. divergent task) and participant factors (e.g. gender, familiarity, power vs. solidarity). Though assuming that task complexity could be controlled and learner abilities measured in advance, some interactions between the three parts of the model can still occur. In this way, task complexity could interfere with learner's perception of task difficulty. Or task condition, such as performing a task in a one-way fashion versus a two-way fashion, may also affect learner's perception of its difficulty.

Later, Robinson and Gilabert (2007) updated the existing version of the Triadic Componential Framework by adding some new elements to it. One of the objectives of the article was to create an operational taxonomy for task type classification suitable for task designers, who would further adapt them for their particular classroom contexts. Therefore, the items selected to be included in the new framework were intended first, to be adequate for pedagogic design and use in classroom settings, and, second, to be theoretically justified.

Here again, Robinson reconfirmed his predictions regarding L2 production and L2 development as affected by task complexity. As claimed in previous descriptions of the model (2001a, 2001b, 2003, 2005), increased task complexity along resource-directing dimensions will promote L2 development of newly learned target items. In contrast, manipulating task complexity along

Task Complexity (Cognitive factors)	Task Condition (Interactive factors)	Task Difficulty (Learner factors)
(Classification criteria: cognitive demands)	(Classification criteria: interactional demands)	(Classification criteria: ability requirements)
(Classification procedure: information-theoretic analyses)	(Classification procedure: behaviour-descriptive analyses)	(Classification procedure: ability assessment analyses)
(a) Resource-directing variables making cognitive/conceptual demands	*(a) Participation variables* making interactional demands	*(a) Ability variables* and task-relevant resource differentials
+/– here and now	+/– open solution	h/l working memory
+/– few elements	+/– one-way flow	h/l reasoning
–/+ spatial reasoning	+/– convergent solution	h/l task-switching
–/+ causal reasoning	+/– few participants	h/l aptitude
–/+ intentional reasoning	+/– few contributions needed	h/l field independence
–/+ perspective-taking	+/– negotiation not needed	h/l mind/intention-reading
(b) Resource-dispersing variables making performative/ procedural demands	*(b) Participant variables* making interactant demands	(c) Affective variables and task-relevant state-trait differentials
+/– planning time	+/– same proficiency	h/l openness to experience
+/– single task	+/– same gender	h/l control of emotion
+/– task structure	+/– familiar	h/l task motivation
+/– few steps	+/– shared content knowledge	h/l processing anxiety
+/– independency of steps	+/– equal status and role	h/l willingness to communicate
+/– prior knowledge	+/– shared cultural knowledge	h/l self-efficacy

Figure 2.1 The Triadic Componential Framework for task classification – categories, criteria, analytic procedures, and design characteristics (from Robinson and Gilabert, 2007)

resource-dispersing variables will contribute to further automatization of already learned language features. In this way, both manipulating along resource-directing and resource-dispersing variables is crucial for L2 development.

For the present study, a resource-directing variable was chosen, i.e. spatial reasoning demands, motivated by a number of reasons: (1) almost on a daily basis we have to reason in spatial terms, such as when reading a map trying to find our way to some place or helping someone else to get from one place to another; (2) in the classroom context where this research study was to be conducted work on spatial expressions is part of the curriculum; (3) many learners and users of English have to eventually deal with the problem of the correct use of spatial expressions, due to the dissimilarity of some of the spatial forms between English and other languages; (4) there is considerable psychological research on spatial reasoning so manipulation of cognitive task complexity along the spatial reasoning dimension could be easily supported by already existing studies in cognitive psychology.

Research questions

Based on the theoretical background related to task sequencing in task-based language learning and some of the assumptions mentioned in the previous section, the present chapter aims at answering the following research questions:

1. Does task sequencing affect the learning of new target L2 items related to the expression of spatial relations when tasks are organized from cognitively simple to cognitively complex as opposed to other sequences?
2. Does task sequencing contribute to the longer-term retention of learned target items after treatment and over a two-week period when tasks are organized from simple to complex as opposed to other sequences?

Due to the fact that no previous studies on task sequencing in the field of task-based language teaching have been carried out, no directional hypotheses are advanced here. The results obtained from the experiment will, however, be discussed in the light of the prediction of the SSARC model proposed by Robinson (2010), as it stands out as the most explicit and precise model of task sequencing applicable to empirical research. The predictions drawn from such a model would be that new input forms will be better learned and retained when performing tasks in a simple to complex sequence than in any other kind of sequence.

Experimental design

In order to answer the two research questions, a simple pre-, post- and delayed post-test design with a focus on prepositional expressions of space was applied. Students in the study, 48 participants from two intact groups, did two control tasks (a receptive and a productive one) before the treatment in order to establish their knowledge of target spatial items (pre-test). Then they were randomly organized into three groups according to three different task sequence organizations: (1) from simple to complex – which was the target sequence, proposed by Robinson (2003, 2007, 2010); (2) from complex to simple; (3) and randomized.[3] Right after the treatment they did an immediate post-test (with the same control tests) and a delayed post-test after a two-week period in order to analyse the retention of the newly learned input. The design took into consideration the classroom conditions in which the experiment was to be carried out, and so minimal interference with regular classroom procedures was sought.

Participants

Forty-eight students enrolled in the summer intensive course in English organized by the School of Modern Languages at the University of Barcelona, Spain, volunteered for the study. The participants were recruited via their teachers who later explained the objective and the organization of the study. They completed all the parts of the experiment within their regular classroom sessions. Their proficiency level was assessed by a school internal placement test, which established their initial proficiency in English at an intermediate level (B1). Students had had approximately the same number of years (M=14.56, SD=2.12) of instruction in English as a foreign language and their ages ranged between 18 and 23 (M=20.52, SD=1.74). Since the experiment was carried out within their classroom sessions and attendance fluctuated, not all the students did all parts of the experiment and, therefore, five (5) participants had to be excluded from the final statistical analysis of the collected data. The final number of participants included in the statistical analysis was 43.

Materials

As the experiment consisted of a pre-test, treatment, post-test and delayed post-test design, two blocks of materials were designed: control tests, on the one hand, in order to analyse (1) initial level of knowledge of target items by the participants; (2) immediate learning of the received target input by means of its practice with a series of tasks; (3) retention of the acquired target information from input and treatment after a two-week period; and, on the other hand, input and treatment tasks were used.

Regarding the control tests, two different tasks were used to assess participants' L2 development in the study: a descriptive task (a productive knowledge task) and a two-part vocabulary task (part I – translation of target expressions from Spanish into English; part II – multiple-choice test for receptive knowledge). The descriptive task was a simple picture description task (see Appendix A). In the instructions participants were told that they had recently arrived in London and they had found a flat. In order to find ideas for decorating their own flat, they had been to their friend's fabulously decorated flat and had been highly impressed by its stylish refurbishment. So, once at home they decided to write an e-mail to their boyfriend/girlfriend who was about to come to join them in London in order to describe exactly what they saw in their friend's flat. It was a writing task (to facilitate data collection), with no reasoning demands (as the students only needed to describe the picture).[4] The task had a list of 12 items (i.e. furniture and décor objects) to be mentioned in the description, those being placed in a way that was designed to elicit each of the target items.

The vocabulary test was provided after the productive descriptive task to avoid exposing the participants to some target items which they could then use in the descriptive task. Only one version of the task was created and used to avoid some possible differences in final results. The first part of the test consisted of a simple translation from Spanish into English of the target items together with three distractors,[5] a total of 12 expressions to translate (e.g. 'encima de la mesa' – 'on top of the table', 'en el lado derecho de la cama' – 'on the right-hand side of the bed').

The second part of the test was a multiple-choice task, which also included the same number of items to deal with (i.e. a total of 12 items). For each gap, the students had four options where only one was correct. The focus of this part of the test was on the use of forms of a given prepositional expression. The test was previously revised by native speakers and piloted to ensure its reliability (α=.71 for Part I and α=.70 for Part II). The example of a sentence is given below:

The stools will go just _____ *stove.*
a) opposite to the   b) opposite   **c) opposite the**   d) opposite of the

The treatment session consisted of two parts: the first one was designed to provide input (see Appendix B) and the second one was a sequence of three practice tasks designed on the basis of their cognitive complexity. Students worked in pairs. During the input session conducted by the teacher, the students were offered three tasks. The objective was always the same: to imagine that they were delivery men and they had just come to their client's place and now, by following the instructions of the client, they had to furnish the required space. Each of them was given a photocopy of the input tasks with three descriptions, and three floor plans (empty and then furnished). On an empty floor plan of a flat they had to draw the furniture items (just to draw a box with the name, not a full drawing, to save time and effort). As an example, first the teacher was asked to give the instructions for the first task and to make sure the students understood these. The subsequent instructions were given by the students (Task 2 – Student A, and Task 3 – Student B), in such a way that each student gave the instructions for one task and then also followed one of the instructions of his/her peer for the other task. That was an information gap activity, since the student that had to

Table 2.1 Three task sequences

	Task 1	Task 2	Task 3
Sequence 1 (from simple to complex)	simple	+ complex	++ complex
Sequence 2 (from complex to simple)	++complex	+ complex	simple
Sequence 3 (randomized)	+ complex	simple	++ complex

follow the instructions did not have any access to the furnished map, but had to fill an empty map with the furniture items according to the instructions of his/her peer. Importantly, the three texts of the input had an equal number of items (9 target items + 3 distractors) that appeared three times each throughout the texts. This was done to balance the number of potential exposures to each target item.

The treatment part itself (see Appendix C and Appendix D) also consisted of three tasks created on the basis of spatial reasoning demands (a resource-directing variable of cognitive task complexity), which were organized from simple to complex (Group 1), from complex to simple (Group 2) and randomized (Group 3) (see next section).

These tasks were done in pairs. As in the input session, the students were engaged in the same type of task, where they were asked to imagine they had just moved to London and they needed to furnish their newly rented flat. The whole space had a double room (simple task), a living room (+ complex task), a kitchen (++ complex task), and a single room. One by one, except for the single room, they had to furnish the whole space. To do so, in each case they were provided with a list of items to put inside (the number of items was always eight), and again they were designed to elicit the use of the target spatial expressions.

Operationalization of task complexity

At the level of theoretical construct definition the reference here is Robinson's (2001a) definition of task complexity as the conceptual, attention, memory and reasoning demands that the structure of the task imposes on the learner's processing. And so a more complex task is one which imposes higher processing demands on the learner. At the specific level of task variable operationalization, in order to manipulate the complexity of the tasks along +/− spatial reasoning, first the general cognitive psychology literature on spatial reasoning was consulted, and this was followed by a pilot in which several factors (e.g. perspective, the number of objects, the amount of space, etc.) were tested. An affective variable questionnaire (Robinson, 2001b, 2007) was used during piloting to make sure that the learners' perception of task difficulty actually matched the cognitive complexity of the task.

In **Task 1** (simple task) the students were already given the place of the objects drawn on the floor plan they had. So, the only thing they had to do was to explain (to verbalize) the furniture distribution in the double room by giving instructions to a delivery man. Here, no spatial reasoning demands were involved in the task and the task required the simple transmission of information.

In **Task 2** (+ complex task) the students were asked to furnish the living room. This time they had a plan with only half of the objects already distributed on it, but they had to decide whether to put the rest of the items in the living room and then explain where to put all the objects (already drawn on the plan or not). So, here already some spatial reasoning demands were required in the task. Here, however, they did not need to take any specific perspective and they could use the other objects already in the room as a reference.

In **Task 3** (++ complex task) the students again were asked to furnish a new space, a kitchen, but there they did not have an already well-organized floor plan to be described. In terms of spatial reasoning this task was considered to be the most complex one since they did not simply need to transmit information but also to make decisions about the objects and the space available at the same time that they were taking the perspective of the delivery man who was placed by the door (see Table 2.2).

Table 2.2 Distribution of Task Complexity through the three tasks

	Task 1 Simple	**Task 2 +Complex**	**Task 3 ++Complex**
Criteria of task complexity	Space fully furnished Space references already provided Simple information transmission No perspective taking required	Half of the space furnished Partial spatial references provide Analysis and partial use of existing info No perspective taking required	Empty space No other spatial references provided Analysis and decision-making without help from existing info Perspective taking required

GROUP 1, GROUP 2, GROUP 3

Day 1	Pre-tests: a descriptive task, a two-part vocabulary test
one week	
Day 2	Input + three treatment tasks Immediate post-tests: a descriptive task, a two-part vocabulary test
10–14 days	
Day 3	Delayed post-tests: a descriptive task, a two-part vocabulary test

Figure 2.2 Experimental procedure

Procedure

This experiment was carried out in July 2011 during a summer intensive course in English. It was divided into three sessions. On the first day participants were given the two pre-test tasks (a descriptive task, followed by the two-part vocabulary test – translation + multiple-choice). The average time of the session was approximately half an hour. The second day (a week after a pre-test) consisted of a treatment session and an immediate post-test. The duration of the session ranged from one hour and a half to two hours. Ten to fourteen days between the immediate and delayed post-tests were left. Each task was preceded by a teacher's detailed instruction of what they were expected to do (see Figure 2.2).

Scoring procedures

The descriptive task was scored in two ways: (1) by counting the total number of target expressions that appeared in the task (retention of new forms without restricting this only to correct use); (2) by calculating the number of target expressions used *correctly* in the task (retention and correct use of new target forms). In the first scoring procedure, 1 point was assigned to: each target expression of space and each target expression of space used correctly. In the second scoring procedure, 1 point was assigned to each target expression of space used correctly; and 0 was given to target expressions of space used incorrectly. Below is given an example of the two scoring methods:

Dear Elvira,

Yesterday I put all my furniture on my wonderful living room! In this e-mail I sent you a photo.

At the back of (Target Correct, TC) the room there is a big sofa very comfortable. **Above (TC)** the sofa there are 2 pictures. In the middle of the room there is a rug, **on the top (Target Incorrect, TI)** a coffee table and a laptop and **above (TC)** the table there is a red lamp. **On the right-hand side (TC)** in front of the coffee table there is an armchair, and another armchair **on the left side (TC)**. Also **near (TC)** the sofa **on the left side (TC)** there is a plant. **On the right-hand side (TC)** there is a table with white chairs.

Finally there is a wooden chair behind the sofa. What do you think about my living room?

Bye

	TOTAL	Correct target expressions	Incorrect target expressions
Score 1	9	8	1
Score 2	8	8	1

For both parts of the vocabulary test, 1 point was given to each correct answer, whereas 0 points were assigned to incorrectly translated, not translated or unanswered items in the first part and to incorrectly answered or unanswered items in the second part. The total maximum score obtained for each of the parts was 12. As will be seen in Appendix A, the raw numbers of the two parts were added together and so scores are out of 24 possible items. Although they tap into different constructs, for our calculations it was decided to collapse both the results of the productive test (part I) and the results of the receptive test (part II) to obtain a global measure of their vocabulary knowledge.

Statistical instruments

Due to the relatively small number of participants (13 to 15 per group) and the fact that some of the variables did not meet standards for normality of distribution, it was decided to use non-parametric tests with all variables for all tests. Therefore, the statistical instruments used in the present study include descriptive statistics, Kruskal-Wallis tests, and non-parametric Wilcoxon signed ranks tests which are used to: 1) compare means between pre-test, post-test and delayed post-tests for each of the groups; 2) compare differences between the groups at any of the three points.

Results

Research question 1

With our first question we tried to understand if task sequencing affected the learning of new target items related to the expression of spatial relations when tasks are organized from cognitively simple to cognitively complex as opposed to other sequences.

For all groups the improvement after the treatment is statistically significant for both control tests: the receptive vocabulary test (Gr.1 = .006, Gr.2 = .001, Gr.3 = .001), and productive descriptive task (Gr.1 = .001/.003,[6] Gr.2 = .001/.001, Gr.3 = .001/.001) (see Appendix E). That means that immediately after treatment all groups significantly improved their knowledge of target items. Next, it was necessary to look at any possible between-group differences to figure out whether sequence played any significant role in the learning of spatial prepositions as a consequence of cognitive task complexity manipulation. Before that, a Kruskal-Wallis analysis of pre-test results was carried out in order to ensure group comparability and as seen in Appendix F (Vocabulary Test and Descriptive Task) no significant differences were found, so any significant differences yielded after treatment could be attributed to the effects of the sequence. When comparing the results of the groups after treatment, it could be observed (see Appendix G) that Group 2 (from complex to simple) learned significantly more target items than Group 1 (from simple to complex) or Group 3 (randomized) in the immediate post-test. Moreover, these differences proved to be statistically significant between Group 1 and Group 2 for the results of the vocabulary test and between Group 2 and Group 3 for the results of the descriptive task (all targets). Group 1 also significantly outperformed Group 3 in the descriptive task (correct targets). Nevertheless, in the overall results Group 2 still scored higher for this measure too.

Looking at the gains immediately after treatment, statistical analysis showed no significant difference between the groups as measured by the Descriptive task and the vocabulary test (see Appendix I). However, descriptive statistics showed that Group 2 retained more target information compared to its initial state both doing the descriptive task and the vocabulary test (see Table 2.3).

Research question 2

With the second question we asked if task sequencing contributed to the retention of new target items after treatment and over a two-week period

Table 2.3 Descriptive statistics of tasks: means, standard deviations, skewness and kurtosis

			Group 1 (N=13)				Group 2 (N=15)				Group 3 (N=15)			
			M	SD	Sk	K	M	SD	Sk	K	M	SD	Sk	K
Descriptive Task	Pre-Test	All Targets	2.31	1.32	-.15	-1.05	1.53	1.13	.08	-1.33	1.20	.94	.14	-.85
		Correct Targets	2.00	1.41	.42	-1.45	1.13	.834	.58	.51	1.20	.99	.21	-1.12
	Post-Test	All Targets	7.85	2.58	.93	1.66	7.50	1.29	.38	-.72	6.46	1.76	.67	-.22
		Correct Targets	5.15	2.60	-.44	-.87	6.07	1.39	-.55	.32	4.77	2.09	.62	-.49
	Delayed Post-Test	All Targets	7.00	2.61	.50	-.66	7.00	1.48	.41	-.06	5.1	1.79	.97	1.48
		Correct Targets	5.82	2.60	-.22	-.62	5.83	1.64	.61	-.53	4.3	1.83	-.42	-1.95
Vocabulary Task	Pre-Test		12.08	2.66	-1.16	1.11	13.27	4.64	-.02	-.82	14.33	2.77	.42	-.62
	Post-Test		16.15	3.96	-.001	-1.11	19.27	2.66	-.65	1.30	18.80	2.60	-.030	-1.11
	Delayed Post-Test		20.27	2.15	-.58	.01	18.85	2.48	-.38	-1.15	18.50	2.55	-.31	.73

when tasks were organized from simple to complex as opposed to other sequences.

As seen in Appendix E, after a two-week period all groups remembered a statistically significant amount of new target information as measured by both control tests: vocabulary test (Gr.1 = .003, Gr.2 = .005, Gr.3 = .005) and descriptive task (Gr.1 = .003/.007, Gr.2 = .002/.002, Gr.3 = .005/.005) in comparison with their initial knowledge before the treatment. When comparing groups, the only significant difference was found between Group 2 and Group 3 in the descriptive task – all targets (p = 0.41). However, when looking at the descriptive statistics it is clearly seen that both Group 1 and Group 2 obtained similar higher results compared to Group 3 (see Table 2.4).

Regarding the retention of target information, noteworthy is the fact that none of the groups show any significant loss of target information after a two-week period, which is shown by the lack of significant differences between the results in the post-test and in the delayed post-test for both control tests (see Appendix E), except for one score. Very interestingly, the participants from Group 1 (from simple to complex) scored significantly higher in the delayed vocabulary post-test than in the immediate post-test (see Appendix E, p=.028), which suggests that the treatment sequence for Group 1 promoted further retention of spatial target items over time.

Regarding the gains the groups obtained during the treatment session as measured after a two-week break, it is confirmed that Group 1 retained and even continued improving their knowledge of target items after treatment which is clearly seen in their improved result after two weeks in comparison to their results immediately after treatment (see Appendix I).

Discussion

Research question 1

When analysing the results of research question 1, two main conclusions can be drawn. Firstly, and independently of the type of sequence, all groups significantly improved their knowledge of target spatial expressions (ranging from 4 to 6 new items being learned on average) when comparing their initial results in the control tests with their immediate post-test results. This suggests that the provision of input followed by intense oral practice (the three tasks in the treatment) seems to lead to learning. Secondly, despite our prediction

Table 2.4 Descriptive statistics of tasks – gains: means, standard deviations, skewness and kurtosis.

			Group 1 (N=13)				Group 2 (N=15)				Group 3 (N=15)			
			M	SD	Sk	K	M	SD	Sk	K	M	SD	Sk	K
Descriptive Task	Pre-Test vs. Post-Test	All Targets	5.54	3.26	.472	-.429	5.93	1.54	.43	-.49	5.46	1.94	1.16	1.18
		Correct Targets	3.15	2.73	.498	-.951	4.93	1.82	-.33	-1.15	3.85	2.19	1.07	1.16
	Pre-Test vs. Del. Post-Test	All Targets	4.64	2.91	.292	-1.16	5.50	1.24	.85	-.09	4.01	2.21	1.23	2.42
		Correct Targets	3.64	3.08	.041	-1.95	4.75	1.48	1.11	1.07	3.30	1.83	.26	-1.05
	Post-Test vs. Del. Post-Test	All Targets	1.27	2.45	.509	-.33	.67	1.83	-.05	-1.18	1.40	1.96	-.04	.77
		Correct Targets	-.27	2.25	-.823	.86	.50	1.93	-.41	-.77	.50	2.80	-.30	-1.51
Vocabulary Task	Pre-Test vs. Post-Test		4.08	3.99	.41	-.56	6.01	4.42	.01	-1.12	4.47	3.54	.68	-.47
	Pre-Test vs. Del. Post-Test		8.27	2.37	-.01	-1.12	5.01	4.02	.02	.04	4.50	2.99	1.23	1.30
	Post-Test vs. Del. Post-Test		-4.00	4.29	-.11	-1.31	.08	3.25	-1.15	.37	.01	2.54	-.87	.07

based on the SSARC model, the target sequence (from simple to complex) did not seem to be more efficient in helping L2 learners learn spatial expressions than the two other sequences, at least in the short term. The participants in Group 2 (from complex to simple) scored unexpectedly higher for all the measures of spatial expressions than the two other groups. When we look at the sequence itself, the participants in Group 2 started with the most complex task. It may be speculated that by doing so their attentional resources may have been enhanced and geared towards how those high demands (having to decide on the objects, their best location and the explanation of where to place them from the point of view of the delivery man) could be met linguistically. In this way, learners may have detected the gaps in their interlanguage which they may have later filled with the subsequent input provided in the two following tasks presented to them in decreasing complexity. A potential immediate effect of this enhanced attention directed towards conceptualization may have been the higher number of target items detected and learned (as shown by both the receptive and the productive control tests) from the input by the learners in Group 2.

Research question 2

The results of the delayed post-test showed significant differences in gains of target vocabulary compared to pre-test for all groups with no significant differences in results among the groups. Firstly, this showed that the task treatment also had significantly positive effects in the long run. In the descriptive task all participants used significantly more target items both immediately after the treatment and two weeks after the treatment. This was also true for the receptive vocabulary knowledge task, which showed that after two weeks learners could still recognize the items they had learned. Noteworthy is the fact that there were no significant losses of the vocabulary learned in any of the groups. But probably the most interesting result with regard to this second question is that Group 1, who performed the sequence from simple to complex, is the only group that produced a significantly higher number of target items two weeks after the treatment as compared to the results obtained in the immediate post-test (4 new items on average right after the treatment as opposed to 8 new items on average two weeks after the treatment). We may speculate that the sequence itself may have played a role by helping learners better allocate their attentional and memory resources during the treatment. If we use the explanations provided by the SSARC model as a reference, the simple-to-complex sequence may have helped learners to liberate resources and so may have helped them engage in deeper semantic processing and into more rehearsal and elaboration of input which may have contributed to better retention of the new target items. It may be the case that in the other two sequences too many resources may have been geared towards conceptualization during highly complex task performance (either by dealing with the most complex task first or second), leaving less resources for input rehearsal and elaboration.

Limitations and conclusions

There are many limitations to this study but we will focus on the three main ones. The first one has to do with the classroom conditions in which the data were collected. Given the small number of participants no control group was used and no generalizations of the findings to other populations can be made. A larger number of participants should be involved in future experimental research to confirm whether there indeed exists a relationship between the type of sequence and any gains for L2 development. Secondly, interactions between sequencing and individual differences are likely to be at play during task performance. It is reasonable to believe that sequence may play a much more important role for learners with lower aptitude or working memory capacity than for more cognitively talented learners, and no data from individual differences were obtained from the participants. Future research should consider individual differences if a more complete picture of learning in relation to task sequencing is to be provided. Thirdly, the explanations of the results in this study are speculative in nature since no techniques have been used to tap into the actual mental processes taking place during task performance under different sequences. Future research should also consider the use of techniques such as think aloud protocols or stimulated recall to tap into the way resources are allocated during performance on the basis of different task sequences.

By way of conclusion, it should be pointed out that even if many of our explanations are speculative two facts emerge from this study. Firstly, oral task practice following input leads to the learning and retention of new L2 items and, secondly, sequencing tasks from simple to complex has the potential to help students retain newly learned input more efficiently than other sequences. These two findings render the exploration into the effects of task sequencing on L2 learning worth continuing.

Appendix A[7] Descriptive task

Imagine that you've just moved to London and now you have to furnish your new flat. Today you went to visit a friend of yours and you loved her/his living room.

Here is the living room.

What do you have to do? . . .

Now you're already at home and you want to share your impressions with your friend who is still in Spain. Write him/her an e-mail describing the living room you've just seen. Remember that you have to mention where each of the following objects was in the living room (as you see them in the photo):

1. a sofa
2. two green armchairs
3. a carpet
4. a set of three small white candles
5. a plant

6. two pictures
7. a coffee table
8. a dining table with two red chairs
9. a window
10. one lamp

You have got **15 minutes** to write your e-mail.

Appendix B Input – Test 1

Please follow the instructions of the teacher and draw the pieces of furniture on the plan.

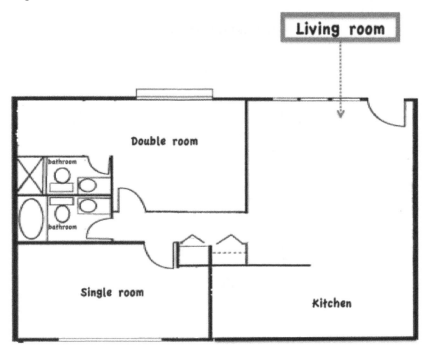

There are two windows in the living room. The first one is **at the back** and the second one is **on the right-hand side** of the room.

On the right-hand side of the room there is also a sideboard and a TV, which is **on** the wall **above** the sideboard.

There are two sofas in the room. One of them is **along** the left-hand side wall **opposite** the sideboard. Three paintings are **on** the same wall **above** the sofa.

The other sofa is **along** the window with two small coffee tables on each side of it.

A big rug is right **in the middle of** the room **in front of** the sofa with two small tables. There is a coffee table on the rug with three plates **on top of** it.

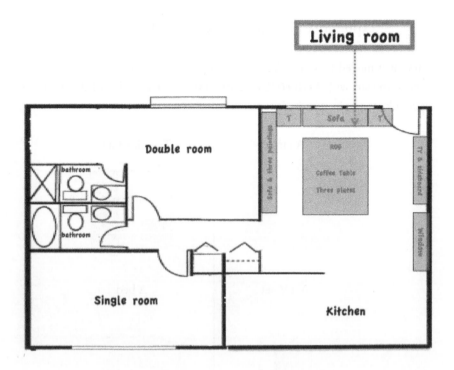

Appendix C Simple task – double bedroom

You've just moved to a new flat in Edinburgh. Now you have to furnish it. You decided to start with **THE DOUBLE ROOM**. You've got a list of the items you would like to put in your bedroom:

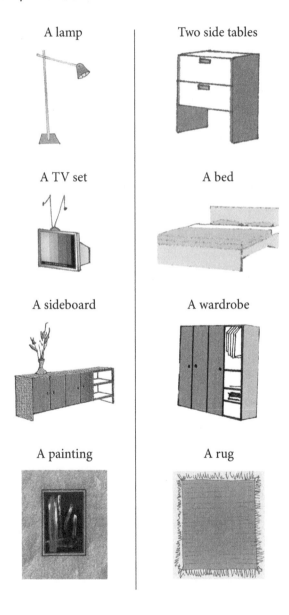

A lamp	Two side tables
A TV set	A bed
A sideboard	A wardrobe
A painting	A rug

YOUR TASK as A CLIENT

Imagine that you are at the furniture shop.

You'll work **IN PAIRS**.

First, you'll be **THE CLIENT** and then **THE DELIVERY MAN**.

As a client you have to explain to the delivery man as precisely as possible where you want **each of the objects** given above in the room.

Here you've got the plan of your flat where you've already got the places of these objects. So, the only thing to do is to explain it.

You've got 1 minute to prepare.

PLAN OF YOUR NEW FLAT 1.A

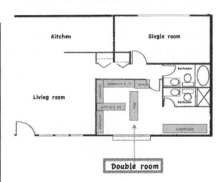

Appendix D Complex task – kitchen

You're almost done. The only space to furnish is your KITCHEN. Here again you've got a list of the items you would like to put in it:

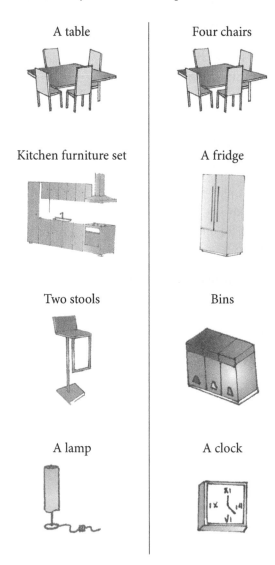

A table	Four chairs
Kitchen furniture set	A fridge
Two stools	Bins
A lamp	A clock

YOUR TASK as A CLIENT

The last thing to do at the furniture shop.

To explain to the delivery man as precisely as possible where you want **EACH** of the **EIGHT** objects in the kitchen.

This time you have to furnish the kitchen completely.

You've got 1 minute to prepare.

Appendix E Within-group comparison (Wilcoxon paired ranks test): Descriptive task and vocabulary test

			Group 1 (N =13)		Group 2 (N =15)		Group3 (N =15)	
			Z	Sig.	Z	Sig.	Z	Sig.
Descriptive Task	Pre-Test vs. Post-Test	All Targets	−3.184	.001*	−3.309	.001*	−3.194	.001*
		Correct Targets	−2.987	.003*	−3.310	.001*	−3.190	.001*
	Pre-Test vs. Delayed Post-Test	All Targets	−2.940	.003*	−3.104	.002*	−2.823	.005*
		Correct Targets	−2.684	.007*	−3.084	.002*	−2.816	.005*
	Post-Test vs. Delayed Post-Test	All Targets	−1.530	.126	−1.257	.209	−1.911	.056
		Correct Targets	−.211	.833	−.902	.367	−.616	.536
Vocabulary Test	Pre-Test vs. Post-Test		−2.756	.006*	−3.303	.001*	−3.187	.001*
	Pre-Test vs. Delayed Post-Test		−2.938	.003*	−2.828	.005*	−2.814	.005*
	Post-Test vs. Delayed Post-Test		−2.199	.028*	−.566	.571	−.239	.811

Appendix F Between-group comparison (Kruskal-Wallis test): vocabulary test and descriptive task

		×2 value	df	Sig.
Vocabulary Test	Pre-test	2.799	2	.247
	Post-test	4.696	2	.096
	Delayed Post-test	3.348	2	.187
Descriptive Task	All targets (Pre-test)	5.330	2	.070
	Correct targets (Pre-test)	3.255	2	.196
	All targets (Post-test)	3.626	2	.163
	Correct targets (Post-test)	2.783	2	.249
	All targets (Delayed Post-test)	6.460	2	.040*
	Correct targets (Delayed Post-test)	2.527	2	.283

Appendix G Between-group comparison (Wilcoxon paired ranks test): Descriptive task and vocabulary test

			Group 1 vs. Group 2		Group 1 vs. Group 3		Group 2 vs. Group 3	
			Z	Sig.	Z	Sig.	Z	Sig.
Descriptive Task	Pre-Test	All Targets	−2.013	.074	−.840	.401	−1.724	.085
		Correct Targets	−1.724	.085	−1.628	.103	−.061	.951
	Post-Test	All Targets	−.052	.959	1.357	.175	−1.897	.058
		Correct Targets	−1.075	.282	−2.015	.044*	−.170	.865
	Delayed Post-Test	All Targets	−.170	.865	−1.826	.068	−2.047	.041*
		Correct Targets	−.256	.798	−1.378	.168	−1.577	.115
Vocabulary Test	Pre-Test		−.630	.529	−2.054	.060	−.850	.395
	Post-Test		−2.050	.040*	−1.855	.061	−.704	.481
	Delayed Post-Test		−1.204	.229	−.931	.352	−.276	.783

Appendix H Between-group comparison – gains
(Kruskal-Wallis test): Vocabulary test and descriptive task

	Test		Comparison	×2 value	df	Sig.
Descriptive Task	Vocabulary Test		Pre-test vs. Post-test	1,475	2	.478
			Pre-test vs. Delayed Post-test	8.296	2	.016*
			Post-test vs. Delayed Post-test	8.051	2	.018*
		All targets	Pre-test vs. Post-test	.822	2	.663
			Pre-test vs. Delayed Post-test	4.538	2	.103
			Post-test vs. Delayed Post-test	4.138	2	.126
		Correct targets	Pre-test vs. Post-test	2.212	2	.331
			Pre-test vs. Delayed Post-test	.661	2	.719
			Post-test vs. Delayed Post-test	.832	2	.660

Appendix I Between-group comparison – gains (Wilcoxon paired ranks test): Vocabulary test and descriptive task

	Test	Comparison	Group 1 vs. Group 2		Group 1 vs. Group 3		Group 2 vs. Group 3	
			Z	Sig.	Z	Sig	Z	Sig.
Descriptive Task	Vocabulary Test	Pre-test vs. Post-test	−1.376	.169	−.394	.694	−1.016	.310
		Pre-test vs. Delayed Post-test	−.653	.514	−1.442	.149	−.351	.725
		Post-test vs. Delayed Post-test	−1.544	.123	−1.992	.046*	−.070	.944
	All targets	Pre-test vs. Post-test	−.714	.475	−.051	.959	−1.382	.184
		Pre-test vs. Delayed Post-test	−.562	.574	−.736	.462	−1.552	.121
		Post-test vs. Delayed Post-test	−1.17	.24	−1.29	.20	−.74	.46
	Correct targets	Pre-test vs. Post-test	−1.38	.17	−.63	.53	1.80	.07
		Pre-test vs. Delayed Post-test	−1.03	.302	−.27	.79	−1.36	.17
		Post-test vs. Delayed Post-test	−.509	.611	−.420	.674	.001	1.00

Notes

1 SSARC: SS – 'simple/stabilizing interlanguage'; A – 'automatizing access to interlanguage'; RC – 'restructuring and complexifying of the learner's current level of interlanguage'.

2 Fluency, complexity and accuracy are dimensions of task performance that are largely used in the TBLT literature. Although there is some reconsideration of how exactly to measure these three dimensions (e.g. whether by means of general or specific measurements), there is general agreement that these dimensions are valid ones for the analysis of the products of both oral and written tasks (see Housen, Kuiken and Vedder, 2012).

3 No control group was used because of limitations regarding the number of students that could be accessed within the institution. It is therefore assumed, but not confirmed by data, that no learning took place without the treatment.

4 The decision not to include reasoning demands in the control tests had been made to avoid any possible effect of the preliminary task on the main sequence (by potentially moving the treatment series to the pre-test set).

5 The distractors were included in the text so as not to discourage participants by the high number of unknown items to be translated.

6 All target items / correct target items.

7 Pictures were drawn by Irving Diaz Ortega.

References

Becker A. and Carroll, M. (1997). *The Acquisition of Spatial Relations in a Second Language*. Amsterdam: John Benjamins.

Berman, R. and Slobin, D. (1994). *Relating Events in Narrative: A Cross-linguistic Developmental Study*. New Jersey: Lawrence Erlbaum.

Brindley, G. (1987). Factors affecting task difficulty. In D. Nunan (ed.), *Guidelines for the Development of Curriculum Resources*. Adelaide: National Curriculum Resource Centre.

Candlin, C. (1987). Towards task based language learning. In C. Candlin and D. Murphy (eds) *Language Learning Tasks*. Englewood Cliffs, NJ: Prentice Hall.

Housen, A., Kuiken, F. and Vedder, I. (eds) (2012). *Dimensions of L2 Performance and Proficiency: Complexity, Accuracy and Fluency in SLA*. Amsterdam: John Benjamins.

Long, M. H. (1985). A role for instruction in second language acquisition: task-based language teaching. In Hyltensham, K. and Plenemann, M. (eds), *Modelling and Assessing Second Language Acquisition* (pp. 77–9). Clevedon: Multilingual Matters.

Long, M.H. and Crookes, G. (1992). Three approaches to task-based syllabus design *TESOL Quarterly*, 26, 1, 27–56.

Long, M. H. (2005). Methodological issues in learner needs analysis (pp. 19–76). In Long, M. H. (ed.), *Second Language Needs Analysis*. Cambridge: Cambridge University Press.

Niwa, Y. (2000). Reasoning demands of L2 tasks and L2 narrative production: Effects of individual differences in working memory, intelligence, and aptitude. Unpublished M. A. dissertation, Aoyama Gakuin University, Tokyo.

Nunan, D. (1989). *Designing Tasks for the Communicative Classroom*. Cambridge: Cambridge University Press.

Prabhu, N. S. (1987). *Second Language Pedagogy*. Oxford: Oxford University Press.

Robinson, P. (2001a). Task complexity, cognitive resources, and syllabus design: a triadic framework for examining task influences on SLA. In P. Robinson (ed.), *Cognition and Second Language Instruction* (pp. 287–318). Cambridge: Cambridge University Press.

—— (2001b). Task complexity, task difficulty and task production: Exploring interactions in a componential framework. *Applied Linguistics*, 22, 1: 27–57.

—— (2003). The cognition hypothesis, task design, and adult task-based language learning. *Second Language Studies*, 21, 2, Spring, 45–105.

—— (2005). Cognitive complexity and task sequencing: studies in a componential framework for second language task design. *International Review of Applied Linguistics in Language Teaching*, 43, 1, 1–32.

—— (2007). Task complexity, theory of mind, and intentional reasoning: effects on L2 speech production, interaction, and perceptions of task difficulty. *International Review of Applied Linguistics in Language Teaching*, 45, 3, 191–213.

—— (2010). Situating and distributing cognition across task demands: The SSARC model of pedagogic task sequencing. In M. Putz and L. Sicola (eds), *Cognitive Processing in Second Language Acquisition: Inside the Learner's Mind* (pp. 243–69). Amsterdam/Philadelphia, PA: John Benjamins.

Robinson, P. and Gilabert, R. (2007). Task complexity, the Cognition Hypothesis and second language learning and performance. *International Review of Applied Linguistics in Language Teaching*, 45, 3, 161–76.

Skehan, P. (1996). A framework for the implementation of task based instruction. *Applied Linguistics*, 17 (1), 38–62.

—— (1998). *A Cognitive Approach to Language Learning*. Oxford: Oxford University Press.

Taylor, H. A. and Tversky, B. (1996). Perspective in spatial descriptions. *Journal of Memory and Language*, 35, 371–91.

3

The Role of Task Sequencing in Monologic Oral Production

Aleksandra Malicka
University of Barcelona

Introduction

Developing a new skill, whether it is learning to play a new instrument, learning to drive a car or learning to speak a foreign language, is made up of multiple components. Some of these are easier to master and others pose more of a challenge to the learner. It is logical to assume that in order to master these skills, a certain organization in the way unfamiliar content is presented to the learner is a necessary condition. It is also reasonable to assume that in the acquisition process the learner is first to be exposed to uncomplicated, easily manageable elements before the more sophisticated and elaborate ones are presented. Straightforward as it may seem, a few issues have to be decided upon: 1. When learning a particular skill, or acquiring new material, which components are 'simple' and which are 'complex'? 2. On the basis of what criteria are these components considered 'simple' and others 'complex'? 3. Does there exist an optimal order in which the different elements should be presented so as to generate an environment which promotes the development of a particular skill? Finding answers to these basic questions is a challenging task, yet a fundamental one if progression from absolute unfamiliarity to a certain degree of proficiency is the goal of exposure.

The aforementioned questions, which potentially apply to developing a level of expertise in an area of daily life, can be extended far beyond a particular skill: they are pertinent to any training program, instructional setting or educational framework. In any approach or framework, the constituents which the syllabus or program consists of, need to be sequenced on the basis of some logical, systematic and empirically based criteria which will create the most favourable opportunities for learning to occur.

In the field of education these questions are of interest to multiple communities: syllabus designers, textbook authors, teachers or school head teachers. In the field of Second Language Acquisition, in the subdomain of task-based language learning and teaching (TBLT), researchers have long sought to find answers to the aforementioned issues. The objective of this pursuit has been that of discovering an optimal environment for creating opportunities during oral performance of pedagogic tasks. Some of the specific questions pertinent to the TBLT context have been, what is a simple and a complex task? How much difference is sufficient to design two tasks of clearly distinguishable levels of difficulty? Finally, how should tasks be presented in a sequence so that performance is boosted, and so that exposure to a sequence potentially leads to L2 development? In the line of research particularly relevant to this issue, the cognitive one, researchers have suggested the idea of task complexity, and more specifically, *cognitive complexity*, as a benchmark for establishing complexity levels of a task, and *task* itself as an organization unit of a syllabus. Two main theoretical frameworks have informed the research into Task Complexity: Robinson's Cognition Hypothesis (2001, 2003, 2005) and Skehan's (1996) Trade-off Hypothesis. The upcoming paragraphs will present key issues in both hypotheses relevant to this chapter.

The construct of Task Complexity has been defined as the 'result of the attentional, memory, reasoning, and other information-processing demands imposed by the structure of the task on the language learner' (Robinson, 2001, p. 28). In light of both hypotheses, cognitive complexity is, broadly speaking, the amount of thinking required for successful task completion. The multidimensional nature of task complexity is evidenced in two competing taxonomies of task demands proposed by the two scholars, which influence overall task performance. Skehan (1998) suggests a distinction between code complexity, cognitive complexity and communicative stress, whereas Robinson, in the Triadic Componential Framework (Robinson, 2007) associated with the Cognition Hypothesis, differentiates between cognitive factors, interactive factors and learner factors. In both frameworks it is the cognitive complexity of tasks which is the factor that is subject to a deliberate manipulation, the other factors, such as L2 proficiency, motivation, etc., being the reality the researcher or teacher encounters. As Robinson argues, learner factors can be determined *in situ* and in progress (Robinson, 2001) but are, as yet, difficult to diagnose in advance of task performance and engagement.

Within the factor of cognitive complexity, Robinson in his conceptual framework makes a further distinction between two complementary groups of factors, resource-directing and resource-dispersing dimensions, each placing different kinds of demands on the learner. The former group are 'those dimensions in which the demands on language use made by increases in task complexity and the increased conceptual demands they implicate, can be met by specific aspects of the linguistic system' (Robinson, 2005, p. 4). Resource-dispersing dimensions, on the other hand, by dividing attention, lead to 'consolidation and fast real-time access to existing interlanguage resources' (Robinson, 2010, p. 248). A pedagogic task can be manipulated along one group of factors or the other, or both simultaneously.

However, cognitive complexity is not only a means to manipulate the complexity level of an individual task; from a broader perspective, cognitive complexity also serves as a principle for sequencing tasks in a syllabus. According to Skehan and Foster (2003, p. 93), '[an] individual task has to be located, in a principled way, in longer-term instruction sequences which seek to promote balanced development, such that improvements in one area will be consolidated by improvements in others'. Along similar lines, Robinson (2001, p. 27) claims that [sequencing decisions are] 'theoretically motivated, empirically substantiable, and pedagogically feasible'.

Robinson went on to develop these theoretical ideas into a framework for sequencing pedagogic tasks, the SSARC model of pedagogic task sequencing (Robinson, 2010). It posits that tasks should be sequenced in an order from simple to complex as such sequencing facilitates development due to the fact that different complexity levels of tasks have different functions. The role of simple tasks is to stabilize the current state of the interlanguage by dealing with familiar material and to consolidate the present state of knowledge about the L2. As complexity increases, access to L2 forms is automatized as it becomes speedier. Finally, complex tasks force the learner to stretch their existing L2 repertoire to meet the demands of those tasks. Learners are therefore forced to test new, not-yet-internalized forms, an operation unnecessary in a simple task, as it is doable without referring to advanced unfamiliar L2 forms.

Although Robinson and Skehan agree that tasks need to be sequenced according to principled criteria, where they do not coincide is when it comes to the effect of such manipulation on production. More specifically, the core difference between these two positions lies in how they explain the distribution of attention during performance of a complex task, where *performance* is understood as the interplay between the dimensions of fluency, accuracy and complexity. Although they agree on the fundamental issue that increased task demands are bound to exert an influence on production, they see cognitive complexity as affecting production in contradictory manners. The Cognition Hypothesis claims that, as human attentional resources are potentially unlimited in capacity, during task performance accuracy and complexity can receive the same amount of attention since they draw on separate resource pools. Complex tasks, therefore, have the potential to lead to qualitative changes in performance, and it is possible for the complexity and accuracy of speech to be simultaneously augmented. According to the Trade-off Hypothesis, since the pool of attention is limited, complexity and accuracy enter into competition for attentional resources during task performance. As a result, 'tasks which are cognitively demanding in their content are likely to draw attentional resources away from language forms' (Skehan and Foster, 2001, p. 189). Therefore a trade-off effect is expected between the dimensions of accuracy and complexity.

These conflicting theoretical models of attention allocation have been extensively investigated in task-based research in recent years (e.g. Niwa, 2000; Lee, 2002; Nuevo, 2006; Gilabert, 2007; Kuiken, Mos and Vedder, 2007; Kuiken and Vedder, 2007; Michel, 2011; Michel, Kuiken and Vedder, 2007; Robinson, 2001, 2005; Sasayama and Izumi, 2012). Despite a relatively long tradition in investigating the phenomenon of task complexity, two problematic issues in research carried out so far can be observed: some lack of uniformity when it comes to operationalizing the construct of complexity, and a practice of assuming differences between the designed complexity levels based on theoretical rationales from other areas of cognitive psychology, as well as learners' testimony to the added 'difficulty' of complex tasks, rather than investigating them directly. As a consequence, the body of research carried out so far has yielded largely mixed, and frequently contradictory, findings. Where fluency, accuracy and complexity measures have been employed to track changes in performance, while some studies have indicated a pattern following the predictions of Robinson's Cognition Hypothesis, other studies contributed evidence in favour of Skehan's Trade-off Hypothesis, with the different areas of performance being affected in intricate, frequently quite unpredictable ways. In the case of both hypotheses, only partial, rather than complete, rejection or confirmation has been the case. Also, despite the considerable interest task-based pedagogy has received, the issue of sequencing, in this case sequencing pedagogic tasks, is an under-researched area. Most studies have employed tasks in their simple and complex conditions (as a dichotomy between simple versus complex tasks, rather than operationalizing task demands along a continuum of increasing complexity), and they therefore provided only partial insights into patterns of performance emerging as a result of engaging in a pedagogic task. As a consequence, little is known about whether longer sequences of tasks affect performance, and, if so, the potential qualitative changes such sequencing brings about. The current study aims to shed light on the issue of sequencing by measuring performance on a sequence of three tasks. It inquires about the ostensibly facilitative nature of the simple–complex sequence, as is advocated in the main theoretical framework of sequencing pertinent to the current study.

Literature review

Investigating the variables ±number of elements and ±reasoning demands

The studies reviewed in this section share two features. First, the tasks used in them were manipulated along the variables *number of elements* and *reasoning demands* from Robinson's Triadic Componential Framework, which are the variables manipulated in the task design in the current study. Second, in all the studies reviewed here, except for one (Révész 2011), three task conditions have been employed: a simple task, a complex task, and a +complex task; a pattern observed in this study. Despite this basic similarity, however, none of these studies reported here, or in general, have directly investigated sequencing. That is, what they investigated is the effects of these three task complexity levels on performance as measured by complexity, accuracy and fluency (CAF) measures, and on development of specific forms, but sequencing *per se* was not the object of the study.

One more similarity between previous research and the current study is that a joint effect of manipulating these variables was investigated, rather than measuring the impact on performance of a single variable. Such an approach is not uncommon in task complexity studies; for instance the variables ±here-and-now and ±contextual support have mostly been investigated jointly, within the same task design. It must be noted, however, that ±here-and-now and ±contextual support are, respectively, a resource-directing variable and a resource-dispersing one, whereas ±number of elements and ±reasoning demands are both resource-directing variables.

We now turn to specific examples of studies which have employed the conditions described above, the tasks they used and the results they produced.

In two studies by Ishikawa (2008, 2011) three tasks were used: a no reasoning task (control task), a simple reasoning task and a complex reasoning task.

Whereas the 'no reasoning' task required the participants to merely describe relations between people, and therefore reasoning demands were null, in both simple and complex reasoning tasks the participants were supposed to attribute intentions and mental states to others in a situation in which human relationships changed in the workplace. In the simple task, 2 section members were involved in the change, and in the complex task 4 members were involved. Regarding the operationalization of complexity, the simple and complex tasks, as opposed to the control or 'no reasoning' task, required the participants to successfully understand the psychological and other mental states which brought about a change in relationships between people. Increased intentional demands did not have an effect on fluency, except for one measure, but they triggered accuracy and complexity (with one measure used per each dimension). This last result is in line with the Cognition Hypothesis.

The same task was used in a study by Ishikawa (2011), and it revealed similar patterns to those of the 2008 study in the case of two dimensions. Namely, increased intentional reasoning fostered accuracy and complexity (again, only one measure was used for each). Following the predictions of the Cognition Hypothesis, fluency decreased on the complex task. However, this result was found for only one of the employed measures (dysfluency), but not for the other one (speech rate).

A study by Kim (2009) investigated the impact of task complexity on between-learner interaction and the development of question formation and past tense in English. Three levels of complexity were used and these are referred to in the study as: 'simple', '+complex' and '++complex'. The simple task version consisted of two-way narrative tasks, whereas the +complex and ++complex versions were two-way decision-making tasks. The difference between +complex and ++complex tasks was operationalized as the number of considerations to bear in mind when taking a decision (2 in the simple version versus 4 in the complex one). Participants, by collaborating in pairs, were asked to suggest the best part-time job for students presented on the prompt sheet. The tasks were designed to elicit question formation and the occurrence of past tense in English. Compared to the simple condition, high complexity tasks turned out to be good stimuli for interaction and they led to L2 development.

In a study by Kim and Ventura (2011), four different tasks related to university life were used: describing events at a university festival, hosting an American friend, sharing an experience from university orientation, and preparing for a mayoral election campaign. In the simple task the participants were only required to exchange information, in the +complex task they were asked to take a decision, and in the ++complex task they had to take a decision bearing in mind certain considerations (which is the variable ±number of elements). However, no information was provided regarding the exact difference in the number of considerations between the complex and the +complex task. The two complex tasks, compared to the simple one, resulted in further development of past tense morphology. However, no significant statistical difference was found between +complex and ++complex tasks. The authors report that this could be due to insufficient differences between +complex and ++complex task versions.

In a classroom-based study by Révész (2011) a simple and a complex version of an argumentative task were used. In this task the participants played the role of members of a personal trust foundation board and they had to assess two proposals for funding. The difference between the simple and the complex task was operationalized as the available economic resources ($500,000 versus $10,000,000) and the number of projects the resources could be allocated to (three versus six). The complex task version required the learners to justify the reasons for their choice. This study employed one measure per lexical and structural complexity (in the latter case one specific measure was used) and three for accuracy. The results of the study are broadly in line with the Cognition Hypothesis: accuracy and lexical complexity were boosted on the complex task, with mixed results found for structural complexity (it was confirmed for the specific measure and for one of the global measures).

In the study by Nuevo, Adams and Ross-Feldman (2011) a narrative (targeted at past tense) and a decision-making task (targeted at locatives) were used, with three complexity levels each. In the narrative task, the participants were required to collaboratively write up a story. In the simple task, they were given pictures arranged in the correct order, and in the complex one plot information was not available. In the decision-making task the participants had to come up with the best sitting arrangement for guests. In the simple version there was one obvious sitting arrangement which clearly matched the information about the guests. By contrast, in the complex version there were several imperfect solutions in addition to having to deal with more guests. Increased complexity did not foster modified output. The only area in which a significant effect was found was that of self-repair in the case of locative forms.

Malicka and Levkina (2012) investigated the influence of increased task demands on the production of speakers of different EFL proficiency levels. The tasks were oral instruction-giving tasks and were manipulated along ±number of elements and ±spatial reasoning demands. The tasks required the participants to explain where in an apartment they wanted certain furniture items to be placed.

Regarding the variable ±number of elements, in the simple task there were 6 pieces of furniture and in the complex one there were 15, out of which the subjects were asked to choose 5. As for ±spatial reasoning demands, these were operationalized as the presence of two points of reference in the simple task, and absence of points of reference in the complex one. In the case of the high proficiency speakers, increased demands led to an improvement in accuracy on 1 specific measure, 2 lexical complexity measures, and 2 structural complexity measures. Regarding low proficiency subjects, increased complexity led to an improvement in fluency to the detriment in the other dimensions except for 1 specific accuracy measure, where performance was worse on the complex task. The results indicate a pattern whereby the Cognition Hypothesis holds true for higher proficiency speakers, whereas the Trade-off Hypothesis is pertinent to the low-proficiency ones.

Sasayama and Izumi (2012) measured the impact of cognitive task complexity and pre-task planning time on learner production. The authors used a simple and a complex task manipulated along ±number of elements, which referred to the number of characters involved in a story (2 characters in the simple task and 6 in the complex one). High cognitive demands of the complex tasks were operationalized as the ability to distinguish between the various characters. While the complex task negatively affected fluency, structural and lexical complexity and accuracy remained intact as a result of increased cognitive complexity. The Cognition Hypothesis was therefore partially confirmed.

Summary of findings of previous research

Regarding the manipulated variables, ±number of elements refers to these elements of a task which can be counted, and it is the instances of that element that mark the difference between a simple and a complex task condition. Regarding reasoning demands, the simple condition mostly required the participants to perform the action of narrating or describing, as opposed to decision-making or justifying their choices in the complex version.

The manipulation of elements and reasoning demands within the same task was predicted by Robinson as 'likely to require a wider range of language than simpler tasks, e.g. greater use of lexical connectors, subordination, complex noun phrases, and a wider variety of attributive adjectives' (Robinson, 2001, p. 38). The studies reviewed above have generally confirmed this prediction: the simultaneous manipulation of two variables, in this case ±number of elements and ±reasoning demands, seems to be conducive to changes in performance and the results obtained are generally more systematic than in the case of studies which manipulated these variables separately. Another noteworthy fact is that in this kind of manipulation the effect of cognitive complexity was found for all three dimensions, fluency, accuracy and complexity. However, in none of the studies did the differences between all three complexity levels reach statistical significance, with some studies revealing differences between the simple and the most complex version, and others between the simple and the complex one, but not between all three. The differences in cognitive complexity might therefore not have been stretched enough between the different tasks to bring about predicted qualitative changes. One possible explanation for this finding, in the case of those studies in which a task of 'medium' complexity level was complexified by adding more elements, could be that elements on their own did not have the potential of changing the nature of production. It can be speculated that a simultaneous manipulation of elements plus another variable could have led to an increase.

Research questions

Considering the findings obtained in previous studies, the study reported here aimed to investigate the following research questions:

RQ1. How do the different complexity levels of tasks, as manipulated along ±reasoning demands and ±number of elements, contribute to task performance?

RQ2. Is there interaction between task complexity and sequencing tasks from simple to complex?

These questions are motivated by two factors: 1. The need to further investigate the effect of task complexity on performance, in order to contribute evidence in favour of, or against, the Cognition Hypothesis and the Trade-off Hypothesis; and 2. The need to investigate the way performance is affected by different sequencing conditions.

Methodology

Participants

The participants in the current study (*N*=50) were students in their first, second and third year of tourism at a University College of Tourism in Barcelona. All of them were Spanish and Catalan learners of English and their age ranged from 19 to 25. Their level of proficiency in English was assessed by means of the Oxford Placement Test (a multiple choice with 60 items). The average score of the subjects was 33.7. The participation in the project was voluntary and the participants were randomly assigned to one of the experimental conditions in the study.

Experimental conditions

The study reported here included two experimental sequencing conditions. 'Sequencing' has been operationalized as performing a sequence of three tasks in one sitting and at short intervals. Therefore, sequencing was measured at a certain point of development, and not over time, so only short-term effects of sequencing are measured.

The two experimental conditions present in the study are understood as two sequencing orders of performing tasks: 1. Sequencing tasks from simple to complex (N=25); and 2. Randomized sequencing (N=25). In the simple–complex condition, all participants performed the tasks in the same sequence, that is, first the simple task, then the complex task, and finally the +complex task.

The randomized condition consisted of five sub-conditions, which were operationalized as all possible orders of administering the three tasks employed in the study. The administered orders of the different cognitive complexity levels were the following:

1. simple, +complex, complex (N=5)
2. complex, simple, +complex (N=5)
3. complex, +complex, simple (N=5)
4. +complex, complex, simple (N=5)
5. +complex, simple, complex (N=5)

The tasks

Context and instructions

The tasks used in the current study were designed following the results of a Needs Analysis carried out in the tourism sector. The tasks were three problem-solving scenarios at a hotel reception in which the participant played the role of a receptionist at a hotel. Due to unexpected circumstances, a problem arose in the hotel, and some of the clients had to be relocated to new hotel rooms or to new hotels. Each task consisted of the description of the situation, which offered details about the participant's role, the profiles of the clients involved in the situation, and five options of new rooms or hotels. The participants were instructed that in each task they had to leave a message on the clients' answering machines and they had to choose the option (depending on the task, a new hotel room or a new hotel) which they considered most adequate for the client profile they were faced with. The tasks were designed in such a way that rather than there being one obvious solution for each client, several imperfect solutions were possible, each matching the profile of the client in selected aspects, but not in all of them.

All three tasks were monologic and open tasks. The instructions to all tasks were presented in the L1 Spanish so as to prevent the participants from merely repeating the language of instructions in their own production.

Operationalization of complexity

Elements

The variable ±number of elements embraces two components of tasks: client profiles and hotel or rooms options. Cognitive task complexity does not refer to the number of clients or room options, which are kept constant across the three task versions, but rather to *the number of characteristics thereof.* That is to say, only those components of the tasks the number of occurrences of which changes across the different task versions have been labelled 'elements'. Therefore, the number of the clients being three, or the number of room and hotel options being five across the task versions, is not referred to as ± number of elements. Specific components which the variable number of elements refer to are described below.

Reasoning demands

In terms of ±reasoning demands, the tasks employed in this study are manipulated along the number of mental operations needed for task completion. These mental operations are understood as a range of speech acts: describing, recommending, apologizing and justifying. Increased cognitive complexity is the function of the number of these acts and their simultaneous occurrence within a task.

Simultaneous manipulation of ±reasoning demands and ±elements in the three tasks

In the simple task the number of elements refers to six characteristics of the rooms, and the only mental operation needed to perform it is describing the provided information. This task does not require the participant to find a room for a particular client profile, but simply to transfer information. Its cognitive complexity is therefore low because it places only a limited amount of reasoning on the learner: mere exchange of information, without taking into account any conditions, is the only necessary condition for the task to be completed.

In the complex and the +complex task, the variable ±number of elements is operationalized as two sets of information: 1. Pieces of information provided about the different clients (i.e. 4 characteristics in the complex task and 8 in the +complex task); and 2. Pieces of information provided about the different rooms and hotels (i.e. their characteristics such as price, view, discounts, availability, options of meal plan, location, etc.; a total of 4 characteristics per option in the complex task and a total of 10 characteristics in the +complex one). Regarding the dimension of reasoning demands, the complex task requires the participants to apologize for the situation, describe the new available options, and recommend one option to each of the three clients. In the +complex task, in addition to the mental operations required in the complex task, the participants must also justify their choice. It is the build-up of elements and mental operations that results in the participants' having to pay attention simultaneously to various aspects of the tasks, which makes the +complex task more demanding than the complex one, and the complex one more demanding than the simple one. In addition, it is the simultaneous rather than individual occurrence of these two variables within the same task that distinguishes the simple task from the two tasks of high complexity levels.

Data collection procedure

The participants were randomly assigned to one of the conditions in the study, that is, simple–complex or randomized sequencing. The participants were informed that their performance would not be evaluated, and that after each task they would fill in a short four-item questionnaire about the task.

For each of the three tasks, the participants had 90 seconds to familiarize themselves with the task. The simple and the complex task were presented as three A4-size sheets, and four A4-size sheets in the case of the +complex task. A pilot study carried out prior to the data collection revealed that 90 seconds was sufficient to get familiar with the content of the task, but not to plan the answer. Online planning time was not restricted. All components of the tasks – instructions, client profiles, and room and hotel options – were available to the participants during task performance.

The recording of the first task then took place, after which the participants were given an affective variables questionnaire in which they assessed the difficulty of the task. This procedure was repeated three times, once for each task. The recording of all three tasks and filling in the questionnaires took from 20 to 30 minutes per participant. No time limit was set for the participants to perform the task. The recordings took place in a quiet room one on one with the researcher.

The corpus of data obtained from the recording sessions consisted of 150 recordings (three per participant) whose duration ranged from 2 to 15 minutes. All data were transcribed using the CLAN version of CHILDES (Child Language Data Exchange System) (MacWhinney, 2000).

Measuring task difficulty: Affective variables questionnaire

In order to independently measure task complexity, an affective variables questionnaire was administered to the participants. The questionnaire consisted of four questions: how difficult the task was, how much mental effort was needed to perform it, how much anxiety it caused, and how well or badly the participants felt they had performed the task. The answers were given on a 9-point scale, where '1' means low difficulty and '9' means high difficulty. Each participant filled in the questionnaire right after performing each task.

Measures

The measures used in the current study are general fluency, accuracy and complexity (CAF) measures of performance used in previous research. Fluency was calculated by means of three measures: a) unpruned speech Rate A (number of syllables obtained from an unpruned transcription divided by the total number of seconds and multiplied by 100), b) pruned speech Rate B (number of syllables obtained from a pruned transcription divided by the total number of seconds and multiplied by 100), and c) dysfluency ratio (total number of repetitions, restarts, and self-repairs divided by the total number of seconds and multiplied by 100). Two global measures employed for accuracy are Errors per AS-unit (the Analysis of Speech Unit) and Errors per 100 words. Structural and lexical complexity were each measured using two measures: Words per clause and Words per AS-unit were used for structural complexity and D and Guiraud's index for lexical complexity.

Statistical test

Three statistical tests were employed in the current study: a) descriptive statistics to retrieve information about means and standard deviations, b) one-way repeated measures ANOVA to check for statistical significance in the effect of cognitive complexity and sequencing, and c) pairwise comparisons detected differences between the three tasks. Alpha levels were set at $p < .05$.

Results

Research question 1: How do the different complexity levels of tasks, as manipulated along ±reasoning demands and ±number of elements, contribute to task performance?

This section presents the results obtained in the study. Table 3.1 presents results of the descriptive statistics found for all the measures. As can be observed in Table 3.1, cognitive complexity had an influence on performance in all dimensions of production. Gradual patterns of improvement from the simple, complex to +complex task can be observed in the case of 4 measures (*D*, Words/ ASU, and two accuracy measures). The other measures revealed intricate patterns of performance: in fluency, both in speech rate A and speech rate B, there was an improvement from the simple task to the complex task, but on the most complex task fluency decreased again. In dysfluency ratio and Guiraud's index, the speech was, respectively, least fluent and least complex on the complex task.

A closer look at the results for sequencing order reveals an intriguing pattern. Whereas the pattern of results is the same for the simple–complex and randomized group in fluency, lexical complexity and accuracy, the opposite pattern can be observed in structural complexity. On both measures employed in this dimension, structural complexity gradually increased in the simple–complex group, and it gradually decreased in the randomized group. In other words, in the simple–complex group *the complex task triggered most structural complexity*, and in the randomized group it was *the simple task that generated most structural complexity*.

The results from one-way repeated measures ANOVA show the performance between simple, complex, and +complex tasks (Table 3.2).

The results revealed that there was a significant effect of task complexity on all measures ($p < .05$) except for one structural complexity measure, Words/AS-unit. The effect size (partial eta squared) revealed that according to effect size benchmarks suggested by Cohen (1988), the effect sizes in the case of all measures are large (over .14) except for one accuracy measure, Errors/100 words, which is almost large (.11).

Table 3.1 Descriptive statistics for all measures: Means and standard deviations

| | | SIMPLE TASK | | | | | | COMPLEX TASK | | | | | | +COMPLEX TASK | | | | | |
| | | Simple-complex | | Randomized | | TOTAL | | Simple-complex | | Randomized | | TOTAL | | Simple-complex | | Randomized | | TOTAL | |
Category	Dependent variable	M	SD	M	SD	M	SD	M	SD	M	SD	M	SD	M	SD	M	SD	M	SD
Fluency	Rate A	120.75	27.29	122.27	23.27	121.51	25.11	129.87	45.29	128.21	33.58	129.04	39.46	116.34	34.44	109.68	34.47	113.01	34.27
	Rate B	112.51	26.61	114.54	22.50	113.53	24.41	117.83	42.01	118.64	30.96	118.24	36.52	105.65	31.62	102.00	33.74	103.82	32.41
	Dysfluency ratio	4.36	2.03	3.68	1.60	4.02	1.84	9.63	5.40	8.01	4.10	8.82	4.81	4.57	2.04	4.02	1.75	4.29	1.90
Lexical complexity	Guiraud's index	2.45	.39	2.47	.27	2.46	.33	2.24	.32	2.26	.30	2.25	.31	2.59	.63	2.36	.37	2.47	.52
Structural complexity	D	44.79	12.01	45.78	14.19	45.29	13.06	47.93	12.32	51.05	12.83	49.49	12.55	53.34	12.68	57.18	12.40	55.26	12.56
	Words/clause	7.43	1.27	7.63	.78	7.53	1.04	6.88	1.56	7.00	.98	6.94	1.29	7.99	1.97	7.25	1.14	7.62	1.64
	Words/AS-unit	9.29	1.25	9.63	1.67	9.46	1.47	9.41	2.11	9.62	1.49	9.52	1.81	9.59	1.46	9.54	1.43	9.56	1.43
Accuracy	Errors/AS-unit	1.01	.63	1.11	.51	1.06	.57	.96	.76	1.10	.52	1.03	.65	.84	.62	.95	.43	.90	.53
	Errors/100 words	11.05	7.12	11.78	5.70	11.41	6.40	10.06	5.81	11.68	5.81	10.87	5.81	8.91	6.22	10.42	6.29	9.66	6.24

Table 3.2 One-way repeated measures ANOVA (all measures): Degrees of freedom, sum of squares, F-value, p-value, effect size

Dependent variable		Df	Sum of squares	F-value	p-value	Partial eta squared
Fluency	Rate A	2	6430.30	4.229	.020*	.153
	Rate B	2	5401.00	4.463	.017*	.160
	Dysfluency ratio	2	727.274	41.870	.000*	.641
Lexical complexity	Guiraud's index	2	1.543	7.492	.001*	.242
	D	2	2506.92	26.730	.000*	.532
Structural complexity	Words/clause	2	13.734	4.853	.012*	.171
	Words/AS-unit	2	.261	.122	.885	.005
Accuracy	Errors/AS-unit	2	.765	5.164	.009*	.180
	Errors/100 words	2	80.232	2.994	.040*	.113

Table 3.3 presents the results of the differences between the simple task and the complex one, the complex one and the +complex one, and the simple and the +complex one. The results reveal that for all dimensions and measures except for one (Words/AS-units) statistically significant differences were yielded between the different tasks. In all measures these can be observed comparing at least two

Table 3.3 Pairwise comparison between the three tasks

Dependent variable		Simple-Complex	Complex-+Complex	Simple-+Complex
Fluency	Rate A	.110	.006*	.045*
	Rate B	.275	.006*	.017*
	Dysfluency ratio	.000*	.000*	.216
Lexical complexity	Guiraud's index	.001*	.025*	.896
	D	.009*	.000*	.000*
Structural complexity	Words/clause	.011*	.026*	.776
	Words/AS-unit	.842	.813	.648
Accuracy	Errors/AS-unit	.656	.008*	.034*
	Errors/100 words	.348	.026*	.030*

tasks. On one lexical complexity measure, D, the differences can be observed between all three cognitive complexity levels of tasks. More specifically, the differences between the simple task and the complex one were found on four measures, between the complex task and the +complex task on eight measures, and between the simple task and the +complex one on five measures. Regarding research question 1, the results indicate that an increased cognitive complexity level did have an influence on production: all three dimensions, fluency, accuracy and complexity, were affected by an increase in complexity.

Research question 2: Is there interaction between task complexity and sequencing tasks from simple to complex?

Table 3.4 presents the results obtained for the relationship between task complexity and sequencing tasks from simple to complex versus randomized sequencing. It shows that no statistically significant difference was found for the sequencing condition, simple–complex versus randomized ($p > .05$). Therefore no interaction was found between cognitive complexity and different sequencing orders. Regarding research question 2, it can therefore be stated that the sequencing order in which the participants performed the tasks (simple–complex versus randomized) did not have an influence on their production.

Table 3.4 One-way repeated measures ANOVA (sequencing): Degrees of freedom, sum of squares, F-value, p-value, effect size

Dependent variable		Df	Sum of squares	F-value	p-value	Partial eta squared
Fluency	Rate A	2	424.10	.448	.617	.020
	Rate B	2	223.361	.254	.777	.011
	Dysfluency ratio	2	8.640	.551	.580	.023
Lexical complexity	Guiraud's index	2	.536	.895	.416	.037
	D	2	55.326	.430	.653	.018
Structural complexity	Words/clause	2	6.775	1.168	.320	.047
	Words/AS-unit	2	· 1.019	.568	.570	.024
Accuracy	Errors/AS-unit	2	0.13	.090	.914	.004
	Errors/100 words	2	5.842	.298	.744	.013

Discussion

Research question 1: How do the different complexity levels of tasks, as manipulated along ±reasoning demands and ±number of elements, contribute to task performance?

The first research question inquired about whether there are differences in how cognitive task complexity affects performance as measured by global fluency, accuracy, and complexity measures. The results of the study suggest that overall performance was *heavily affected by cognitive complexity* between the different designed cognitive complexity levels.

The major finding from the study at hand is that the *complex task condition* led to a *decrease in fluency*, with a simultaneous increase in *lexical complexity and accuracy*. The results for structural complexity are mixed because different patterns were revealed for the two measured employed in the study. However, a closer look at the descriptive statistics reveals that even though statistical significance was not reached in the case of one structural complexity measure, the increase in structural complexity is proportional to that in cognitive complexity. These results confirm the fundamental claim behind the Cognition Hypothesis that increased cognitive complexity triggers higher levels of complexity and accuracy to the detriment of fluency.

As the current study explored the effect of cognitive complexity on a sequence of tasks rather than a simple–complex dichotomy, intricate patterns have emerged which shed some light on how the different dimensions of production change over time, and that some are more susceptible to variation over a sequence than others, before regression or progression takes place. The major finding for fluency is that it deteriorates on the +complex task. The dysfluency ratio revealed an intricate pattern in which temporary deterioration was observed in the complex task, but performance on the +complex task was as fluent as on the simple one, according to this measure. In the case of complexity of speech, both structural and lexical, on one measure per each of these dimensions, before speech production was boosted on the +complex task, it went through an intermediate stage of destabilization on the complex one. This means that cognitive complexity leads to an improvement but through a stage of decline. Accuracy is the only dimension in which gradual improvement from the simple to the +complex task can be observed. Accuracy seems to be the most firm of the dimensions in the sense that improvement in the +complex task was not preceded by a lower score on the complex one.

These patterns show that performance, even on a sequence of as few as three tasks, possibly goes through similar stages as the ones discovered to take place in the process of acquisition of a second language. When analysing performance on different tasks within the same measure, it can be observed that a range of different phenomena take place such as U-shaped behaviour, backsliding and generally sudden shifts in production (Kellerman, 1985). Linear progression from the simple task to the most complex one, which was the case in accuracy, is an exception rather than a rule. Nonlinear patterns are much more common, as was observed in the case of fluency. Even on such a short-term sequence, curves in production are far more common than continuous progression or regression, which illustrates the multifaceted nature of speech production. Performance shows quite unpredictable patterns when measured over a sequence, and it is noteworthy that if only the simple and the complex tasks had been taken into account, very different outcomes would have been revealed.

These patterns, or maybe lack thereof, reveal potentially interesting facts about how attention is allocated during task performance. Some dimensions of production are more susceptible to alterations over a sequence, due to an increase in cognitive complexity, than others. It may be the case that attention switches between the different complexity levels, and different cognitive complexity levels of tasks promote greater attention paid to one area than the other, but the different areas do not necessarily compete between each other.

Despite the intricate lines of performance, most noticeable differences were found between the complex task and the +complex task, which may suggest that it is between these two tasks that the differences in cognitive complexity were most salient. However, differences between the simple task and the complex one were also found, which confirms that generally in the task design employed in the current study the differences in the cognitive complexity were distinguishable enough to trigger changes in performance.

This piece of research confirmed a finding from previous research in the area of task complexity that a simultaneous manipulation of two variables, in this case reasoning demands and elements, leads to changes in performance and these are largely in line with the Cognition Hypothesis. Regardless of where exactly the differences lie, generally a considerable impact on speech was found for all the dimensions, which perhaps confirms that jointly operating variables have a more profound impact on performance than manipulating cognitive complexity along one single variable. Except for the results obtained for one structural complexity measure, this study also contributed evidence to the major claim behind the Cognition Hypothesis, that is, that increased cognitive complexity leads to increased accuracy and complexity, with fluency being negatively affected.

Research question 2: Is there interaction between task complexity and sequencing tasks from simple to complex?

The second research question aimed to investigate whether there is a relationship between cognitive complexity and the simple–complex sequencing order. This study did not find any short-term effects of sequencing on performance: no differences were found between the two sequencing groups investigated in the study, the simple–complex or the randomized one. It can therefore be stated that it is cognitive complexity of tasks, rather than the sequencing order in which tasks are administered, that leads to short-term qualitative changes in performance. Surprisingly, the current study revealed that a complex task, regardless of whether it is administered as the first, the second, or the third one over a sequence, still leads to qualitative changes, and the pattern of performance it triggers largely follows that predicted in the Cognition Hypothesis.

This finding is rather counter-intuitive insofar as it seems logical to assume that performing a simple activity prior to a more complex one should attenuate the burden of the complex one: in this study, the simple task could be expected to have a facilitative effect on performing the complex one. However, the results of this study suggest that learners stretch their linguistic repertoire so as to meet the demands of very complex tasks regardless of the kind of exposure immediately preceding the complex task, i.e. with no task performed prior to performance of a simple task. This result may suggest that the linguistic resources can be stretched and language can be restructured, and be more precise, when less of such support is available, or even when it is not available at all.

To my mind, however, this finding does not necessarily question the alleviative function of the simple–complex sequence but rather reveals potentially intriguing ways in which learners distribute their attention when faced with a randomized sequence of tasks. Dealing with complex activities, irrespective of where they are placed in a sequence, releases the linguistic potential inside the learners, leads to more testing potential hypotheses, and trying out new L2 forms. This, in turn, in the long run potentially leads to the internalization and development of new forms. Consequently, speech becomes more sophisticated at the lexical and structural level. At the same time, dealing with simple tasks, again, whichever their place in a sequence, makes learners stay in their linguistic comfort zone, using familiar forms and showing less risk-taking behaviour.

Surprisingly, it also makes them more subject to using non target-like forms, unlike in the case of complex tasks.

Conclusion

This study attempted to investigate two phenomena: the contribution of different complexity levels of tasks on performance, and the influence of sequencing (simple–complex versus randomized) on performance. Two major findings from this study are that: 1. Designed differences in cognitive task complexity affected the performance of speakers in the ways predicted by the Cognition Hypothesis; and 2. The order of administering tasks did not have a short-term influence on performance, as measured by general CAF measures. Regarding the first finding, the current study raises the issue of the importance of measuring performance beyond a dichotomy. In the current study, had the simple and the complex tasks been employed, the pattern of performance would have been quite different from the one observed when three tasks have been used. Regarding sequencing, although the current study did not find an effect of sequencing on performance, intricate patterns of performance can be observed over a sequence of tasks (e.g. patterns revealed in fluency). Overall, the results of this study therefore lend support to the Cognition Hypothesis when it comes to the contribution of the different complexity levels of tasks to production. However, regarding sequencing, the study failed to provide support to the idea that simple–complex sequencing necessarily facilitates performances. The role of sequencing in task-based teaching is an underresearched area, and in order to see how sequencing affects production over time, longer sequences of tasks would have to be employed, such that changes in performance can be tracked over time rather than in a short-term manner.

References

Cohen, J. (1988). *Statistical Power Analysis for the Behavioral Sciences*. Hillsdale, NJ: Erlbaum.

Ishikawa, T. (2008). *Investigating the Effect of Intentional Reasoning Demands on L2 Speech Production*. Unpublished Ph.D dissertation, Aoyama Gakuin University, Tokyo, Japan.

—— (2011). Examining the influence of intentional reasoning demands on learner perceptions of task difficulty and L2 monologic speech. In P. Robinson (ed.),

Second Language Task Complexity: Researching the Cognition Hypothesis of Language Learning and Performance (pp. 307–30). Philadelphia/Amsterdam: John Benjamins.

Kellerman, E. (1985). Input and second language acquisition theory. In S. Gass and C. Madden (eds), *Input in Second Language Acquisition* (pp. 345–53). Rowley, MA: Newbury House.

Kim, Y., and Tracy-Ventura, N. (2011). Task complexity, language anxiety, and the development of the simple past. In P. Robinson (ed.), *Second Language Task Complexity: Researching the Cognition Hypothesis of Language Learning and Performance* (pp. 287–308). Philadelphia/Amsterdam: John Benjamins.

Kuiken, F., Mos, M. and Vedder, I. (2005). Cognitive task complexity and second language writing performance. In S. Foster-Cohen, M. P. García-Mayo and J. Cenoz (eds), *Eurosla Yearbook*. Vol. 5 (pp. 195–222). Amsterdam: John Benjamins.

Lee, Y.-G. (2002). *Effects of Task Complexity on the Complexity and Accuracy of Oral Production in L2 Korean*. Unpublished doctoral dissertation, University of Hawai'i at Manoa, USA.

Malicka, A. and Levkina, M. (2012). Measuring task complexity. Does EFL proficiency matter? In A. Shehadeh and C. Coombe (eds) *Task-based Language Teaching in Foreign Language Contexts. Research and Implementation*. Amsterdam, Philadelphia: John Benjamins.

MacWhinney, B. (2000). *The CHILDES Project: Tools for Analyzing Talk*. Mahwah, NJ: Lawrence Erlbaum Associates.

Michel, M. (2011). *Cognitive and Interactive Aspects of Task-based Performance in Dutch as a Second Language*. 's-Hertogenbosch: Uitgeverij BOXPress.

Michel, M. C., Kuiken, F., and Vedder, I. (2007). The influence of complexity in monologic versus dialogic tasks in Dutch L2. *International Review of Applied Linguistics*, 45(3), 241–59.

Niwa, Y. (2000). *Reasoning Demands of L2 tasks and L2 Narrative Production: Effects of Individual Differences in Working Memory, Intelligence and Aptitude*. Unpublished M.A. dissertation, Aoyama Gakuin University, Tokyo, Japan.

Nuevo, A. (2006). *Task Complexity and Interaction: L2 Learning Opportunities and Development*. Unpublished doctoral dissertation, Georgetown University, USA.

Nuevo, A.-M., Adams, R., and Ross-Feldman, L. (2011). Task complexity, modified output, and L2 development in learner-learner interaction. In P. Robinson (ed.), *Second Language Task Complexity: Researching the Cognition Hypothesis of Language Learning and Performance* (pp. 175–202). Amsterdam, Philadelphia: John Benjamins.

Révész, A. (2011). Task complexity, focus on L2 constructions, and individual differences: A classroom-based study. *The Modern Language Journal*, 95, 162–81.

Robinson, P. (2001). Task complexity, task difficulty and task production: Exploring interactions in a componential framework. *Applied Linguistics*, 22(1), 27–57.

—— (2003). Attention and memory during SLA. In C. Doughty and M. H. Long (eds), *The Handbook of Second Language Acquisition* (pp. 631–78). Malden, MA: Blackwell.

—— (2005). Cognitive complexity and task sequencing: Studies in a componential framework for second language task design. *International Review of Applied Linguistics*, 43(1), 1–32.

—— (2007). Criteria for classifying and sequencing pedagogic tasks. In Maria del Pilar Garcia Mayo (ed.), *Investigating Tasks in Formal Language Learning* (pp. 7–26). Philadelphia, PA: Multilingual Matters.

—— (2010). Situating and distributing cognition across task demands: The SSARC model of pedagogic task sequencing. In L. Sicola and M. Putz (eds), *Cognitive Processing in Second Language Acquisition: Inside the Learner's Mind* (pp. 246–69). Amsterdam: John Benjamins.

Sasayama, S. and Izumi, S. (2012). Effects of task complexity and pre-task planning on Japanese EFL learners' oral production. In A. Shehadeh and C. Coombe (eds) *Task-based Language Teaching in Foreign Language Contexts. Research and Implementation*. Amsterdam, Philadelphia: John Benjamins.

Skehan, P. (1996). A framework for the implementation of task-based instruction. *Applied Linguistics*, 17, 38–62.

—— (1998). *A Cognitive Approach to Language Learning*. Oxford: Oxford University Press.

Skehan, P., and Foster, P. (2001). Cognition and tasks. In P. Robinson (ed.), *Cognition and Second Language Learning* (pp. 183–205). Cambridge: Cambridge University Press.

4

Task Complexity and Task Sequencing in Traditional Versus Online Language Classes

Melissa Baralt
Florida International University

Introduction

The primary claim of the Cognition Hypothesis is that cognitive complexity is the sole determining factor for which decisions on how to sequence tasks in the classroom should be made. Language learners should first carry out tasks that are cognitively simple (i.e., tasks that pose few demands on attention and memory), and then progress by carrying out tasks that gradually increase in complexity. So far, researchers have compared how learners' interaction and second language (L2) development may differ as a result of carrying out simple versus complex tasks (e.g., Baralt, 2013; Gilabert, Barón, and Llanes, 2009; Kim, 2012; Kim and Tracy-Ventura, 2011; Nuevo, 2006; Révész, 2009, 2011). To date, however, there is very little research on how cognitive complexity should be dispersed across a sequenced implementation of tasks, i.e., looking at which task sequencing orders are most effective. Also in need of empirical investigation is how task sequencing mediates learning in the online environment. A significant number of language learning courses are now online (e.g., Blake, 2011), yet research into task cognitive complexity has been almost exclusively limited to the traditional, face-to-face environment. The present chapter aims to contribute to this gap by examining the effects of cognitive complexity and task sequencing on learner interaction and L2 development in traditional and online Spanish foreign language courses.

Theoretical background: Cognition Hypothesis of task-based language teaching

For the past two decades, Robinson (e.g., 1995, 2001a, 2001b, 2007, 2011; Robinson and Gilabert, 2007) has developed his theory on how to design and sequence tasks.[1] The Cognition Hypothesis of Task-Based Language Teaching details a taxonomy of task design features, to include cognitive, interactive, ability and affective factors that mediate the efficacy of tasks. Robinson argues that cognitive complexity, or the 'attentional, memory, reasoning, and other information-processing demands' that are required of the language learner as a result of a task's design (Robinson, 2001b, p. 29), is the basis on which tasks should be designed to maximize language learning. There are two task design variables that comprise this construct. The first, resource-dispersing variables, mediate the way in which learners' attentional resources are allocated across non-linguistic aspects of the task. These task design features affect how learners access their developing L2 system, and can promote quicker retrieval and automatization of this access. An example is the task design feature '+/-planning time'. A simple task version (+planning time) would allow learners to have planning time before carrying out the task. They can think beforehand of the words they want to say and prepare for their task performance. The more complex version (-planning time) would eliminate this opportunity for planning time: learners would then have to carry out the task without being able to pre-plan their linguistic output.

The second variable, resource-directing features, has to do with how learners' attention can be directed to language during task performance. For example, '+/-intentional reasoning' is a design feature of a task that instills a functional need to use certain linguistic forms. No intentional reasoning would be the cognitively simple version of the task. Learners would simply have to relay information of an event without having to reflect on the intentions or reasons that caused people to do certain actions (i.e., 'John pushed Barry.'). Making the task more complex, '+intentional reasoning', would require this reflection (i.e., 'John pushed Barry because . . .'). Having to express why an event occurred in addition to reporting the event itself can channel learners' attention to the linguist features needed to express others' intentions. These kinds of functional task demands require attention to aspects of the L2 grammar system that make performing the task possible (i.e., reporting an emotion, conveying conjunctions with syntactic embedding, etc.), thereby encouraging awareness of forms.

Both resource-dispersing and resource-directing variables play a critical role in learning another language: L2 forms and the rapidity and ease with which these variables are accessed and communicated in real time. They form the foundation of the Cognition Hypothesis, which references interaction, uptake and learning opportunities (all essential constructs that facilitate language learning) as a result of their implementation:

> ... complex tasks lead to more interaction and uptake of linguistic forms that are relevant to the cognitive/conceptual demands of the task when these are made salient in the input, compared to simpler task versions, and so to more learning opportunities ...

> (Robinson, 2007, p. 195)

This claim on the differential effects of cognitively simple, versus cognitively complex, tasks has been empirically ascertained in a handful of studies (e.g., Baralt, 2013; Kim, 2012; Révész, 2009; Kim and Tracy-Ventura, 2011). In classroom contexts, Robinson argues that language learners be given an opportunity to perform a cognitively simple task first, and then perform a cognitively complex version of that same task. This will best set them up for target-like task performance and L2 development. A teacher should thus progressively increase the complexity level of pedagogic tasks, and such a sequence will prepare learners for the full complexity level of target tasks in the real world.

SSARC model of task sequencing

So far, this proposed *sequencing* of tasks, the real heart of the Cognition Hypothesis, has yet to be extensively researched. The gradual disbursement of cognitive complexity to prepare the learner to best perform real world tasks is where, theoretically speaking, language learning will be maximized. In 2010, Robinson laid out suggestions for how to design and sequence tasks in the classroom with his SSARC model of pedagogic task sequencing. SSARC,[2] in sum, implies giving learners tasks that are cognitively simple on all accounts first; then making them more complex along resource-dispersing lines (such as eliminating planning time) to promote control over what is already established in the L2; then making the task as complex as possible by implementing a resource-directing requirement to encourage form-meaning connections. Each stage should be replicated as many times as needed by learners until fully complex versions of the pedagogic task are performed successfully.

With the absence of empirical support for the SSARC model, some researchers have suggested that varying sequences of task complexity may be best, perhaps depending on the task type, learner and saliency of forms needed to successfully carry out the task. Nuevo, Adams and Ross-Feldman (2011), for example, suggest a 'spiral syllabus model' when sequencing tasks for learners (p. 198). This was based on their mixed findings of task complexity efficacy and how it differentially mediates learner modified output with different task types. Robinson has also highlighted the possibility that non-linear sequences, or even U-shaped sequences of complexity (i.e., complex, simple, complex), may be more effective (Robinson, 2011, p. 18). Clearly, research is needed on different sequencing orders to inform second language acquisition and L2 syllabus design.

Considering tasks and task sequencing for online language learning

In addition to more examinations of how to sequence tasks, researchers have called for investigations on the online language learning environment, and how this mediates task design and task sequencing efficacy (see Lai and Li, 2011, for an excellent review on technology and task-based language teaching). Given the rapid increase in post-secondary course enrollment in the United States, with over 25 percent of university-level classes online (Blake, 2011), this is an essential empirical need. Ortega (2009) has even called the inclusion of synchronous online communication in language teaching an 'ethical imperative' (p. 248). In response to this, universities are now offering web-facilitated courses, fully online courses, and even hybrid options that might include both traditional and online interaction (Blake, 2011). One platform in the online environment that has gained particular attention for foreign language teaching is synchronous computer-mediated communication, or SCMC chat. SCMC is a real-time written conversation over the Internet. It is a medium during which interaction, focus on form, and feedback take place – all mechanisms of interaction that facilitate second language acquisition. In fact, SCMC can even be more effective at focus on form than face-to-face, often resulting in more accurate production by learners (e.g., Böhlke, 2003; Lai and Zhao, 2006; Yilmaz and Yuksel, 2011; see discussions by Chun, 2013, and Lai and Li, 2011). This is because its written nature often provides additional processing time for learners to formulate their output. Another benefit of SCMC is the alleviation it can pose to working memory capacity constraints. While face-to-face interaction requires that input be held and processed in working memory, input provided in SCMC (to include corrective feedback) is there to stay, and can be revisited by scrolling up in the chat (e.g., Ayoun, 2004; Baralt, 2013; de la Fuente, 2003; González-Lloret, 2003; Lai and Zhao, 2006; Lee, 2001; Shekary and Tahririan, 2006; Smith, 2008).

Inherent to this benefit is one particularly unique characteristic of SCMC: delayed interaction-based turn-taking, which Ortega (2009) refers to as 'disrupted turn adjacency' (p. 228). This feature does have some benefits; for example, learners can take advantage of the delay in having to respond to input and formulate (as well as modify) their message before sending a response. A disadvantage of delayed turn-taking is the way it sets up corrective feedback as a response to learner errors. Learner noticing and awareness of forms is essential for second language acquisition (Schmidt, 1995), and SCMC's delayed turn-taking can result in learners' missing the correction. Lai and Zhao (2006) discuss this in detail, referring to the phenomenon observed in their data as 'non-contingent recasts' (see Lai, Fei and Roots, 2008; Smith, 2003). For online language classes, delayed turn-taking may render large-group chats particularly difficult because the teacher cannot maintain control of the interactions (e.g., Loewen and Erlam, 2006) or ensure the contingency of feedback after errors.

So far, there is very little research on how cognitive complexity is realized in online language learning, and specifically, how SCMC's delayed turn-taking works alongside more complex tasks. Only one study (Baralt, 2013) has examined the efficacy of feedback in conjunction with simple versus complex tasks in both the face-to-face and SCMC environments. In a pre-test-post-test-delayed post-test design, 84 learners of intermediate-level Spanish FL carried out two cognitively simple or cognitively complex tasks one-on-one with the researcher. Cognitive complexity was operationalized as +/-intentional reasoning, and all participants received recasts on the form essential to the task's demands: the Spanish past subjunctive. Baralt found that in the face-to-face mode, the complex task resulted in significantly more learning (measured by two interactive tasks and a multiple-choice test). In the SCMC mode, the complex task resulted in hardly any development. Rather, the cognitively *simple* task worked best in SCMC. Increased cognitive complexity in SCMC therefore did not have the same positive effects on learning as it did in face-to-face, and this was due to feedback episodes misplaced in noncontingent turn-taking, coupled with cognitive overload due to the task demands. Judging from these results, it could be argued that during a cognitively simple task in SCMC, attention to form is indeed amplified. During a cognitively complex task in SCMC however, attention is too dispersed to be allocated to form. If it is the case that cognitive complexity does not work in online environments, this must be attested in order to inform task design for online language teaching. As more online courses are being developed for language teaching, researchers and practitioners must examine tasks that are theorized to promote second language acquisition in the face-to-face mode, and test how they work differently online. To reiterate Lai and Li's (2011) point, this may also require a reevaluation of theoretical paradigms most appropriate for language teaching tasks in the SCMC mode.

Research on the construct of cognitive complexity in the face-to-face environment

In line with this goal, a quick summary of research on how cognitive complexity affects the language learning process is necessary. Note that almost all of these studies have been done in the face-to-face mode only. Two lines of research have examined (1) how cognitive complexity mediates L2 development (e.g., Baralt, 2013; Kim, 2012; Kim and Tracy-Ventura, 2011; Nuevo, 2006; Révész, 2009), and (2) how it mediates features of interaction theorized to promote second language acquisition (e.g., Gilabert, Barón and Llanes, 2009; Kim, 2009, 2012; Nuevo et al., 2011; Révész, 2011; Robinson, 2001b, 2007). The findings of these two strands of literature will be briefly summarized here, followed by a more detailed summary of the investigations by Nuevo et al. (2011), Révész (2011), and Kim (2012), given their direct relevance to the present study.

Cognitive complexity and L2 development

Of the five studies published on cognitive complexity and L2 development, four found that more cognitive complex tasks result in statistically more learning than cognitively simple tasks (Baralt, 2013; Kim, 2012; Kim and Tracy-Ventura, 2011; Révész, 2009). Nuevo (2006) did not find an effect for more complex tasks. These studies' contexts, means of operationalization of cognitive complexity, dependent variables, and interactive factors are summarized below in Table 4.1. In general, these results show support for Robinson's claims about cognitive complexity's capacity to enhance attention to and internalization of form inherent to a task's demands.

Table 4.1 Studies examining the effects of cognitive complexity on L2 development

Study	Context	Task made more complex by	Interactive set-up	Results
Baralt (2013)	Spanish as a FL	+ intentional reasoning	Learners paired with researcher	Complex groups in FTF and simple groups in SCMC achieved greatest gains in past subjunctive
Kim (2012)	EFL	+ causal reasoning (+C); + causal reasoning and +few elements (++C)	Learners paired with learners	++Complex groups had greatest gains in question formation and past tense
Kim and Tracy-Ventura (2011)	EFL	+ reasoning, - few elements	Learners paired with learners	++Complex group had highest gains on past tense
Nuevo (2006)	ESL	+ causal reasoning	Learners paired with learners	No difference in groups' acquisition of past tense or locative prepositions
Révész (2009)	EFL	– here-and-now	Learners paired with researcher	Complex groups with recasts achieved highest gains in past progressive

Cognitive complexity and interaction

The second group of studies has examined how increased cognitive complexity differentially mediates features of conversational interaction. In general, this line of research has shown that increasing the cognitive complexity of a task will generate more 'learning opportunities', as Robinson predicts. 'Learning opportunities' have been operationalized in several ways, including learners' language-related episodes (LREs), metalinguistic talk, and hypothesis formation during a task. In general, learners appear to do more of this during interaction as a task's level of cognitive complexity increases, but it may depend on task type (Nuevo et al., 2011). Table 4.2 below provides a visual summary of this research strand.

Of all of the studies reviewed above, Nuevo et al. (2011), Révész (2011) and Kim (2012) were the only ones conducted in natural classroom environments. Nuevo et al. (2011) examined how cognitive complexity mediates modified output (whether self-initiated or collaboratively with a peer), and whether or not modified output predicted L2 development. Seventy-nine learners of ESL carried

Table 4.2 Studies examining the effects of cognitive complexity on interaction

Study	Context	Task made more complex by	Interactive set-up	Results
Kim (2009)	EFL	+ reasoning, - few elements	Learners paired with learners	Significantly more LREs in +reasoning task, more resolution of LREs in complex tasks overall
Kim (2012)	EFL	+ reasoning, - few elements	Learners paired with learners	Significantly more LREs and more advancement in ESL question formation in most complex tasks
Gilabert, Barón and Llanes (2009)	EFL	- here-and-now, - few elements, + causal reasoning	Learners paired with learners	Significantly more LREs and repairs, and significantly more clarification requests in complex tasks, but task type made a difference
Nuevo (2006)	ESL	+ causal reasoning	Learners paired with learners	Significantly more hypothesis formation in complex tasks (on one task type)
Nuevo, Adams and Ross-Feldman (2011)	ESL	+ causal reasoning, + intentional reasoning, + spatial reasoning	Learners paired with learners	Significantly more individual self-repair in complex tasks (decision-making task only)
Révész (2011)	EFL	+ reasoning, - few elements	Learners paired with learners	Significantly more LREs and metalingustic task in complex tasks
Robinson (2001b)	EFL	- few elements	Learners paired with learners	Significantly more confirmation checks in complex tasks
Robinson (2007b)	EFL	+ intentional reasoning	Learners paired with learners	Significantly more turns, clarification requests, confirmation checks, and partial uptake in complex tasks

out three different tasks with a peer in class. The tasks included a decision-making task (placing people at a table based on their personalities and likes) and a narrative task (sequencing the correct order of pictures). Cognitive complexity was operationalized as +/-intentional reasoning and +/-spatial reasoning for the decision-making task, and +/-causal reasoning for the narrative task. Learning was measured with an oral performance task and a grammaticality judgment test. Nuevo et al. found that performing the cognitively complex task resulted in more self-repair, but for the decision-making task only. And, if learners produced more self-repair, they were more likely to show development on the grammaticality test. There were no differences found for the narrative task, however. The researchers concluded by suggesting that the different types of modified output may make a difference, and perhaps some work best congruently with cognitively simple tasks, while others work best with cognitively complex tasks.

Révész (2011) as well as Kim (2012) looked at the occurrence of language-related episodes (LREs), which are 'any part of a dialogue where the students talk about the language they are producing, question their language use, or correct themselves or others' (Swain and Lapkin, 1998, p. 326). LREs are a conscious reflection on language that emerges from learners' collaborative task-based work together, making them an effective way to operationalize learning opportunities as a result of more complex tasks. In both studies, the researchers found that more cognitively complex tasks in the classroom result in more LREs. In Révész's (2011) study, 43 learners of ESL worked in self-selected groups (3–4 people per group) in class and had to complete two decision-making tasks. For the simple task, learners had to decide upon three charity programs to which they would give $500,000. The complex version was double the amount of money and involved choosing between six programs, with harder decision-making factors involved. Cognitive complexity was thus operationalized as +reasoning and -few elements. Révész found that the more complex task in class resulted in significantly more LREs and metalinguistic talk (i.e., students focusing explicitly on language during the task, which can be beneficial for learning), lending support to the Cognition Hypothesis.

Kim's (2012) study examined how resolved LREs during class time resulted in L2 development. One of the only longitudinal studies on cognitive complexity, she looked at the effects of cognitive complexity on interaction and learning in four intact EFL class across an entire semester. In a pre-test-post-test design, Kim operationalized cognitive complexity along a continuum: simple, +complex, and ++complex. She developed 12 different tasks (four for each class) in relation to the course themes. Learners performing the simple task only had to exchange information. The +complex version required learners to suggest appropriate part-time jobs for each student, considering only a few background variables (+few elements). Learners performing the ++complex version also had to suggest part-time jobs, but they had to base their decision on more factors (-few elements). In all, 191 learners of EFL paired with a partner in class and were recorded each time they performed the tasks. Kim found that the most complex task version resulted in significantly more LREs during class time, and led to significantly more advancement in their production of English question formation.

The data from these studies suggest that more cognitively complex tasks in the FL classroom may push learners to pay more attention to language, leading to more learning and thus confirming predictions of the Cognition Hypothesis. This could be dependent on task type (e.g., Nuevo et al., 2011). It is still not known, however, whether tasks of increased complexity will have this same positive result on student-produced LREs and learning in online FL classes.

The one study published so far on how cognitive complexity works in the online environment suggests that the predictions of the Cognition Hypothesis may not hold in the SCMC mode (Baralt, 2013). As Baralt's study was laboratory-based, its generalizability to natural classroom contexts, to include online classes, is limited. In addition, there is no research as yet on how tasks should be sequenced in a classroom setting, both traditional and online.

Justification for the present study

The goal of the present study is to address this gap by examining the effects of cognitive complexity and task sequencing in both online and traditional (face-to-face) classrooms. Following the SSARC model, this study examines the effects of different sequences of task complexity, as well as U-shaped sequences (simple, complex, simple, and vice-versa), via the following research questions.

Research questions

1. How do different sequences of cognitive complexity impact students' learning opportunities for the Spanish past subjunctive during task-based, learner-learner interaction in:

    (a) traditional, face-to-face classrooms versus
    (b) online classrooms?

2. How do different sequences of cognitive complexity impact students' L2 development of the Spanish past subjunctive in:

(a) traditional, face-to-face classrooms versus
(b) online classrooms?

Method

Participants

Ninety-four students of intermediate-level Spanish FL at a large, public university in the eastern United States participated in the study. Four sections of the same course, Spanish Intermediate II, were selected for the study. Two of the classes were taught traditionally (i.e., face-to-face) and met three times a week in a classroom. The other two classes were taught online. Students in these classes had to log on three times a week for online class 'meetings', while the remaining half of the course requirement (such as online exercises) could be completed individually. The online class students had to meet in person for their class assessment days (i.e., all oral and written exams had to be taken in a classroom on campus); these were their only face-to-face meetings. Total enrollments for each class were: 32 students (traditional class), 16 (traditional class), 24 (online class) and 22 (online class). Both traditional and online classes used the same textbook and followed the same syllabus. The classes were taught in a foreign language department that promoted communicative language teaching.

Operationalization and sequencing of task complexity

The tasks chosen for this study were story retells, where students first read a section of a story in their L1 (English) and then had to retell that section together in the target language (Spanish). The task input was 12 small cards: six that had a brief blurb of a story written on them in English (students' L1), and six that were a comic strip picture. The tasks were two-way in that they required participants to read the L1 story blurb silently to themselves, and then go on to the comic strip picture to retell the story as accurately as possible in the past and in Spanish with their partner.[3]

To operationalize cognitive complexity, +/- intentional reasoning was implemented as a task demand in three interactive tasks for students to perform in pairs during class time. Two versions of each task were created: a cognitively simple and a cognitively complex one. In the simple task version, characters' intentional reasons (such as emotions, mental states, etc.) were already provided in both the L1 blurb and in the comic picture. Learners simply had to retell the story and the intentional reasons given. In the complex version, the intentional reasons were not provided. Learners who performed the complex task were informed that for some of the characters' actions in the story, they would also have to think about and express the cause behind that action. Intentional reasoning was elicited with an empty yellow thought bubble in the comic strip. +/-Intentional reasoning is resource-directing because it directs learners' attention to aspects of linguistic code that are needed in order to communicate such reasons: *was angry that, was jealous that, wanted,* etc., followed by the complex syntactic embedding that comes with communicating these mental states. In the Spanish language, expressing the intentional reasons of others in the past is naturally accompanied by the past subjunctive. Subjunctive marking (mood) is required on verbs in the dependent clause position when modality expressed in the primary clause verb mandates its use. Intentional reasons or verbs of volition are one example of how modality is realized, i.e., *Estaba molesto de que Juan **dijera** una mentira* (He was angry that John **told** a lie).

As opposed to earlier studies where learners completed a simple *or* a complex task (e.g., Baralt, 2013; Kim, 2012; Révész, 2009) learners in the present study performed both simple and complex tasks in one of four sequences: (1) simple, simple, complex (SSC); (2) complex, complex, simple (CCS); (3) complex, simple, complex (CSC); and (4) simple, complex, simple (SCS). This was for the purpose of testing the SSARC model, as well as Robinson's (2011) proposition on the possible differential effects of complex sequences, simple sequences, and/or even U-shaped sequences.

It is important to point out here that at the onset of the study, students in all four classes had spent three lessons carrying out tasks that naturally required the present subjunctive in Spanish. They had had one lesson on the present subjunctive (with explicit explanation done in class on the concept of modality, followed by mood), and had completed several communicative tasks in class (or online) that required the present subjunctive. With their instructor, students had briefly reviewed the past subjunctive in the class lesson before the experiment began, but had not done any communicative tasks with the form yet. Thus, a key difference between the participants in this study versus the participants in Baralt's (2013) study is prior exposure of the form. In Baralt's (2013) study, participants had never covered the past subjunctive and received discrete-item feedback in the form of recasts by an expert interlocutor (the researcher) during the experiment. Participants in the present study had reviewed the past subjunctive in class with their teacher, and for the tasks, were paired with a peer (one of their classmates).

Assessment materials

To measure students' use of the Spanish past subjunctive, two tasks, one paired oral production task and one paired written production task, were designed. Three different versions of each were created for the pre-test, post-test 1, and post-test 2. The assessment tasks were also story retell tasks in which students had to read a short blurb in their L1 and then retell it as best as they could collaboratively. The stories were different from the treatment tasks so as to avoid task repetition effects. The oral production tasks were recorded with a digital recorder, while the written production tasks were written out on a piece of paper. For both, the task outcome was successful completion of retelling the entire story, collaboratively, with an MP3 recording or a written out story to show for it.

Equipment

Equipment for this study included 16 Olympus© digital audio recorders which were used to record students' pair interaction in the traditional classes. For the online classes, one of the university's computer laboratories was used. The lab contained 32 PCs computers all equipped with the Genesis™ Language Lab System software.[4] This software has several educational tools; for the present study, the SCMC text-based chat tool as well as the Genesis™ virtual recorder were used. The chat tool was the platform with which students in the online classes interacted with each other, and the virtual recorder captured and recorded each student's screen activity during the tasks.

Procedure

The study was carried out over two weeks and during class time. On the first day, each classroom teacher guided students in their class to carry out the oral production task and the written production task in pairs. This data served as the pre-test. The traditional classes met in their regular classrooms, while the online classes met in the computer lab for the duration of the experiment.[5] Days two, three, and four of the experiment were three class meetings in a row during which students performed the experimental tasks with their partner in class. These three meetings served as the treatment. Learners in the traditional classes did all three retell tasks in person with a classmate, while learners in the online classes did all three tasks online via SCMC chat with a classmate. All learners worked with the same partner throughout the duration of the study. On day four, after the treatment task had been completed, students carried out an oral production and a written production task with their partner, which served as the

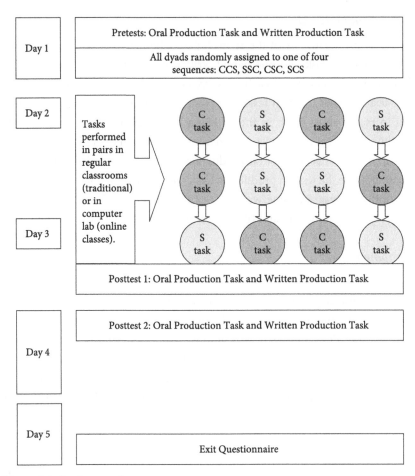

Figure 4.1 Study procedure

post-test 1 data. The final day of the study took place one week later, where students, in the same pairs, completed the last version of the oral and written production tasks (post-test 2 data). They then filled out a brief exit questionnaire. The study procedure can be seen in Figure 4.1.

Coding and analyses

Two dependent variables were coded for and analyzed in this study: learning opportunities, operationalized as language-related episodes (LREs), and L2 development. First, LREs were identified in the transcribed recordings from the face-to-face interaction and from the SCMC chat transcripts. Following Kim (2012), only those LREs that involved the targeted linguistic item, the Spanish past subjunctive, were coded for. This was for the purpose of identifying those collaborative learning opportunities in which learners paid attention to the past subjunctive and that would presumably affect L2 development of that form. An example of an LRE between two students from the present study is provided below in example 1.[6]

1. A. *Sra. Martínez dudaba que . . .* (Sra. Martínez doubted that . . .)

   B. *. . . que ella roba?* (that she steals-IND?)

   A. Wait but it has to be past tense. *¿Robó?* (She stole-IND [preterite]?)

   B. Or maybe *robaba?* (stole-IND [imperfect])?

   A. But wait . . . it's doubt . . . 'cause *dudaba* (doubted) . . . do you think this has to be the subjunctive?

   B. Hmmm. *¿Robe?* (she steals-SUB?)

   A. So then it'd be *Sra. Martínez dudaba que ella robe.* (Sra. Martínez doubted that she steals-SUB.)

   B. Yeah.

L2 development was determined by learners' use of the past subjunctive on the oral and on the written production tasks (at post-test 1 and post-test 2). As is suggested in Norris and Ortega (2009), a developmentally sensitive coding system was employed for the coding of this variable. For each obligatory instance on the assessment tests, zero points were given if students used indicative verb forms, half a point was given if the students used the present subjunctive, and a full point was assigned if students produced the past subjunctive.[7] This weighted system of coding is suggested to more robustly account for interlanguage development and emergence of forms in a learner's linguistic system, as opposed to scoring their production against native-like use (Baralt, 2013; Norris and Ortega, 2009; Révész, 2009).

For inter-rater reliability, 20 percent of the LRE and L2 development data (selected randomly) was coded by another rater. The rater was an applied linguist with three years of experience conducting research in second language acquisition. She was also bilingual in English and Spanish. Cohen's kappa for LREs on the past subjunctive was .86, and for L2 development, .96.

Factorial ANOVAs were performed to statistically compare the number of LREs produced by the different task sequence groups in each classroom environment (traditional and online), while repeat-measures ANOVAS were performed to statistically compare L2 development. All analyses were done with the statistical program SPSS version 21, and normal distribution of data was confirmed before carrying out parametric tests. Effect sizes are reported for each analysis.

Results

Descriptive statistics for LREs

The first research question asked how different task sequences affect learning opportunities – operationalized as learner-produced LREs targeting the Spanish past subjunctive during task performance – in a traditional versus an online class setting. Table 4.3 below presents the descriptive statistics for the average number of student-produced LREs according to the task complexity sequence they were assigned. A visual inspection of the data shows a marked difference in LRE production depending on the classroom environment. While a range of LREs was produced in the different task sequences in the traditional face-to-face classroom, not a single LRE was produced by any of the learners in the online classes, regardless of task sequence order. Looking at the face-to-face data more closely, additional patterns were present according to the specific task sequence completed: learners who carried out the face-to-face task sequence complex-complex-simple (CCS) produced the highest average of LREs: 17. The next highest were those students who did the complex-simple-complex (CSC) sequence, with an average of 15. The remaining two sequences, simple-complex-simple (SCS) and then simple-simple-complex (SSC), produced less than half of that amount, at six and four average LREs, respectively. This indicated that the classroom environment, traditional versus online, differentially mediated

Table 4.3 Descriptive statistics for LREs

Classroom environment	Task sequence performed	Average number of LREs produced across entire task sequence
Traditional, face-to-face	SSC: simple-simple-complex ($N = 12$)	4
	CCS: complex-complex-simple ($N = 12$)	17
	SCS: simple-complex-simple ($N = 12$)	7
	CSC: complex-simple-complex ($N = 12$)	15
Online	SSC: simple-simple-complex ($N = 12$)	0
	CCS: complex-complex-simple ($N = 12$)	0
	SCS: simple-complex-simple ($N = 12$)	0
	CSC: complex-simple-complex ($N = 10$)	0

students' LREs during task performance. Second, it appeared that performing the complex task version more (i.e., task sequences with more opportunities to do the complex task version SCC, or the CSC) is what generated the most LREs, as opposed to any specific task sequence order.

Statistical analyses for LREs

Statistical analyses confirmed these observed differences. Results from a 2×2 factorial ANOVA examining the effects of classroom environment and task sequence on students' production of LREs found a statistical effect for the interaction between the two independent variables $(F, (3, 86) = 59.1, p = 0.0,$ partial eta-squared = .67, power = 1.0). This interaction effect implied that only when the classroom environment was traditional (i.e. face-to-face), the task sequence order that students performed made a difference in how many learning opportunities (i.e. LREs) were generated. In face-to-face, those students who did either the CCS or the CSC task sequences produced significantly more LREs than students who performed the SSC or SCS sequences (compare the group means of M = 17 and 15, to M = 4 and 6, respectively). However, there were no statistical differences between the CCS and CSC sequences, nor between the SSC and SCS sequences. When the classroom environment was online, the task sequencing effect on the production of LREs was null, because no such learning opportunities took place amongst learners in this environment. Thus, to answer research question 1, the task sequences with two complex tasks (CCS and CSC) generated significantly more production of LREs in student pair-work, but in traditional, face-to-face classrooms only.

Descriptive statistics for L2 development

The second research question investigated how different task sequences affect learning in a traditional versus online class setting. The descriptive statistics for students' use of the Spanish past subjunctive on the oral and written post-test 1 and 2 are provided below in Table 4.4. Once again, a visual inspection of this data shows a discrepancy between the traditional versus online class environment. In the traditional classrooms, those learners who performed the complex-complex-simple (CCS) and complex-simple-complex (CSC) task sequences with a partner demonstrated slightly more use of the Spanish past subjunctive on both the oral and written post-tests (at time 1 and 2) than the other two sequence groups, though overall, their production of the form was low. Students in the online

Table 4.4 Descriptive statistics for L2 development

Classroom environment	Task sequence performed	Oral production		Written production	
		Post-test 1	Post-test 2	Post-test 1	Post-test 2
Traditional, face-to-face	SSC: simple-simple-complex (N = 12)	0.5	0.5	0.5	0.5
	CCS: complex-complex-simple (N = 12)	2.0	1.0	2.5	1.5
	SCS: simple-complex-simple (N = 12)	1.0	0.5	1.0	0.5
	CSC: complex-simple-complex (N = 12)	1.5	1.0	2.0	1.0
Online	SSC: simple-simple-complex (N = 12)	0	0	0	0
	CCS: complex-complex-simple (N = 12)	0	0	0	0
	SCS: simple-complex-simple (N = 12)	0	0	0	0
	CSC: complex-simple-complex (N = 10)	0	0	0	0

classes, regardless of the sequence in which tasks were performed, did not produce the subjunctive form on any of the assessments.

Statistical analyses for L2 development

To see if these group differences were statistical, repeat-measures ANOVAs were run with class environment and sequence option set as the independent variables.

Oral post-tests

The ANOVA results showed a statistical triple interaction effect for class environment and sequence option on the oral post-test (F, $(6, 172) = 6.84$, $p = 0.0$, partial eta-squared = .19, power = .99). On the oral post-test 1 and post-test 2, students' use of the subjunctive depended on both class environment and task sequence order. Only in the face-to-face traditional classes, students who performed the complex-complex-simple (CCS) or complex-simple-complex

(CSC) task sequences attempted to use the Spanish past subjunctive statistically more than those who did the two sequence options with more of the simple tasks (SSC and SCS). Post-hoc Scheffé tests confirmed differences between each of the CCS and CSC task sequence groups and the two SSC and SCS groups (with mean scores of 2.0 and 1.5 on post-test 1, compared to 0.5 and 1.0, respectively). In general, group scores lowered slightly by post-test 2 (with mean scores at 1.0 for both the CCS and CSC groups, and 0.5 for both the SSC and SCS groups), however, the pattern of more use of the form in both the CCS and CSC groups stayed the same. There were no statistical differences between these two groups (CCS and CSC), which meant that the task sequencing order did not lead to differential learning. Rather, it was having the opportunity to carry out more complex tasks within a sequence (either CCS or CSC) that resulted in more L2 development of the subjunctive. Lastly, if students were in the online class, the task sequence did not make a difference: in the online classroom environment, students did not produce the subjunctive on the oral post-tests.

Written post-tests

Results from the repeat-measures ANOVA also showed a statistical triple interaction between class environment, task sequence order, and scores from the written post-tests (F, $(6, 172) = 17.37$, $p = 0.0$, partial eta-squared = .38, power = 1.0). As with the oral assessment tasks, students' use of the past subjunctive on the written post-tests depended on both their classroom environment and the task sequence order that they performed in class. Only in the traditional face-to-face classrooms were there differences. Those students who performed either the complex-complex-simple (CCS) or complex-simple-complex (CSC) tasks used the past subjunctive statistically more than those who did the simple-simple-complex (SSC) or simple-complex-simple (SCS) task sequences. Post-hoc Sheffé tests showed that the CCS resulted in significantly more uses than both the SSC and SCS sequences, and that performing the CSC sequence resulted in more uses of the subjunctive than the SSC and SCS groups, respectively. There were no statistical differences between the CCS or CSC groups. This implied that once again, there was no difference between the task sequence order of CCS versus CSC; rather, it was performing more versions of the cognitively complex tasks in a sequence than cognitively simple tasks. Finally, the order of task sequencing made no difference in the online classes, because students who interacted in that environment did not use the subjunctive on either of the written post-tests.

Results summary

An effect for task sequencing on learning opportunities and subsequent L2 development was found in this study. However, as opposed to a specific task sequence, those sequences that contained more complex tasks (CCS, CSC) generated the most production of LREs (compared to sequences with more options to perform simple tasks: SSC, SCS). This same finding applied to learning outcome as well. Critically, this finding was exclusive to the face-to-face, traditional classes. The online class learners who performed the tasks in SCMC – regardless of task sequence – did not produce any LREs or show any subsequent L2 development of the past subjunctive on the assessments.

Discussion

This study sought to examine if different sequences of cognitive complexity would differentially affect interaction-based learning opportunities and resultant L2 development, and whether or not a task sequencing effect would be the same in traditional compared to online classrooms. In the traditional face-to-face classes, two task sequences resulted in the highest number of LREs and L2 development on the oral and written post-tests: complex-complex-simple (CCS) and complex-simple-complex (CSC). There were no significant differences between these sequences. This implied that it was in-class performance of the greatest number of cognitively complex task versions (either CCS or CSC), as opposed to a specific sequence, that made a difference. In the online class environment, it did not matter which task sequence was performed by students. Regardless of sequence (CCS, CSC, SSC, SCS), not one LRE, or any use of the subjunctive, emerged from their interaction. This finding suggests that a cognitively complex task, theorized and shown to generate more learning opportunities and uptake of form in the face-to-face mode, does not have the same effect in the online environment.

In a review on SCMC research, Ortega (2009) has highlighted the fact that negotiation sequences are not as abundant in SCMC as we may think. She exemplified this with reviews of studies finding very low (e.g., Warschauer, 1996) and very high levels of negotiation in SCMC (e.g., Tudini, 2007), leading Ortega to conclude that contextual factors such as task type and interactant set-up (i.e., dyads versus groups) may be one reason for this variability. The findings reported here support Ortega's conjectures. First, when it comes to design effects in SCMC for learning opportunities, tasks that are more cognitively complex are not effective in the SCMC environment. Second, the participant set-up (peers interacting with peers) could have also mediated the results due to various factors (discussed below).

The data from this study also corroborate Baralt's (2013) finding that cognitive complexity does not appear to work in SCMC in the same way as it does face-to-face. In both the present study and in Baralt (2013), the cognitively complex tasks generated more observed negotiation work, heightened attention to form, and incorporation of the form necessary to complete the task (i.e., learning), but in the face-to-face mode only. One major difference between the studies, however, is the efficacy of the *simple* task in the online environment. In Baralt (2013), the cognitively simple task was very effective in the SCMC mode, and led to the most learning of the past subjunctive. In the present study, learners who performed more of the simple tasks online (sequences SSC or SCS) did not produce a single LRE together, nor attempted to use the targeted form on the assessments. These discordant results are surprising. A possible explanation for these differences has to do with how learners perceive their interlocutor's proficiency level, supporting Ortega's point on interactant set-up for SCMC. In Baralt (2013), learners interacted one-on-one with an expert (the researcher), who provided them with corrective recasts. This power relationship, alongside SCMC's capacity to enhance focus on form during a simple task (visual, re-visitable corrections that stay permanently on the screen), greatly amplified noticing of the form. In the present study, it may be the case that learners did not view each other as providers of feedback, or did not know enough about the form to be able to give feedback, and/or were not socially comfortable correcting a peer. Lai and Zhao (2006) reported on similar perception factors in their study as well, based on their participants' reports of disliking their peers' inability to provide corrections. Lai and Zhao have called for more research on how learners' perceptions of their interlocutor's capacity to give feedback can affect noticing of feedback, and the data reported on here certainly support this idea and need.

In regard to Robinson's Cognition Hypothesis and SSARC model for task sequencing, this study found that sequence options with the highest instances of complex tasks were the most effective. So far, there has been no research on cognitive complexity dispersed across different task sequence orders. Rather, a plethora of studies has compared the efficacy of simple versus complex tasks, and in general, the more complex tasks have had a consistent effect on learning opportunities (e.g., Kim, 2009, 2012; Révész, 2011) and L2 development (Kim,

2012; Révész, 2009; Baralt, 2013). The present study appears to support this strand of research, that more complex tasks – and not necessarily a specific sequence of tasks – are more effective for interaction-based language learning. What's more, the results reported here support Robinson's suggestion that U-shaped sequences may also be effective; perhaps such sequences (or even 'spiral' sequences, e.g., Nuevo et al., 2011) are particularly advantageous because they resemble learners' own developing interlanguage trajectories. It would be intriguing to pursue this notion in future empirical investigations.

Limitations

This study does not go without limitations. The first has to do with the previously discussed topic of interlocutor. As discussed above, it is possible that same-proficiency partners did not see themselves as being providers of feedback, and this could have affected the results. All dyadic partners were learners' classmates as well as their social peers. On the exit questionnaire, 'Lack of feedback', 'I never knew if I was making a mistake or not', and 'I hated not being corrected' were the common complaints of students who performed the tasks online. Contrarily, learners from the traditional, face-to-face classrooms had zero complaints, and, overall, reported enjoying the tasks. This finding underscores the importance of considering interlocutor roles and interactant-related variables that, arguably, may mediate the way in which task demands (to include cognitive complexity) and learning opportunities work in tandem.

That not one LRE emerged from the online students' collaborations was a surprising result from this study. However, this conventional construct so often researched in face-to-face TBLT literature may need to be expanded in the SCMC environment. For example, students' familiarity with interaction – which is heavily encouraged in the traditional classes – may have something to do with their comfort and habit about talking about language. The face-to-face, traditional classroom learners may have been much more comfortable and familiar with interactive tasks, resulting in their capacity to focus on language together (in the form of LREs). As one reviewer pointed out, these learners may have also viewed face-to-face tasks as more institutionalized traditional classroom activities, where attention to form and LREs are encouraged. On the other hand, the online language learners could have seen their SCMC tasks as more of a communicative medium, less constrained by classroom walls and a place where focus on form, at least in the way it realizes itself in traditional mediums, is not germane to the SCMC environment. Lai and Li (2011) have argued that communicative competence in technology-enhanced TBLT may also need to refer to institutional and environmental competences inherent to using SCMC. They, as well as Ortega (2009), point out the need to extend the theoretical paradigms(s) we use to define and operationalize online constructs that can promote second language acquisition. Examples include digital literacies, learner identity development, and play (Lai and Li, 2011, p. 10). It is possible that these SCMC-specific constructs were acquired but were not accounted for or measured in this study.

Another possible limitation has to do with the targeted linguistic item. The Spanish past subjunctive has very low saliency and does not exist in English (students' L1). Albeit non-target-like, learners can still get their meaning across by retelling a story in the past without marking the verbs with subjunctive morphology. This raises the question of functional need of the form versus a focus on form. Following the Cognition Hypothesis, increased cognitive complexity in tasks should instill a functional need for a specific form, and use of this form is the only means by which the task can be successfully performed. For grammatical forms such as the Spanish subjunctive, however, an external focus on form (as opposed to a learner-generated recognition of a linguistic deficiency) may be imperative to promote awareness of it. That may explain why the task worked differently in SCMC in Baralt (2013), because learners were paired with an expert interlocutor who provided them with recasts in the form of discrete-item feedback after each erroneous usage (i.e. verbs not marked with the subjunctive). For learner-learner interaction, even if learners are being encouraged by a cognitively complex task theorized to channel their attention to a form, there are certain linguistic items that may still need additional focus on form to foster target-like use. A form's amenability to feedback has been shown to depend on the type and saliency of that linguistic item (e.g., Havranek, 2002), and even student level (e.g., Chaudron, 1983). These factors may resonate regardless of task type or even cognitive complexity.

Thus, the present study may have yielded very different findings if students had been paired with an expert interlocutor, and/or if the task required the use of a different type of grammatical form. At the same time, we need more research on tasks' efficacy for student-student interaction, because this is the most ecological interactant-set-up to classroom contexts. A critical area for future research, then, is to examine what task types and task sequences work best in classroom contexts where learners are paired with learners. See Kim (2012) for initial work in this area.

Conclusion

The study reported here found that in traditional face-to-face classrooms, performing task sequences that contained more cognitively complex tasks resulted in better learning opportunities and more L2 development. The implications are that, in traditional classrooms, performing cognitively complex tasks right from beginning may be best. Another option could be for teachers to do cognitively simple tasks in the pre-task phases of a task in their lesson plan, to serve as a task model, and/or order tasks in U-shaped sequences with more complex than simple task options in their classrooms. Online language courses, on the other hand, require a fundamentally different theoretical scope that should inform designing and sequencing tasks. The present study showed that researchers and teachers cannot assume that tasks that work in face-to-face are transferrable to the SCMC mode. Cognitively simple tasks may work best for this medium. In order to ensure that tasks in SCMC take on the affordances of the online medium so as to best promote second language acquisition, it is essential that we research how learners are using the technology to interact with one another. This may involve training students on the learner-centred nature of SCMC, and how they can make the most of its features (Lamy, 2004). Doing so will inform task design and task sequencing, a benefit for online language teaching and for the advancement of the field.

Notes

1   Other taxonomies for the implementation and investigation of tasks have included foci on task operations (Willis, 1996); cognitive classifications (Prabhu, 1987); task interactant roles and information exchanged (Pica, Kanagy and Falodun, 1993); input, condition, processes and outcomes of a task (Ellis, 2003); and cognitive complexity in the areas of language, cognition and performance condition (Skehan and Foster, 2001). Another example includes Samuda and Bygate's (2008) taxonomy, which provides a very holistic list of task elements to consider, such as teachers' and learners' procedures and processes, individual differences, and task, lesson and curriculum applications.

2   The first letters of SSARC, 'SS' stand for simple task demands, and these are done first on both resource-dispersing and resource-directing variables before giving the learner more complex versions (thus 'simple simple', on all accounts). 'A' refers to automaticity, because after making the task more complex along resource-dispersing lines, faster and more automatic retrieval of linguistic resources will be promoted. 'R'

implies the next step: restructuring. This will happen once the task is made complex along all lines: resource-dispersing and resource-directing features are performed at the most complex versions, or 'C'.

3 Please see Baralt, 2013, for a more detailed description and examples of the tasks.

4 Genesis™ 11.0 is software that allows the 'teacher' computer to oversee the activity of all student computers in a laboratory.

5 Due to complications in a pilot version of this study, it was decided that, logistically, it would be best for students in the online classes to participate in the study by coming to campus and carrying out the tasks together during a class 'meeting' time in the laboratory.

6 Note here that 'IND' implies indicative morphological marking on the verb, while 'SUB' implies subjunctive marking.

7 One of the reviewers rightfully asked how verbs with correct aspect/time, but incorrect person marking (i.e., first person, second person), might have been coded for in the study. As no such cases existed in the dataset, these were not coded for.

References

Ayoun, D. (2004). The effectiveness of written recasts in the second language acquisition of aspectual distinctions in French: A follow-up study. *The Modern Language Journal,* 88, 31–55.

Baralt, M. (2013). The impact of cognitive complexity on feedback efficacy during online versus face-to-face interactive tasks. *Studies in Second Language Acquisition,* 35, 689–725.

Blake, R. J. (2011). Current trends in online language learning. *Annual Review of Applied Linguistics,* 31, 19–35.

Böhlke, O. (2003). A comparison of student participation levels by group size and language stages during chatroom and face-to-face discussions in German. *CALICO Journal,* 21, 1, 67–87.

Chaudron, C. (1983). Research on metalinguistic judgments: A review of theory, methods, and results. *Language Learning,* 33, 343–77.

Chun, D. (2013). Contributions of tracking user behavior to SLA research. In Hubbard, P., Schulze, M. and Smith, B. (eds), *Learner-Computer Interaction in Language Education: A Festschrift in Honor of Robert Fischer* (pp. 256–62). San Marcos, TX: CALICO.

De la Fuente, M. J. (2003). Is SLA interactionist theory relevant to CALL? A study on the effects of computer-mediated interaction on L2 vocabulary acquisition. *Computer Assisted Language Learning,* 16, 47–81.

Gilabert, R., Barón, J. and Llanes, À. (2009). Manipulating cognitive complexity across task types and its impact on learners' interaction during oral performance. *International Review of Applied Linguistics in Language Teaching,* 47, 367–95.

González-Lloret, M. (2003). Designing task-based CALL to promote interaction: En busca de esmeraldas. *Language Learning and Technology*, 7, 86–104.

Hampel, R. (2006). Rethinking task design for the digital age: A framework for language teaching and learning in a synchronous online environment. *ReCALL*, 18, 105–21.

Havranek, G. (2002). When is corrective feedback most likely to succeed? *International Journal of Educational Research*, 37, 255–70.

Kim, Y. (2009). The effects of task complexity on learner-learner interaction. *System*, 37, 254–68.

—— (2012). Task complexity, learning opportunities and Korean EFL learners' question development. *Studies in Second Language Acquisition*, 34, 627–58.

Kim, Y. and Tracy-Ventura, N. (2011). Task complexity, language anxiety and the development of the simple past. In P. Robinson (ed.) *Second Language Task Complexity: Researching the Cognition Hypothesis of Language Learning and Performance* (pp. 287–306). Philadelphia: John Benjamins.

Lai, C., Fei, F. and Roots, R. (2008). The contingency of recasts and noticing. *CALICO Journal*, 26, 70–90.

Lai, C. and Li, G. (2011). Technology and task-based language teaching: A critical review. *CALICO Journal*, 28, 498–521.

Lai, C., and Zhao, Y. (2006). Noticing and text-based chat. *Language Learning and Technology*, 10, 102–20.

Lamy, M. N. (2004). Oral conversations online: Redefining oral competence in synchronous environments. *ReCALL*, 16, 520–38.

Lee, L. (2001). Online interaction: Negotiation of meaning and strategies used among learners of Spanish. *ReCALL*, 13, 232–44.

Loewen, S. and Erlam, R. (2006). Corrective feedback in the chat room: An experimental study. *Computer Assisted Language Learning*, 19, 1–14.

Norris, J. and Ortega, L. (2009). Towards an organic approach to investigating CAF in instructed SLA: The case of complexity. *Applied Linguistics*, 30, 555–78.

Nuevo, A. (2006). Task complexity and interaction: L2 learning opportunities and interaction. Unpublished doctoral dissertation, Georgetown University, Washington, DC.

Nuevo, A.-M., Adams, R. and Ross-Feldman, L. (2011). Task complexity, modified output, and L2 development in learner–learner interaction In P. Robinson (ed.), *Second Language Task Complexity: Researching the Cognition Hypothesis of Language Learning and Performance* (pp. 175–202). Amsterdam: John Benjamins.

Ortega, L. (2009). Interaction and attention to form in L2 text-based computer-mediated communication. In A. Mackey and C. Polio (eds), *Multiple Perspectives on Interaction in SLA: Research in Honor of Susan M. Gass* (pp. 226–53). New York: Routledge.

Pica, T., Kanagy, R. and Falodun, J. (1993). Choosing and using communication tasks for second language teaching and research. In G. Crookes and S. Gass (eds), *Tasks in*

Language Learning: Integrating Theory and Practice (pp. 9–34). Philadelphia: Multilingual Matters.

Prabhu, N. S. (1987). *Second Language Pedagogy.* Oxford: Oxford University Press.

Révész, A. (2009). Task complexity, focus on form, and second language development. *Studies in Second Language Acquisition,* 31, 437–70.

Révész, A. (2011). Task complexity, focus on L2 constructions, and individual differences: A classroom-based study. *The Modern Language Journal,* 95, 162–81.

Robinson, P. (1995). Task complexity and second language narrative discourse. *Language Learning,* 45, 99–140.

—— (2001a). Task complexity, cognitive resources, and syllabus design: A triadic framework for examining task influences on SLA. In P. Robinson (ed.), *Cognition and Second Language Instruction* (pp. 287–318). Cambridge: Cambridge University Press.

—— (2001b). Task complexity, task difficulty, and task production: Exploring interactions in a componential framework. *Applied Linguistics,* 22, 27–57.

—— (2007). Task complexity, theory of mind, and intentional reasoning: Effects on L2 speech production, interaction, and perceptions of task difficulty. *International Review of Applied Linguistics in Language Teaching,* 45, 191–213.

—— (2010). Situating and distributing cognition across task demands: The SSARC model of pedagogic task sequencing. In M. Putz and L. Sicola (eds), *Cognitive Processing in Second Language Acquisition: Inside the Learner's Mind* (pp. 243–69). Philadelphia, PA: John Benjamins.

—— (2011). Second language task complexity, the Cognition Hypothesis, language learning, and performance. In P. Robinson (ed.), *Second Language Task Complexity: Researching the Cognition Hypothesis of Language Learning and Performance* (pp. 3–38). Amsterdam: John Benjamins.

Robinson, P. and Gilabert, R. (2007). Task complexity, the Cognition Hypothesis and second language learning and performance. *International Review of Applied Linguistics in Language Teaching,* 45, 161–76.

Samuda, V. and Bygate, M. (2008). *Tasks in Second Language Learning.* Hampshire/New York: Palgrave Macmillan.

Schmidt, R. (1995). Consciousness and foreign language learning: A tutorial on the role of attention and awareness in learning. In R. Schmidt (ed.), *Attention and Awareness in Foreign Language Learning* (pp. 1–63). Honolulu, HI: University of Hawai'i, Second Language Teaching and Curriculum Center.

Shekary, M. and Tahririan, M. H. (2006). Negotiation of meaning and noticing in text-based online chat. *The Modern Language Journal,* 90, 557–73.

Skehan, P., and Foster, P. (2001). Cognition and tasks. In P. Robinson (ed.) *Cognition and Second Language Instruction* (pp. 183–205). Cambridge: Cambridge University Press.

Smith, B. (2003). Computer-mediated negotiated interaction: An expanded model. *The Modern Language Journal,* 87, 38–58.

—— (2008). The relationship between scrolling, negotiation and self-initiated self-repair in an SCMC environment. *CALICO Journal*, 26, 231–45.

Swain, M. and Lapkin, S. (1998). Interaction and second language learning: Two adolescent French immersion students working together. *The Modern Language Journal*, 82, 320–37.

Tudini, V. (2007). Negotiation and intercultural learning in Italian native speaker chat rooms. *The Modern Language Journal*, 91, 577–601.

Warschauer, M. (1996). Comparing face-to-face and electronic discussion in the second language classroom. *CALICO Journal*, 13, 7–26.

Willis, J. (1996). *A Framework for Task-based Learning*. Harlow, UK: Longman.

Yilmaz, Y. and Yuksel, D. (2011). Effects of communication mode and salience on recasts: A first exposure study. *Language Teaching Research*, 15, 457–77.

5

The Effects of Guided Planning, Task Complexity and Task Sequencing on L2 Oral Production

Colin Thompson
Shimonoseki City University

Introduction

The past twenty years has seen a significant amount of research on the role of task planning as a means for improving learners' L2 speech (for a review of studies, see Ellis, 2009). One type of planning, 'strategic planning', takes place before the performance of a task, allowing learners time to prepare what they are going to say (Ellis, 2005). Numerous studies such as Kawauchi (2005) and Sangarun (2005) have shown how strategic planning that incorporates some sort of guidance, for example attention to form or meaning, can benefit different aspects of L2 speech such as fluency. Mochizuki and Ortega (2008) investigated strategic planning that targeted specific linguistic forms which led to improvements in learners' accuracy. The majority of these studies, however, are limited in that they consist of 'one-off' experiments that do little to tell us about the effects of task planning *over time*. This is where the claims of Cognition Hypothesis come into play which provides guidelines on how tasks can be *sequenced* to promote optimal conditions for language learning. The purpose of this chapter is to investigate the combined effects of strategic planning with tasks that are sequenced according to the claims of the Cognition Hypothesis in order to facilitate complex L2 output.

Strategic planning and L2 oral production

Researchers have investigated the way strategic planning can be manipulated in order to influence different aspects of L2 speech. For example, 'guided planning' involves focusing learners' attention in some way as they prepare for a task, for example, attending to language or content, while 'unguided planning' allows learners time to plan independently (Ellis, 2009). Guided planning has been shown to facilitate more structurally complex speech (see Sangarun, 2005). Unguided planning has also produced gains in grammatical complexity (see Yuan and Ellis, 2003) although in other studies it has not (Gilabert, 2007) but did in terms of lexical complexity. Consequently, research to date has shown that different planning conditions influence learners' output in different ways.

Of theoretical importance here is Kormos' (2011) bilingual model of oral production which is adapted from Levelt's (1989; Levelt, Roelofs and Meyer, 1999) model of L1 production. Kormos' (2011) model outlines four main components for L2 speech production. First is conceptualization which involves 'activating the relative concepts to be encoded' (Kormos, 2011, p. 42), i.e. planning the goal of a communicative message, referred to as 'macro planning' and then deciding on the viewpoint to express it, known as 'micro planning'. This initial planning of a message is not yet linguistic but comprises all the information necessary to be converted into language, acknowledged as the 'preverbal plan'. Second is formulation which concerns the lexical, grammatical and phonological encoding of the preverbal plan. The specifications of the plan activate the required lexical items within a learner's mental lexicon. The lexicon consists of 'lexemes' which represent a learner's knowledge of L1 and L2 vocabulary, and 'lemmas' which relate to their morphological and syntactic properties. Syntactic encoding begins with the activation of the appropriate lemma, followed by encoding of phrases and clauses. Third is articulation which receives and executes the intended message as spoken language. Finally, there is a self-monitoring component which checks each of the above stages for errors as speech is generated and processed, and can lead to the re-phrasing of utterances.

In terms of L1 speech, conceptualization involves planning, i.e. thinking of what to say, whereas formulation and articulation are carried out automatically due to the speaker's automatized L1 system. This allows all three stages to operate in parallel with the capacity to produce L1 speech with no time delays (Kormos, 2011). In terms of L2 production, learners typically do not have automatized knowledge, and so it takes more time to encode messages particularly with words which are rarely used (Bygate and Samuda, 2005). Consequently, formulation and even articulation may require conscious attention for lower proficiency learners (Kormos, 2011). L2 communication breakdowns can therefore occur when a learner has to process or respond in the L2 under the normal time constraints of everyday speech.

Skehan (1998) argues that learners have limited attentional resources which have adverse effects on learners' L2 fluency, accuracy and complexity when task demands are high, for example when there is no planning time. Attention capacity limits force the learner to prioritize one aspect of speech over another when performing complex tasks which results in a 'trade-off' of attention usually between complexity and accuracy. As a result, tasks can bring gains in accuracy or complexity but not both. Bygate and Samuda (2005) argue that it is possible to 'free-up' attentional resources by providing strategic planning 'which reduces the processing load of subsequent on-line performance: speakers may have mentally organized the content; and/or worked on the formulation of aspects of the communication' (p. 39). In other words, strategic planning provides time for learners to attend to conceptualization (message content) and/or formulation (grammar encoding) which is then stored in memory and later produced during task performance as more fluent, complex and/or accurate L2 speech.

Robinson (2011), on the other hand, argues against limited capacity processing and a trade-off between accuracy and complexity. He believes both aspects of speech can be improved by having learners perform more cognitively demanding tasks. For example:

> ... increasing the amount of reasoning a task requires, promotes greater effort at controlling production and more vigilant monitoring of output. This increased complexity leads to greater accuracy and complexity of L2 production when compared to performance on simpler task versions that require little or no reasoning.
>
> (Robinson, 2011, p. 12)

According to Robinson (2011), a complex task which may involve learners explaining the reasons behind other people's actions will increase the attention learners pay to their speech and their efforts at producing complex syntax, for example, cognitive state terms – *he thinks that . . . she believes that*, compared to simple tasks that require no reasoning. In terms of Kormos' (2011) model, 'complex task demands lead to greater effort at conceptualization and elicit the morphologically richer and structurally more complex syntactic mode' (Robinson, 2011, p. 14). Complex tasks therefore generate more elaborate communicative concepts at conceptualization which in turn results in more complex *and* accurate L2 speech. In order to determine which of these two competing theories is the more convincing, more research is needed.

Guided planning and L2 oral production

Mochizuki and Ortega (2008) investigated whether guided planning that included grammar assistance towards English relative clauses would improve L2 production of Japanese high school students. This type of planning allowed time for the learners to focus on the target structure while preparing to perform an oral narrative. The task was specifically designed to elicit relative clauses by containing seven obligatory contexts within the story. A total of 112 students participated in dyads and were split into three groups; a guided planning group which received five minutes planning time with written examples of relative clauses and instructions to try and use the grammar in the task, an unguided planning group which received five minutes planning time with no assistance, and a control group with no planning time. To ensure the students produced relative clauses, an aural L2 stimulus of the narrative was played before the students began planning. Accurate use of relative clauses was measured using a six-point rating scale. The results of the study showed significant gains for the guided planners compared to the unguided planners and the control group in terms of accuracy and one complexity measure involving relative clauses per T-unit but not for other global complexity measures and fluency. These findings therefore lend weight to both Robinson's and Skehan's predictions.

A limitation of Mochizuki and Ortega's (2008) study, however, and that of many planning studies (for example, Yuan and Ellis, 2003; Kawauchi, 2005) is that they only address the immediate effects of planning at certain points in time (Ellis, 2005). According to Ellis (2009), the only study that has investigated the long-term effects of planning on L2 production appears to be Bygate (2001) in which oral tasks were repeated every two weeks over a ten-week period. A limitation of this study was that it did not account for changes in specific linguistic features but focused on general linguistic changes for fluency, accuracy and complexity. In order to monitor the effects of strategic planning on specific language forms, it is necessary to use 'focused tasks' designed to elicit their use (Ellis, 2005). According to Loschky and Bley-Vroman (1993), a focused task should make the use of a targeted form as essential as possible to ensure learners use it. Mochizuki and Ortega's (2008) study attempted to design such a task for eliciting relative clauses; however, the participants' production of the form was lower than expected which led these authors to conclude, in line with Loschky and Bley-Vroman (1993), that task essentialness may be unattainable but that task usefulness would be more realistic.

In order to facilitate learners' use of a linguistic structure over time, a focused task would need to be sequenced with similar focused tasks. To ensure maximum conditions for L2 language use, a theoretically grounded proposal for sequencing tasks is therefore required.

Task sequencing and the Cognition Hypothesis

The Cognition Hypothesis (Robinson, 2010) claims that:

> ... optimal task-based language use and learning opportunities over time, i.e. task *sequencing*, is done by designing and having learners perform tasks simple on all the relevant parameters of task demands first, and then gradually increasing their cognitive complexity on subsequent versions.
>
> (Robinson, 2010, p. 242)

Robinson (2010) provides a framework for designing tasks which includes a full taxonomy of task features and procedures for sequencing tasks. The purpose of this study concerns two aspects of the model: 'task complexity' and 'task difficulty'.

Task complexity

Task complexity relates to the cognitive demands of tasks, of which there are two main influences; 'resource-dispersing' and 'resource-directing' dimensions (Robinson, 2010, p. 245). The former relates to the *performance* demands that tasks place on learners, for example the availability of planning time. Robinson (2010) favours reducing planning time when sequencing tasks as this helps promote 'greater *control* over, and faster access to existing interlanguage systems of knowledge' (p. 248), and primes learners to perform tasks under normal time constraints. The latter concerns the *conceptual and linguistic* demands that tasks place on learners and can vary in their cognitive complexity. For example, as we saw earlier, tasks that involve intentional reasoning require the use of complex L2 syntax as well as additional L2 structures that accompany them such as relative clauses, for example, *she thinks that she likes the dog which has long hair*. As a result, increasing the complexity of tasks along resource-directing dimensions, by increasing intentional reasoning demands, can facilitate greater use of this language. Robinson (2007) illustrated this with 42 Japanese learners who were required to perform one simple, medium and complex task in dyads. The first task involved narrating a story about a character who decided to build a house. The subsequent tasks involved the same storyline but increased in complexity because the character reacted more to other people's opinions. The study used specific measures for cognitive state terms and the results showed that these terms were produced more frequently using ratio measures of 'cognitive state terms per clause' in the complex task compared to the other two versions, confirming that complex tasks elicit more complex language.

Tasks that are sequenced according to an increase in their intentional reasoning demands could therefore be expected to facilitate form–function mappings of the associated language, such as relative clauses, thus leading to improved use of the form.

Task difficulty

Another claim of the Cognition Hypothesis concern learners' *perceptions* towards the cognitive demands of tasks, referred to as 'task difficulty' (Robinson, 2010). It states that 'more cognitively complex tasks will be perceived by all learners to be more difficult than less complex counterparts' (Robinson, 2007, p. 196). This claim was also confirmed in Robinson's (2007) study in which the participants completed a five-item questionnaire that focused on task difficulty after they had performed the simple, medium and complex tasks. The results of the questionnaires showed that learners rated the complex task as being significantly more difficult than the medium task, which in turn was rated significantly more difficult than the simple version. Robinson (2007) concluded that 'task complexity, and task difficulty are clearly distinct, but related constructs' (p. 210). Task *complexity* relates to the cognitive demands of tasks and can therefore justify 'within' learner variation in performing two different tasks for example, performing a simple versus complex task. Task *difficulty*, on the other hand, helps to explain 'between' learner differences in the performance of a task. Robinson (2007) encouraged future studies to investigate the relationship of learners' perceptions towards task difficulty with that of task complexity to explain how *both* factors influence language production.

Research questions and hypotheses

This study addresses the following three questions:

1. To what extent can oral narratives facilitate task usefulness of relativization (in Mochizuki and Ortega's 2008 sense) for Japanese second-year University learners of English?
   Hypothesis 1. Oral narratives designed to elicit relative clauses and sequenced with guided planning and task complexity will make production of the form useful for task completion.
2. To what extent does guided planning and task complexity facilitate L2 oral production in terms of structural complexity compared to guided/unguided planning and task complexity?
   Hypothesis 2. Guided planning and task complexity will facilitate L2 oral production to a greater extent than guided/unguided planning and task complexity using 'relative clauses per AS-Unit' as a measure of structural complexity.
3. To what extent do Japanese University learners perceive increasingly complex tasks as being more difficult to complete over time?
   Hypothesis 3. Complex tasks will be rated more difficult, stressful and less successfully completed by both groups compared to simpler task versions over time.

Experimental design

The study was carried out using a mixed factorial design that incorporated within-subject and between-subject variables. The within-subject variable was testing with three levels: pre-test, immediate post-test, delayed post-test. An additional feature of the present study was task complexity in which all the students performed a sequence of tasks that increased in complexity along intentional reasoning demands. Finally, the between-subject variable was planning time with two levels: guided planning and guided/unguided planning.

The participants

Twenty-four Japanese University students of English participated in the study. They were all second-year students majoring in economics or international commerce and were enrolled in an English language oral communication program as an additional credit to the courses. The majority of the students did not have TOEIC or TOEFL scores and were placed into different classes based on the results of an internal English placement test. In line with the majority of previous planning studies, the students were recruited from the immediate level classes and above. The participants were aged between 19 and 21 years old, with a mean age of 19. Eight students were male and 26 were female. The participants had studied English for approximately the same length of time: seven to nine years.

The participants were assigned into two even groups: guided planning (GP), and guided/unguided planning (GUP). Both groups were equal according to n-size (n = 12), gender, and placement test score. To ensure both groups were considered roughly equal in terms of proficiency, an independent samples t-test was carried out regarding their placement test scores. The GP group had a slightly larger mean score of 557.50 compared to the GUP score of 544.92 but this difference was not significant, $t(22) = .911, p > .05$.

Materials: Pre- and post-tests

To assess L2 oral production, story-telling narratives were used and were adapted from the task in Mochizuki and Ortega (2008). The pre-test narrative story involved a mother, son (Kevin) and sister (Kate) going to a pet shop to buy a dog. The narrative consisted of eight pictures sequenced in correct order and contained seven obligatory cases of relative clause use. For example, in one picture the daughter is thinking about a dog *which has long hair* (see Appendix A for the seven obligatory contexts). Each participant was asked to narrate the story in a monologue format to the researcher who acted as the listener. To create a communicative incentive, the researcher's pictures were in mixed order and the participants were informed that the pictures would be placed in the order of their narration.

The intermediate and delayed post-test narratives were similar in terms of cognitive difficulty but differed in terms of content (in order to prevent a practice effect). For example, they each contained the same seven obligatory cases of relative clauses but the storylines were different. The intermediate narrative test involved a son, mother and father going to a clothes shop to buy shirts and a dress; the delayed narrative test involved three sisters going to a garden centre to buy different types of plants. Finally, in order to create real-life processing conditions for language use (Robinson, 2005), no planning time was allocated prior to the tests, and unlike Mochizuki and Ortega (2008) no L2 stimulus was provided.

The students also performed pre- and post-grammatical judgment tests which targeted relative clauses (adapted from Izumi, 2003); however, for the purpose of this chapter, only the narrative pre- and post-tests are reported.

Treatment tasks: Increasing intentional reasoning demands

Five narratives were designed for the treatment task sequence, again based on the narrative used in Mochizuki and Ortega (2008); however, these tasks differed in terms of content *and* cognitive complexity. In terms of content, they contained different storylines. In terms of cognitive complexity, the narratives were sequenced according to an increase in intentional reasoning demands by containing additional cases of relative clauses. For example, narrative 2 contains a picture of a girl thinking about a *rabbit which has big ears*, while narrative 3 contains a picture of a boy thinking about a car *which has black windows*, and another car *which has black wheels*. Table 5.1 illustrates the number of obligatory cases of relative clauses per narrative during the treatment.

The first treatment narrative (2) contained seven cases of relative clauses, narratives 3 and 4 contained nine cases, and narrative 5 and 6 contained 10 cases. All the tasks were pre-piloted to ensure they elicited the targeted forms.

Table 5.1 Obligatory cases of relative clauses per narrative

	Task treatment: Increasing intentional reasoning demands				
	Pre-test narrative 1	**Narrative 2**	**Narrative 3 and 4**	**Narrative 5 and 6**	**Intermediate post-test narrative 7**	**Delayed post-test narrative 8**
Relative clauses	7	7	9	10	7	7

Pre-task planning conditions: Increasing resource-dispersing demands

Prior to the first treatment narrative (2), both groups were allocated 10 minutes guided planning time (the standard amount given in studies of planning, see Ellis, 2009) that included grammar guidance notes which contained examples of relative clauses. The students were instructed to try and use the grammar when they performed the task, and in accordance with Ellis and Yuan (2003), they were not allowed to use their notes when speaking. The task in week 2 was therefore simple along *resource-dispersing* dimensions because of the provision of planning time. The subsequent treatment narratives all gradually increased in complexity along resource-dispersing dimensions by containing less planning time. Narratives 3 and 4 consisted of seven minutes while narratives 5 and 6 consisted of four minutes planning time. The GP group continued to receive guided planning throughout the sequence; however, the GUP group were not allocated grammar guidance notes from task 3 onwards and were instead instructed to plan independently (see Table 5.2). The operationalization of the GUP planning condition was based on the assumption that university learners may not require continual grammar guidance with relative clauses but rather practice opportunities to produce the form.

Procedure

The study was carried out in a spare classroom over a seven week period. In week 1, all the participants performed the pre-test narrative. In week 2, the task treatment began. The students were allocated into their respective GP and GUP groups. First, a 10-minute guidance session on relative clauses was provided by the researcher. This involved showing examples of the form and then asking students to describe cartoon pictures using relative clauses. Each group then

Table 5.2 Pre-task planning conditions during the treatment sequence

	Narrative 2	Narrative 3 and 4	Narrative 5 and 6
GP	Guided planning	Guided planning	Guided planning
GUP	Guided planning	Unguided planning	Unguided planning

Length of planning time = narrative 2 (10 minutes), narratives 3 and 4 (7 minutes), narratives 5 and 6 (4 minutes)

performed narrative 2 after 10 minutes guided planning. In week 3, the GP and GUP groups performed narratives 3 and 4 according to their planning conditions: guided and unguided planning respectively. In week 4, both groups performed narratives 5 and 6 under the same planning conditions as week 3 but with less planning time. In each week of the treatment, the students completed a post-task questionnaire regarding their perceptions of task difficulty. Finally, in week 5 and 7, the groups performed the immediate post-test and delayed post-tests respectively (see Table 5.3).

L2 target structure: English relative clauses

English relative clauses (RCs) were chosen following Mochizuki and Ortega's (2008) study which investigated the use of the form with beginner-level Japanese students. Although RCs are instructed at junior high school, Mochizuki and Ortega (2008) expected their participants would still experience difficulty in producing the form, therefore only simple RC types were targeted; 'object-subject (OS, *I like the dog which has long ears*), object-direct object (OO, *I want the dog which the little girl has in her arms*) and subject-subject (SS, *The dog which has long ears looks friendly*' (p. 19). The results in relativization were disappointing, however, as an average of only 2.36 RCs per narrative were produced out of the obligatory seven cases. Mochizuki and Ortega (2008) attributed this to the lack of task essentialness as well as the participants' proficiency which might not have been high enough to benefit from the planning conditions. As this study used higher-level proficiency learners, it was assumed they would be able to capitalize from guided planning, therefore one simple RC type was included (OS) and, in addition, a more difficult RC type was targeted; 'oblique object' or 'object of a preposition' (OPREP, *He wants the dog which the man is looking at*.) This was in response to previous relativization studies such as Doughty (1991), who reported the benefits of OPREP instruction for RC acquisition for intermediate level learners.

L2 Measures

Amount of relative clauses

Following Mochizuki and Ortega (2008), to analyse task usefulness in eliciting relativization, all RC types produced by the entire sample were recorded and

Table 5.3 Schedule

Groups	Pre-test	(+ Intentional reasoning demands and – planning time)			Immediate post-test	Delayed post-test
	Week 1	Week 2	Week 3	Week 4	Week 5	Week 7
GP	Narrative 1 and Grammatical	Narrative 2	Narrative 3 and 4	Narrative 5 and 6	Narrative 7 and Grammatical	Narrative 8 and Grammatical
GUP	Judgment Test	Questionnaire	Questionnaire	Questionnaire	Judgment Test	Judgment Test

GP = guided planning, GUP = guided/unguided planning

compared. Non-target-like attempts at relativization were accepted provided the speaker produced a relative pronoun.

Structural complexity

Complexity, accuracy and fluency measures were used to measure oral performance; however, for the purpose of this chapter, only the structural complexity measure is reported. Mochizuki and Ortega's (2008) study used 'relative clauses per T-Unit', although in this case 'relative clauses per AS-Unit' was preferred following the guidelines in Foster, Tonkyn and Wigglesworth (2000).

Task difficulty questionnaire

An independent measure of cognitive complexity was also used in the form of a post-task questionnaire to determine participants' views regarding the difficulty of the treatment tasks. Following Robinson (2007), a five-item questionnaire was designed which required students to rate on a scale of 1–7 whether the task was difficult (1 strongly disagree, 7 strongly agree), whether the task was stressful, whether the task was interesting, whether they were successful in completing the task, and whether they wanted to participate in similar tasks.

The questionnaire was analysed in Rasch using Winsteps 3.72.0 to check the functionality of the items used. All the items were found to be of acceptable fit for productive measurement purposes (the values fell within the 0.5–1.5 boundaries).

Analysis

Oral data was transcribed and coded using the software program CLAN. Due to the small n-size, only a small number of outliers could be removed, which resulted in the data being non-normally distributed and this prohibited the use of certain statistical analyses concerning structural complexity (see Appendix B for skewness and kurtosis). Consequently, paired samples t-tests were carried out to calculate the difference in mean sizes from the pre-test to the post-tests for the GP and GUP groups. The level of significance was targeted at $p < 0.05$. In addition, effect sizes were calculated to determine the magnitude of the treatment for each group. Cohen's (1988) d value was used to calculate effects sizes with values rated at 0.2, 0.5 and 0.8 for small, medium and large effects sizes respectively. Independent samples t-tests were also used to test for significant differences between the two groups.

Results

Hypothesis 1: Task usefulness for eliciting relativization

Hypothesis 1 is partially confirmed. Attempts at producing the seven obligatory RC contexts for all the participants during the pre-test, the immediate post-test and the delayed post-test are displayed in Table 5.4. It shows the number of speakers who produced the expected RC type, the number of learners who produced an alternative RC type, the number of participants who described the content of the picture without producing the form, and those learners who avoided describing the picture altogether.

The total number of expected RCs for all 24 speakers was 168 (seven contexts per narrative). At the pre-test, the participants as a whole produced a low average mean of 0.29 RCs per narrative. Only three expected RC types were produced and only a further four alternative RC types were produced in total. The vast majority of participants described the contexts without using any relativization while a smaller amount did not describe the contexts. A different story, however, is depicted at the intermediate post-test where the participants produced a much higher mean of 5.29 RCs per narrative. In all, 65.48 per cent of the 168 expected RCs were produced by the participants. RC contexts 1, 2, 3, 4 and 5 were produced by most of the speakers while only contexts 6 and 7 did not elicit the expected RC types at just 13 per cent and 41 per cent respectively, although context 7 managed to elicit alternative RC types (54 per cent). In terms of the delayed post-test, the

Table 5.4 Pre and post-test narrative relativization

Narrative tests	Speakers							
	Avoided	%	Simplified	%	Alternative RC	%	Expected RC	%
Pre-test	21	12.5	140	83.33	4	2.38	3	1.79
Intermediate post-test			41	24.4	17	10.12	110	65.48
Delayed post-test	5	2.98	35	20.83	19	11.31	109	64.88

participants produced a slightly higher average of 5.33 RCs per narrative compared to the intermediate post-test (5.29) and, on the whole, relativization was very similar as 64.88 per cent of the 168 expected RC's were produced. RC contexts 1, 2, 3, 4 and 5 were again produced by most of the participants while contexts 6 and 7 were not (4 per cent and 46 per cent respectively); however, context 7 again successfully elicited alternative RC types (50 per cent).

Hypothesis 2: The effects of guided planning and task complexity compared to guided/unguided planning and task complexity on structural complexity

Hypothesis 2 is partially confirmed. The descriptive results taken from the structural complexity measure are displayed in Table 5.5. It illustrates the mean average of the GP and GUP groups' pre-test and post-test narrative scores, their standard deviations, and the mean variances from the pre-test narrative to the immediate post-test, the pre-test narrative to the delayed post-test, and the immediate and delayed post-test variance.

Both the GP and the GUP groups produced low means at the pre-test narrative (0.06 and 0.04 respectively) in terms of relative clauses per AS-Unit. However, the GP group produced a larger mean gain from the pre-test to the immediate post-test (0.70) compared to the GUP group (0.62). The GP group produced the same mean gain at the delayed post-test with a variance of 0 between both post-tests; however, the GUP group's mean improved by 0.08, thus both groups produced the same mean gain (0.70) at delayed post-test.

Table 5.5 Descriptive statistics for structural complexity

	Relative clauses per AS-Unit					
Group (n=12)	Pre-test	Immediate post-test	Delayed post-test	Pre-immediate post-test difference	Pre-delayed post-test difference	Immediate-delayed post-test difference
GP Mean	0.06	0.76	0.76	0.70	0.70	0
SD	0.17	0.13	0.06	0.22	0.19	0.18
GUP Mean	0.04	0.66	0.74	0.62	0.70	0.08
SD	0.10	0.26	0.35	0.25	0.35	0.26

GP = guided planning, GUP = guided/unguided planning

Table 5.6 Statistical significance and effect sizes for structural complexity

Group	n-size	Pre-intermediate post-test (Sig.)	Pre-intermediate post-test Cohen's d-value	Pre-delayed post-test (Sig.)	Pre-delayed post-test Cohen's d-value
GP	12	.000	4.83	.000	5.74
GUP	12	.000	3.29	.000	2.84

GP = guided planning, GUP = guided/unguided planning

Table 5.7 Statistical significance and effect sizes between the GP group and the GUP group

	Relative Clauses per AS Unit		
	Pre-test intermediate post-test	Pre-test delayed post-test	Intermediate post-test delayed post-test
Sig.	0.417	0.955	0.31
Cohen's d-value	0.35	0	0.37

To determine the statistical significance of the mean gains within each group and the extent of their effect sizes, paired sample t-tests and Cohen's *d*-values were calculated (see Table 5.6).

These results show the mean gains from the pre-test to the immediate post-test for the GP group and the GUP are significant ($p < .05$). The effect sizes were also large for both groups ($d > 0.8$). Similar results are shown for both groups from the pre-test to the delayed post-test; both groups showed significant gains in complexity ($p < .05$) and large effect sizes ($d > 0.8$). To see whether gains *between* the two groups were statistically significant, let us examine Table 5.7.

There were no significant differences between the GP group and the GUP group in terms of gains from the pre-test to the immediate post-test ($p = 0.417$). In addition, Cohen's *d*-value of 0.35 indicated only a small to medium effect between the two groups. Differences between the groups were even smaller regarding the pre-test to the delayed post-test gains ($p = 0.955$), while a *d*-value of 0 indicated there was no effect.

Hypothesis 3: Learners' perceptions of task complexity in terms of task difficulty

Hypothesis 3 is largely confirmed. Regarding the GP group, they viewed the treatment tasks mostly as expected (see Table 5.8). In terms of task difficulty, the

Table 5.8 GP group's task questionnaire responses

	Difficulty (M / SD)	Stress (M / SD)	Success (M / SD)	Interest (M / SD)	Motivation (M / SD)
Week 2 (simple)	3.58 / 1.93	3.50 / 2.02	4.50 / 1.09	5.83 / 1.11	5.58 / 1.08
Week 3 (medium)	4.17 / 1.53	3.42 / 1.93	4.17 / 1.53	5.58 / 1.08	5.83 / 0.83
Week 4 (complex)	4.42 / 1.73	3.50 / 1.98	3.00 / 1.04	5.42 / 1.16	5.75 / 0.97

students on average rated the simple task the least difficult (3.58) compared to the medium task which was rated more difficult (4.17), although paired sample t-tests showed this difference was not significant (t (11) = $-1.048, p > .05$). The complex task at week 4 was rated the most difficult (4.42) compared to the medium task, although again this difference was not significant (t (11) = $-.638$, $p > .05$). The GP group did not consider an increase in task complexity to be more stressful because the medium task was considered less stressful (3.42) than the simple task (3.50), while the most complex task was considered as stressful as the simple version (3.50). There were no significant differences between these values. In terms of successful completion, the GP responses were more in line with their perceptions of task difficulty as their confidence on the complex task (3.00) was significantly less than on the medium task (t (11) = $2.646, p < 0.05$), while they were the most confident performing the simple task (4.50).

The GUP group provided similar results to the GP group (see Table 5.9). In terms of task difficulty, the students rated the simple task the least difficult (4.50) whilst the medium task was rated more difficult (4.75); however, this difference was not significant (t (11) = $-.638, p > .05$). The complex task was rated the most difficult (5.08) compared to the medium task but was not significantly different (t (11) = -1.301, $p > .05$). The GUP group considered an increase in task complexity to be more stressful from simple to medium (3.75 to 4.08 respectively); however, the complex task was considered less stressful (4.00) than the medium task, and again there were no significant differences between these values. In terms of successful completion, the GUP group responded in accordance with their perceptions of task difficulty as their confidence on the complex task (3.42) was lower than on the medium task (3.50) which in turn was lower than on the simple version (3.58) but these differences were not significant (t (11) = $.150, p > 0.05$) and (t (11) = $.200, p > 0.05$) respectively.

Finally, independent sample t-tests showed there were no significant differences between the GP group and the GUP group in terms of task difficulty, stress, and interest during each week of the treatment. The GP group did consider

Table 5.9 GUP group's task questionnaire responses

	Difficulty (mean / SD)	Stress (mean / SD)	Success (mean / SD)	Interest (mean / SD)	Motivation (mean / SD)
Week 2 simple	4.50 / 1.17	3.75 / 1.22	3.58 / 1.00	5.08 / 1.08	5.08 / 0.79
Week 3 medium	4.75 / 1.22	4.08 / 1.83	3.50 / 1.09	4.75 / 1.14	4.58 / 1.08
Week 4 complex	5.08 / 1.08	4.00 / 1.54	3.42 / 1.31	5.17 / 0.72	4.67 / 0.98

themselves significantly more successful in completing the simple task (4.50) compared to the GUP group (3.58), t (22) = 2.154, $p < 0.05$; however, there were no significant differences at the medium task or the complex task.

Discussion

1. Task usefulness for relative clause production

In terms of whether the pre-post test narratives were successful in eliciting the targeted RC types, the findings of this study provided mixed results. Despite efforts in task design, the pre-test narrative was unsuccessful in eliciting the seven obligatory contexts as reflected in the low mean of 0.29 relative clauses per narrative. This result was not too surprising, however, as the purpose of the test was to reflect real-life processing conditions for language use, without any guidance; therefore learners were free to use their full L2 linguistic repertoire, and many speakers completed the narrative without using relativization. However, after both groups had completed their sequencing treatment, the immediate and delayed post-test narratives were much more successful in eliciting the expected RC types, with approximately 65 per cent of them produced on both tests. Average means of 5.29 and 5.33 respectively far outweigh the average in Mochizuki and Ortega's (2008) study of 2.36, and this was accomplished without both groups engaging in planning prior to performance. We can therefore conclude that the oral narratives in this study were useful in eliciting the targeted RC types, thus supporting the view of Mochizuki and Ortega (2008), but only after learners were given practice opportunities where their attention was drawn to the form through guided planning and tasks that increased in intentional reasoning demands. These findings therefore support the claim of the Cognition Hypothesis which states that tasks sequenced according to an increase in their cognitive demands facilitate optimal L2 language use over time

(Robinson, 2010). Furthermore, these results have implications for action research as the benefits of sequencing tasks that increase in complexity can serve as a means for improving the quality of intended pedagogy, as shown in this study's post-test production of the targeted RC types.

2. The effects of guided planning and task complexity compared to guided/unguided planning and task complexity on L2 structural complexity

The results of this study showed that guided planning and task complexity produced significant gains in terms of L2 structural complexity for the GP group, and that guided/unguided planning and task complexity also produced significant gains for the GUP learners. Thus, both treatments were effective and the gains of both groups were essentially the same. These findings therefore support previous planning studies which also reported gains in structural complexity (for example, Yuan and Ellis, 2003; Sangarun, 2005). Let us now turn to discuss how the GUP group produced similar gains in complexity compared to the GP group despite the lack of grammar guidance. Unlike Mochizuki and Ortega's (2008) study, which used beginner level high school learners, the participants in the present study were intermediate university learners of English and were therefore expected to have more stable declarative knowledge of relative clauses. Consequently, these learners may only have needed initial guidance towards the targeted RC types, as the GUP group was able to utilize their existing knowledge to plan effectively and independently during weeks 3 and 4 which enabled them to produce the expected RC types during the post-test narrations. Thus, continuous guidance towards relative clauses may not be necessary with intermediate level learners. What do appear necessary, however, are opportunities to practise using the form during narrative production which is where the benefits of the Cognition Hypothesis come into play. Sequencing tasks according to increasing intentional reasoning demands provides opportunities for learners to direct their attention and efforts at conceptualizing and producing more complex output in order to meet the demands of complex tasks. Given the significant gains in both groups' L2 output, it appears that learners of intermediate proficiency are able to capitalize on the learning opportunities afforded by tasks that increase in resource-directing dimensions.

Let us now examine the psycholinguistic processes that occurred during the task sequence that can help to explain the gains in structural complexity for both groups, bearing in mind there was no planning time during the narrative tests, and they contained the same number of RC contexts. At week 2, the first treatment narrative was simple along resource-directing dimensions (as it contained the same number of relative clauses as the pre-test) and simple along resource-dispersing dimensions (as 10 minutes planning time was allowed). The provision of guided planning for both groups would have drawn learners' attention towards the form as they prepared for the narrative. In weeks 3 and 4, the tasks increased in cognitive complexity along intentional reasoning demands. In terms of Kormos' (2011) bilingual model, 'the complexity of tasks has a large influence on the macro-planning stage, where concepts are selected and relations among them are encoded' (Kormos, 2011, p. 53). Increased reasoning demands would have triggered increased effort at conceptualization and the generation of pre-verbal messages. As message specifications activate the required lemmas and lexemes to encode language, the more detailed the pre-verbal messages became, the more complex syntactic structures were encoded and the more complex L2 language was produced, in this case relative clauses. Furthermore, at weeks 3 and 4 the tasks also increased in complexity along resource-dispersing dimensions as planning time was gradually reduced in order to increase 'the ability to access and deploy knowledge during *performance* of a complex skill' (Robinson, 2005, p. 7). In other words, this facilitated the automatization of the target structures by priming learners to produce complex L2 speech under real-time conditions.

The effect of this task sequence treatment would have resulted in the learners memorizing 'formuliac language'. Kormos (2011) reminds us that 'the majority of our utterances are memorized phrases, clauses and sentences which together are called formulaic language' (p. 46). For native speakers, it typically consists of communicative functions such as apologizing and is initiated in conceptualization as 'chunks' that contain multiple concepts which activate subsequent linguistic chunks stored in the lexicon as one lemma. As a result, formulaic language is 'produced faster and with less conscious effort than creatively-constructed elements of the message' (Kormos, 2011, p. 46). In terms of L2 learners, practice opportunities facilitate the encoding of words and their associated syntactic information in the learners' mental lexicon and this assists the automatization of the formulation process. In the case of this study, repeated attempts at producing relative clauses during the sequence narratives would have strengthened the retrieval links of the required syntactic information which results in 'more efficient message planning and faster lexical access and selection' (Gilabert, 2007, p. 64). By the time both groups performed the post-tests, they had memorized and automatized the L2 structures associated with intentional reasoning speech such as relative clauses into formulaic chunks. At the post-tests, the learners were therefore able to conceptualize intentional reasoning 'chunks' as they attempted to explain the actions of other people which were then encoded by the corresponding lemmas. Consequently, the planning and sequencing of narratives in this study helped facilitate learners' attention and proceduralization of complex L2 structures in the form of relative clauses which allowed them to produce the form under the natural conditions of everyday speech. Although as this study used a small sample size, the findings are limited due to the non-normal distribution of the data.

3. Learners' perceptions of task complexity in terms of task difficulty

In accordance with Robinson (2007) the results of this study's post-task questionnaires largely confirm another claim of the Cognition Hypothesis which is that learners' perceptions of task difficulty coincide with the dimensions of task complexity. As the tasks increased in complexity along intentional reasoning demands both planning groups perceived them to be more difficult, and were also less confident in their ability to complete them. However, the level of statistical difference found in this study was not as high as that reported by Robinson (2007) in his study.

As pointed out earlier, task difficulty can highlight differences *between* learners at particular tasks which is of interest in this case because at weeks 3 and 4, both groups performed the same tasks (medium and complex respectively) but under different planning conditions; guided vs. unguided planning. Despite the different planning conditions, there were no significant differences *between* the two groups in terms of perceptions towards task difficulty, stress and their ability to successfully complete the tasks. We can therefore infer that learners of higher proficiency may not need continual guided planning towards relative clauses as they perform more complex intentional reasoning tasks. The GP group did not perceive the tasks as being any easier nor did they consider themselves any more successful in completing the tasks compared to the guided/unguided group. These findings coincide with the linguistic effects of task complexity and differences *within* the groups as the GUP group produced the same gains in complexity at the delayed post-test compared to the GP group despite the former group planning independently for most of the treatment. Consequently these results show that task complexity and task difficulty are related concepts and together they can help to explain changes in L2 performance.

Conclusion

This chapter demonstrated how English relative clauses can be explicitly instructed during pre-task planning and elicited through the design of focused tasks. Tasks sequenced so that they increase in cognitive complexity provide opportunities for learners to produce more complex syntactic language while simultaneously priming students to perform tasks under real-time conditions. This process ultimately helped to proceduralize their knowledge of the targeted forms. The significant gains in the production of relativization from both groups highlight the powerful combination that guided planning and task complexity are in promoting L2 language use.

Appendix A

Pre-test narrative: possible examples for each relative clause context

Context 1 (OS): The mother thinks she likes the dog which has long ears
Context 2 (OS): She wants the dog which is next to the girl
Context 3 (OS): Kevin thinks he likes the dogs which have long hair
Content 4 (OPREP): He wants the dog which the family is looking at
Context 5 (OS): Kate thinks she likes the dog which has long hair
Context 6 (OS): She also likes the dog which has long ears
Context 7 (OPREP): She wants the dog which the girl is smiling at

Appendix B

Descriptive statistics for structural complexity

	Pre-test	Immediate post-test	Delayed post-test
n-size	24	24	24
Mean	.049	.709	.749
SD	.028	.043	.050
Skewness	3.34	−.442	.422
SD	.472	.472	.472
Kurtosis	11.58	.770	4.63
SD	.918	.918	.918

References

Bygate, M. (2001). Effects of task repetition on the structure and control of oral language. In M. Bygate, P. Skehan and M. Swain (eds), *Researching Pedagogic Tasks: Second Language Learning and Testing* (pp. 23–49). Longman.

Bygate, M. and Samuda, V. (2005). Integrative planning through the use of task repetition. In R. Ellis (ed.), *Planning and Task Performance in a Second Language* (pp. 37–77). John Benjamins.

Cohen, J. (1988). *Statistical Power Analysis for the Behavioral Sciences* (2nd ed.). Hillsdale, NJ: Lawrence Erlbaum.

Doughty, C. (1991). Second language instruction does make a difference. *Studies in Second Language Acquisition*, 13, 431–69.

Ellis, R. (2005). Planning and task-based performance: Theory and research. In R. Ellis (ed.), *Planning and Task Performance in a Second Language* (pp. 3–37). John Benjamins.

—— (2009). The effects of three types of task planning on the fluency, complexity, and accuracy in L2 oral production. *Applied Linguistics*, 30 (4), 474–509.

Foster, P., Tonkyn, A. and Wigglesworth, G. (2000). Measuring spoken language: A unit for all reasons. *Applied Linguistics*, 21, 354–75.

Gilabert, R. (2007). The simultaneous manipulation of task complexity along planning time and [+– Here-and-Now]. In M. D. P. Garcia-Mayo (ed.), *Investigating Tasks in Formal Language Learning* (pp. 44–68). Clevedon, UK: Multilingual Matters.

Izumi, S. (2003). Processing difficulty in comprehension and production of relative clauses by learners of English as a second language. *Language Learning*, 53, 285–323.

Kawauchi, C. (2005). The effects of strategic planning on the oral narratives of learners with low and high intermediate L2 proficiency. In R. Ellis (ed.), *Planning and Task Performance in a Second Language* (pp. 143–65). John Benjamins.

Kormos, J. (2011). Speech production and the Cognition Hypothesis. In P. Robinson (ed.), *Second Language Task Complexity: Researching the Cognition Hypothesis of Language Learning and Performance* (pp. 39–61). Amsterdam: Benjamins.

Levelt, W. J. M. (1989). *Speaking: From Intention to Articulation*. Cambridge University Press.

Levelt, W. J. M., Roelofs, A. and Meyer, A. S. (1999). A theory of lexical access in speech production. *Behavioral and Brain Sciences*, 22, 1–38.

Loschky, L. and Bley-Vroman, R. (1993). Grammar and task-based methodology. In G. Crookes and S. Gass (eds), *Tasks in Language Learning*. Clevedon: Multilingual Matters.

Mochizuki, N. and Ortega, L. (2008). Balancing communication and grammar in beginning level foreign classrooms. *Language Teaching Research*, 12, 11–37.

Robinson, P. (2005). Cognitive complexity and task sequencing: Studies in a componential framework for second language task design. *International Review of Applied Linguistics*, 43, 1–32.

—— (2007). Task complexity, theory of mind, and intentional reasoning: Effects on L2 speech production, interaction, uptake, and perceptions of task difficulty. *International Review of Applied Linguistics*, 45, 193–213.

—— (2010). Situating and distributing cognition across task demands: The SSARC model of pedagogic task sequencing. In M. Putz and L. Sicola (eds), *Cognitive Processing in Second Language Acquisition: Inside the Learner's Mind* (pp. 243–68). John Benjamins.

—— (2011). Task-based language learning: a review of issues. *Language Learning*, 61 (1), 1–36.

Sangarun, J. (2005). The effects of focusing on meaning and form in strategic planning. In R. Ellis (ed.), *Planning and Task Performance in a Second Language* (pp. 111–43). John Benjamins.

Skehan, P. (1998). *A Cognitive Approach to Language Learning*. Oxford University Press.

Yuan, F. and Ellis, R. (2003). The effects of pre-task planning and on-line planning on fluency, complexity and accuracy in L2 monologic oral production. *Applied Linguistics*, 24 (1), 1–27.

Section II

Educationally Situated Studies of Task Sequencing in Natural Classroom Contexts

6

A Pedagogical Proposal for Task Sequencing: An Exploration of Task Repetition and Task Complexity on Learning Opportunities

YouJin Kim
Georgia State University

Caroline Payant
University of Idaho

Introduction

Over the last two decades, a growing body of research has shown a positive role for task-based instruction on second language (L2) development (Ellis, 2003, 2012). While task design features and task implementation conditions have received a large amount of attention in task-based research, determining the interaction between these aspects in terms of task sequencing continues to generate theoretical and pedagogical questions. With regard to task design features, the construct of task complexity has been explored in the current study. Building on cognitive and interactionist perspectives of task-oriented second language acquisition (SLA) research, the Cognition Hypothesis, a triadic componential framework, states that sequencing tasks of increasing complexity promotes attention to linguistic forms during task-based interaction and thus facilitates L2 development (Robinson, 2001c). In a recent task-sequencing proposal, Robinson (2010) claims that cognitive demands are the sole determiner of task sequencing and further argues that task complexity variables that promote automaticity development (e.g., resource-dispersing variables) should be increased first followed by variables that draw attention to linguistic aspects (e.g., resource-directing variables).

From a pedagogical perspective, recycling or repeating parts of teaching materials is common, and previous research provides theoretical support for such practice (Bygate and Samuda, 2005). Drawing on Levelt's (1989) speech processing model, research suggests that cognitive processes become automatized at the different stages of speech production by virtue of repeating tasks (Bygate, 1996, 1999, 2001; Patanasorn, 2010). A consideration for task-based syllabi design lies in identifying the specific task characteristics that need to be repeated in order to promote L2 development while maintaining student interest. Moreover, in order to draw pedagogical implications for Robinson's Cognition Hypothesis in designing task-based syllabi, it is pertinent to investigate how complexity factors interact with other task implementation factors such as task repetition in L2 classroom contexts. The purpose of the current study is thus to explore the role of task complexity and task repetition in promoting learner attention to linguistic forms.

Designing task-based syllabi

In education, syllabi articulate pedagogical decisions and provide external representation and sequence of the units that guide pedagogical decisions. Wilkins (1976, as cited in Robinson, 2009a) distinguished between two types of syllabi design: *synthetic* and *analytic* syllabi. In a synthetic syllabus, items that are perceived as being either easier, more learnable, more frequent, or more important are first introduced (Robinson, 2009a). These items are taught in isolation, are presented in a serial fashion, and are often external to learners' authentic needs (Ellis, 2003). Thus, when engaging with the language in outside-the-classroom situations, the learners' role is to synthesize the isolated linguistic elements.

In the analytic syllabi, language is operationalized as a holistic system used for communicative purposes. In an analytic approach, linguistic elements are made explicit (i.e., focus on form) as they arise in meaning-oriented lessons (Long, 1991; Long and Robinson, 1998). The learners' responsibility is to analyse and notice the key language elements during interaction. Because learners' ability to perform these analyses will reflect their current interlanguage system, it has been argued that analytic approaches are more sensitive to SLA constructs including learnability, teachability and developmental sequences of learners' individual interlanguage development (Ellis, 2003; Robinson, 2009a).

Task-based language teaching (TBLT) pedagogy embraces an analytic approach to syllabi-design (Ellis, 2003; Long and Crookes, 1992). Holistic tasks comprise the basic unit of syllabi content. Although several working definitions of tasks are available, the general consensus is that tasks foster pragmatic processing and reflect real-world needs (Ellis, 2003; Samuda and Bygate, 2008; Skehan, 2003). Through task completion, learners encounter language in meaningful contexts, which promotes L2 development because learners are forced to use language to achieve the task goals (e.g., linguistic and functional goals), engage with grammar, consider pragmatic features, as well as focus on the social aspects of the interaction. Furthermore, during these interactions, implicit and explicit focus on form opportunities arise. Therefore task-based syllabi do not break language into small pieces; rather, they take holistic, functional and communicative tasks as the basic unit for the design of educational activity (Van den Branden, 2006). In the present chapter, tasks are operationalized as authentic and meaningful activities that learners could participate in outside the language classroom.

With the accumulation of empirical data, the focus has shifted from a comparison of the benefits of each syllabus type towards the development of empirically grounded taxonomies to inform task-syllabi sequencing (Ellis, 2003; Robinson, 2001b; Skehan and Foster, 2001). Through a needs analysis (Long, 2005), real-world tasks are identified and target features are then manipulated to increase their inherent complexity. The increases serve to gradually approximate the demands of the authentic target tasks. It is important to note that in an English as a Foreign Language (EFL) context, learners rarely use the L2 beyond their English classes. As a result, in the present study, we considered activities performed outside the language classroom in both their L1 (i.e., Korean) and L2 (i.e., English) when designing tasks. Among the various recommendations for grading and sequencing tasks, one of the most systematically examined and empirically testable theories is Robinson's Cognition Hypothesis (1995, 2001c).

Robinson's Cognition Hypothesis and SSARC model

Robinson (1995, 2001c) put forward the Cognition Hypothesis, a multiple-resource view of processing, as a means to inform task-based syllabi design and sequencing. Robinson's (2007a, 2010) theoretically motivated task design framework comprises a classification with three broad task characteristics: (1) task complexity, (2) task conditions, and (3) task difficulty. This proposal has generated a number of empirical studies (García Mayo, 2007; Gilabert, 2007; Kim, 2009b, 2012; Kim and Payant, forthcoming; Kuiken, Mos, and Vedder, 2005; Révész, 2009, 2011; Robinson, 2000, 2011b). According to Robinson (2009b), tasks should be sequenced based on task complexity which includes two categories: resource-dispersing variables and resource-directing variables.

Resource-dispersing variables place performative demands on learners. This process taps into existing knowledge and may increase access and control over this knowledge. Resource-directing variables direct learners' attention to the linguistic code and promote noticing (Schmidt, 2001). Noticing of the L2 system speeds up the grammaticization in conceptual domains and encourages learners to use more complex syntax. For example, increased reasoning demands require learners to position themselves vis-à-vis a theme and require them to express beliefs. Specific linguistic structures such as subordinate clauses are activated in order to linguistically achieve this goal. In sum, increasing the complexity of resource-directing variables is argued to lead to interlanguage development.

Task conditions include participant variables that make interactional demands (e.g., flow of information, number of participants, outcome of solution) and interactant demands (e.g., proficiency, gender, familiarity) on the learners. Task difficulty includes ability variables (e.g., working memory, aptitude) and affective variables (e.g., motivation, willingness to communicate). Since the original proposal informing the design and grading of tasks, however, researchers have not empirically tested how to sequence tasks in classroom settings widely. Recently, Robinson (2010) proposed the theoretically motivated SSARC model, a sequencing framework based on two key principles. First, Robinson argues that only the cognitive demands, which can be manipulated *a priori*, should form the theoretical basis for task sequencing. Increasing the cognitive demands of tasks, unlike interactive factors or learner factors, is hypothesized to tap into available cognitive resources required for complex processing. These can be manipulated to approximate the exigencies of real world performance. The second principle proposes a sequence within cognitive complexity variables, namely, complexity is manipulated along resource-dispersing variables followed by resource-directing variables. The SSARC model constitutes three steps. First, task complexity features are simple along resource-dispersing and resource-directing variables, which draw on simple, stable states (SS) of interlanguage development. Second, variables along resource-dispersing are increased while maintaining resource-directing variables as simple. Increasing task complexity along resource-dispersing dimensions promotes automatization (A) of interlanguage. Finally, complexity along both complexity dimensions is increased. As a result, the interlanguage undergoes restructuring (R) and new form-function/concept mappings emerge. This highest level of complexity (C) will cause the destabilizing of the interlanguage.

To date, there is growing evidence that complex tasks along resource-directing variables induce more complex and accurate language production (Kim, 2009a; Kim and Payant, forthcoming; Niwa, 2000; Robinson, 2000, 2007b) and positively impact the occurrence of interactional features (Gilabert, Barón, and Llanes, 2009; Kim, 2009a; Révész, 2011). In the present chapter, we focused specifically on the relationship between [+/− reasoning demands] and interaction-driven learning opportunities, operationalized as language-related episodes (LREs) based on the growing body of evidence that this draws learners' attention to the linguistic code. LREs are instances in the interactions where learners talk about, question, and/or self-or-other correct language use (Swain and Lapkin, 1995, 1998). As discussed in Gass and Mackey (2007), LREs have been studied within the context of interaction, representing language learning in process. These instances can relate to a variety of aspects of linguistic issues including lexis and grammar. During interaction, three possible outcomes of LREs include: correctly resolved, incorrectly resolved and unresolved. Previous research shows that the outcomes of LREs correlate with second language development (Payant, 2012; Swain and Lapkin, 1998, 2001).

The benefits of carrying out more cognitively demanding tasks on interaction-driven learning opportunities, especially when learning opportunities were operationalized as LREs, are generally well supported. For instance, Gilabert, Barón, and Llanes (2009) investigated the impact of complexity on interactional features using three unique types of tasks (i.e., narrative reconstruction task, instruction-giving map task, decision-making task). Interactional features included negotiation of meaning, recasts, self-repairs and LREs. Task complexity impacted interactional features across all tasks, with the exception of recasts during the decision-making task. Révész (2011) examined interaction-driven learning opportunities with learners from an intact ESL classroom. The learners completed both a simple and a complex version of an argumentative task. She found that the more complex task caused greater amounts of LREs during learner-learner interaction. In these studies, the quality of LREs and their resolution were not reported. Kim (2009a) examined task complexity and learner proficiency effects on the production and resolution of LREs with 34 ESL learners. She found that with the more proficient learners, the complex version of the picture narration task yielded more LREs than the simple version; however, the opposite pattern was found for the less proficient learners. In this study, although task complexity did not appear to significantly mediate resolution, a slightly higher percentage of LREs was correctly resolved during the complex tasks. In a recent study, Kim (2012) investigated the relationship between three levels of task complexity [+/− reasoning demands], LREs, as well as question development in an EFL task-based instruction context. The results indicated a greater number of LREs during complex tasks that targeted advanced question forms. Overall, although previous studies have generally suggested the positive role of carrying out more complex tasks in the amount of interactional features, particularly operationalized through LREs, the effects of intervening variables such as proficiency have been suggested.

In language classrooms, we often observe that teachers recycle either entire or parts of tasks over the semester. In previous task complexity intervention research, when researchers manipulated task complexity levels for each comparison group, students were often asked to carry out more than one task with the same level of complexity. For instance, Kim (2012) asked students in each task complexity group (simple, +complex, ++complex) to repeat four tasks which followed the sample procedure with different topics to examine the role of task complexity in question development in intact classrooms. Because she only reported the average number of LREs produced during the four tasks, it is not clear whether there were different patterns of the amount of LREs over the course of carrying out four tasks. Additionally, current discussions on task-based syllabi have overlooked the complex interaction between task complexity and task repetition, and no research to date has explored such relationship. Yet, Ellis (2003) argues that task procedures, including task repetition, may impact learner-learner interaction in terms of production and L2 development.

Task repetition

Task repetition has been one of the main implementation variables in TBLT literature. In general, task repetition has been found to positively impact learners' linguistic performance (Bygate, 1996, 2001; Gass, Mackey, Alvarez-Torres, and Fernández-García, 1999; Lynch and Maclean, 2000; Patanasorn, 2010). The rationale for repeating tasks can be best explained by considering Levelt's (1989) model of language processing. To account for speech production mechanisms, Levelt proposed three stages of planning: conceptualization (i.e., planning the content of the message), formulation (i.e., selection of lexical, phonological, and grammatical markers) and articulation (i.e., execution of the message). By repeating a similar task, the cognitive burden of speech production is alleviated given that speakers may focus less on planning the content of the message and thus allocate cognitive resources to plan the formulation and articulation of the message. Research now investigates how specific aspects of task repetition foster language performance in terms of complexity, accuracy and fluency.

Bygate (1996) implemented a story retelling task with one ESL learner on two separate occasions. The participant narrated a video extract with a three-day interval. Findings indicate overall improvement at Time 2, particularly in the areas of lexis and grammar. In later studies, Bygate (2001, 2009) investigated task repetition effects with 48 ESL learners. Two experimental groups and one control group completed a series of narrative and interview tasks which manipulated task repetition (i.e., identical content and task) and task type (i.e., identical task type). With respect to task repetition, findings showed gains in complexity for both tasks, in fluency for the interview task, but no statistical differences were observed for the number of errors per t-units (accuracy).

Patanasorn (2010) further examined the construct of task repetition with past tense morphology during learner-learner interaction with 92 Thai EFL learners in classroom contexts. Three task repetition conditions were investigated: (1) task repetition was operationalized as identical procedure and content, (2) content repetition as identical content but different tasks, and (3) procedural repetition as identical procedure but different content. Global and past simple accuracy and fluency development was measured via film retell tasks. Findings indicated that procedural repetition was more beneficial for promoting past tense accuracy development and content repetition for global fluency at the expense of simple past accuracy. Task repetition did not lead to gains accuracy or fluency. The latter finding was interpreted as lack of engagement with the task as a result of repeating identical tasks.

Kim (2013) recently conducted a partial replication of Patanasorn (2010) with 48 Korean EFL learners. In this study, she investigated task repetition and procedural repetition effects on the production and resolution of LREs in junior high school English classes. Two groups of EFL learners were randomly assigned to the task repetition group or the procedural task repetition group. The results indicated that procedural repetition induced more production of LREs than task repetition.

It can be concluded that both task complexity and task repetition mediate the amount of interaction-driven learning opportunities operationalized as LREs. Studies in the domain of task complexity suggest that increased complexity along resource-directing variables in general positively impacts the production of LREs. With regard to the role of task repetition in the occurrence of LREs, Kim (2013) found that procedural repetition tended to promote more LREs, particularly focusing on vocabulary issues. Therefore, a necessary direction to test the predictions stipulated by the Cognition Hypothesis and the SSARC model (2010), which claim that complexity is the sole determiner of task sequencing, is to examine the interaction between task complexity and task repetition to inform to what extent certain levels of task complexity need to be repeated to maximize task-based language learning. Thus the current chapter investigated the interaction between task complexity along [+/– reasoning demands] and two aspects of task repetition on the amount and resolution of interactional features during learner-learner interaction in a classroom-based context. This was a follow-up study of Kim (2013) by adding a task complexity variable, and the findings can provide pedagogical insights by examining two relevant dimensions believed to impact learners' attention to form during interaction and inform task-based syllabi sequencing. The study was guided by the following research question:

> How do task complexity (simple vs. complex) and task repetition conditions (task repetition vs. procedural repetition) impact the occurrence and the resolution of LREs during collaborative task performance over time?

Based on the predictions of the Cognition Hypothesis, it was hypothesized that learners' attention to linguistic form, namely LREs, would be lower for the simple task than for the complex task group. It was also hypothesized that LREs would be fewer for simple task repetition and greatest for the complex procedural repetition.

Methods

Research design

To test the effects of task complexity and task repetition on interaction-driven learning opportunities, the resource-directing variable [+/– reasoning demands] was manipulated. Drawing on previous task repetition studies (e.g., Patanasorn, 2010), two task repetition conditions were explored: repeating content and procedure of a task on three occasions (i.e., task repetition) and repeating procedure of a task with different content on three occasions (i.e., procedural repetition). Each of the four intact classes was randomly assigned to one of the following conditions:

- Condition 1: simple task content/procedural repetition (task repetition)
- Condition 2: simple task procedural repetition (simple/procedural repetition)
- Condition 3: complexity task content/procedural repetition (complex/task repetition)

- Condition 4: complex task procedural repetition (complex/procedural repetition).

Participants

The study was carried out over three instruction sessions with 92 Korean junior high school female students from four intact classes. The learners' ages were between 13 and 14 years (M=13.51). The learners had received at least three years of mandatory English lessons since elementary school. The regular school curricula required four hours of English lessons per week; three meetings were taught by their regular (Korean L1) English teacher and one meeting was with a native English-speaking teacher. Their regular English lessons addressed the importance of building reading and listening skills, vocabulary knowledge, and grammatical competence. In terms of enhancing oral communication skill, each chapter introduced useful expressions organized by speech acts such as requests and refusals.

Instructional materials

Learners from four intact classes participated in three two-way collaborative tasks during regularly scheduled class times. For the task repetition condition, learners participated in the identical two-way information gap task on the topic of hosting an American friend. For the procedural repetition condition, three comparable versions of the tasks were created based on the following topics: (1) hosting an American friend, (2) describing school events, and (3) discussing mayoral candidates. Based on Samuda and Bygate's (2008) task definition, holistic tasks considering learners' real-world needs were devised. These topics were chosen based on learners' daily language use in Korean and current events that they were familiar with.

Task complexity was manipulated according to the [+/– reasoning demands] variable following Robinson's Cognition Hypothesis (Robinson, 2001c). The simple group was required to simply exchange information about four unique activities in order to make a report of the discussed activities, whereas the complex group was required to select one activity/person that should be continued/elected while exchanging information. The process of evaluating and making a decision about the information was hypothesized to increase the cognitive load. These tasks were implemented in their regular course curricula. Details of the sample task 'hosting an American friend' are provided in Table 6.1.

Table 6.1 Descriptions of simple and complex version of 'Hosting an American Friend' task

Simple	Complex
[– reasoning demand]	[+ reasoning demand]
Task input: Name of a destination with two pictures along with 10 unique verbs Table to report places/events	**Task input:** Name of a destination with two pictures along with 10 unique verbs Table to report places/events
Task outcome: Report activities students did with their American friend in Korea. [- reasoning demands]	**Task outcome:** Suggest one activity that should be continued, and one event that should not be continued next year. [+ reasoning demands]

Procedure

The study was carried out over three days (see Table 6.2). Learners from the simple-task repetition and the complex-task repetition groups repeated the identical task on three occasions. Each time learners worked with partners who had different pictures. This allowed each learner to receive different input but to repeat the same output. Learners from the simple and complex procedural repetition groups worked with new contents on each day as well as with a new partner. Learner-learner interaction while carrying out the tasks was audio-recorded. During the interaction, both researcher and the teacher were present in the classroom; however, in order to control for teacher effects, neither teacher nor researcher initiated any comments. Instead, they responded to student-initiated questions.

Table 6.2 Procedure of task repetition

	Simple/Task Repetition	Complex/Task Repetition	Simple/Procedural Repetition	Complex/Procedural Repetition
Day 1	Task #:1 Hosting an American friend		Task #1: Hosting an American friend	
Day 2	Task #2: Hosting an American friend		Task #2: Describing a school event	
Day 3	Task #3: Hosting an American friend		Task #3: Discussing Mayoral candidate	

Data coding

All task performance recordings were transcribed. Data were analysed in terms of learners' attention to linguistic forms, operationalized as LREs, namely instances in the interactions where learners talked about, questioned, and/or self-or-other corrected language use (Swain and Lapkin, 1995, 1998). Two types of LREs were identified: lexical and grammatical LREs. Lexical LREs included instances where learners discussed word meaning, lexical equivalents/translations, as well as spelling. Grammatical LREs included instances where learners discussed syntactic aspects such as question formation, verb tense and sentence structure. The resolution of LREs was identified as follows: (1) learner-learner correctly resolved LREs, (2) learner-teacher correctly resolved LREs, (3) incorrectly resolved LREs, (4) unresolved LREs. Example 1 illustrates a sample learner-learner correctly resolved grammatical LRE targeting a question form.

Example 1: Correctly resolved grammatical LRE

> L1: ... Finally we went to the top of the mountain. We said bye bye.
> L2: How last your feel?
> L1: What?
> L2: How 기분이 어땠냐고? ([How] did you feel?)
> L1: How did you feel?
> L2: Yeah. How did you feel?
> L1: I was at first. I was very sad.

There are occasions where learners are unable to provide some assistance to their peers and rather than trying other sources, the learners proceed with the task (i.e., unresolved LREs). Example 2 describes an unresolved lexical LRE.

Example 2: Unresolved lexical LRE

> L1: What did you saw in there?
> L2: We walked old way and rest in 한옥? (Korean traditional house) 한옥이 영어로 뭐야? (What do you say 'hanok' in English?)
> L1: 몰라 (I don't know). 그냥 한옥이라고 해 (Just say 'Hanok' in Korean)
> L2: We rest in 한옥. (Korean traditional house)
> L1: What did you do next?

The second coder coded 20 percent of the data, and there was 91 percent simple agreement. Any disagreements were discussed and resolved, often following the opinion of the researcher who was present in the classroom during data collection.

Results

The research question investigated the effects of task complexity and task repetition on interaction-driven learning opportunities, and particularly examined the extent to which each task repetition mediated the role of task complexity on the occurrence and resolution of lexical and grammatical LREs. The total number of LREs was tabulated according to type (i.e., lexical LREs and grammatical LREs) and resolution (i.e., learner-learner correctly resolved, learner-teacher correctly resolved, incorrectly resolved, and unresolved) for each of the four conditions. Table 6.3 provides descriptive statistics for the number of lexical and grammatical LREs produced by the four groups.

As shown in Table 6.3, the mean total of 49.61 and 79.80 LREs were produced by the simple/task repetition group and the simple/procedural repetition group respectively, whereas the complex/task repetition and the complex/procedural repetition produced 51.60 and 78.71 LREs respectively. The two-way ANOVA results indicated that there was no impact of task complexity on both lexical [F $(1, 88)=.66, p=.57$] and grammatical [F $(1, 88)=3.22, p=.32$] LREs. With regard to the role of task repetition, the descriptive statistics showed that the procedural repetition conditions ($M=79.80$ and $M=78.71$) promoted more LREs than the task repetition conditions ($M=49.61$ and $M=51.60$) regardless of task complexity levels. The two-way ANOVAs showed that the characteristics of task repetition

Table 6.3 Descriptive statistics for the number of LREs

	Simple/ Task repetition (n=23)		Simple/ Procedural repetition (n=25)		Complex/ Task repetition (n=20)		Complex/ Procedural repetition (n=24)	
	M	*SD*	*M*	*SD*	*M*	*SD*	*M*	*SD*
Lexical LREs	23.09	6.53	43.28	8.06	27.35	5.89	42.83	7.41
Grammatical LREs	26.52	6.28	36.52	11.39	24.25	9.23	35.88	9.26
Total LREs	49.61	10.21	79.80	13.68	51.60	12.12	78.71	11.01

(i.e., repeating both content and procedure vs. repeating procedure) significantly affected the number of grammatical LREs, F (1, 88)=31.02, p=.00, as well as lexical LREs, F (1, 88)=144.66, p=. 00. In addition, there was no interaction effect of task complexity and task repetition on the total number of lexical LREs, [F(1, 88)=2.52, p=.17] as well as grammatical LREs [F (1, 88)=.18, p=.68].

In order to understand task repetition effects, Figure 6.1 shows the frequency of LREs over time in each condition (i.e., simple/task repetition, simple/procedural repetition, complex/task repetition, complex/procedural repetition).

As shown in Figure 6.1, the two procedural repetition conditions, regardless of task complexity (i.e., simple vs. complex), showed an increase in the total number of LREs over the course of the three task performance sessions. However, the learners from the complex/task repetition group produced fewer LREs during Task 3 compared to Task 1 and Task 2. This is the only group who experienced a drop between Task 2 and Task 3.

Table 6.4 presents the descriptive statistics for the total number of lexical LREs as well as the occurrence of lexical LREs over three task performance sessions. Overall, learners from the procedural repetition groups produced a higher number of lexical LREs than the learners from the task repetition groups. An increase in the number of lexical LREs over time in both simple/procedural repetition and complex/procedural repetition groups was observed, and was especially noticeable between Task 2 and Task 3. On the other hand, the number of lexical LREs decreased consistently in the simple/task repetition group such that by Task 3, learners produced only 5.35 lexical LREs, approximately half compared to Task 1. Finally, the complex/task repetition group produced the greatest number of lexical LREs during Task 2 and the fewest at Task 3.

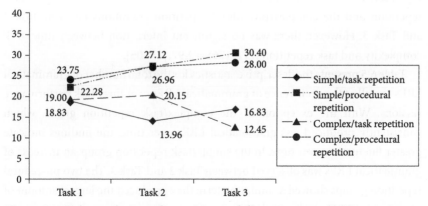

Figure 6.1 Task complexity, task repetition, and the occurrence of LREs over time

Table 6.4 The occurrence of lexical LREs over time

Group	Simple/Task repetition (n=23)		Simple/Procedural repetition (n=25)		Complex/Task repetition (n=20)		Complex/Procedural repetition (n=24)	
	M	**SD**	**M**	**SD**	**M**	**SD**	**M**	**SD**
Task 1	10.96	3.88	11.92	5.74	9.65	2.74	12.21	4.91
Task 2	6.78	3.01	12.96	4.54	11.50	3.72	13.25	4.42
Task 3	5.35	2.95	18.40	4.69	6.20	2.75	17.37	4.51
Total	23.09	6.53	43.28	8.06	27.35	5.89	42.83	7.41

The mixed ANOVA revealed no significant effect for time [$F(2, 176) = .80, p = .45$] on the occurrence of lexical LREs; however, there were significant interaction effects between time and complexity [$F(2, 176)=3.46, p=.03$] and time and repetition [$F(2, 176)=38.69, p=.00$]. For instance, at Task 1, in the simple/task repetition group and the complex/task repetition group, 10.96 and 9.65 lexical LREs were identified respectively. However, at Task 2, in the simple/task repetition group, the amount of lexical LREs decreased (i.e., $M= 6.78$) and they increased in the complex/task repetition group ($M=11.50$). While LREs decreased under both conditions at Task 3, a large decrease was observed for the complex/task repetition group ($M=6.20$). An interaction effect was also identified for time and repetition. In the simple/task repetition and simple/procedural repetition groups, 6.78 and 12.96 lexical LREs were identified at Task 2, respectively. However, at Task 3, while there was an increase in the number of lexical LREs in the simple/procedural repetition ($M=18.40$), a large decrease was observed for simple/task repetition ($M=5.35$). Similar tendencies were observed for the complex/task repetition and the complex/procedural repetition conditions between Task 2 and Task 3. However, there was no significant interaction between time, task complexity and task repetition [$F(2, 176) = 2.97, p = .05$].

Table 6.5 presents the descriptive statistics for the total number of grammatical LREs as well as the occurrence of grammatical LREs over three task performance sessions. With the exception of the complex/task repetition group, which consistently produced less grammatical LREs over time, the findings indicate greater fluctuation over time. In the simple/task repetition group, an increase of grammatical LREs was observed between Task 2 and Task 3. The two procedural repetition groups showed a similar pattern: they produced the largest amount of grammatical LREs during Task 2.

Table 6.5 The occurrence of grammatical LREs over time

Group	Simple/Task repetition (n=23)		Simple/Procedural repetition (n=25)		Complex/Task repetition (n=20)		Complex/Procedural repetition (n=24)	
	M	**SD**	**M**	**SD**	**M**	**SD**	**M**	**SD**
Task 1	7.87	3.24	10.36	4.73	9.35	6.03	11.54	4.73
Task 2	7.17	2.92	14.16	7.23	8.65	4.51	13.71	6.77
Task 3	11.48	4.13	12.00	5.10	6.25	4.71	10.63	3.72
Total	26.52	6.28	36.52	11.39	24.25	9.23	35.88	9.26

The mixed ANOVA revealed no significant effect for time [$F(2, 176)=1.38, p = .25$]; however, there were significant interaction effects between time and complexity [$F(2, 176)=6.04, p=.00$] and between time and repetition [$F(2, 176)=4.33, p=.02$] on grammatical LREs. For instance, at Task 2, in the simple/task repetition group and the complex/task repetition group, 7.17 and 8.65 grammatical LREs were identified respectively. An increase in the number of grammatical LREs (i.e., $M=11.48$) in the simple/task repetition group was observed at Task 3 compared to a decrease of grammatical LREs ($M=6.25$) in the complex/task repetition group. As for the simple/procedural and complex/procedural repetition, while the simple/procedural repetition group produced slightly fewer grammatical LREs than the complex/procedural repetition group at Task 1, (10.36 vs. 11.54), at Task 2, grammatical LREs (i.e., $M=14.16$) in the simple/procedural repetition group outnumbered the complex/procedural group ($M=13.71$). An interaction was also identified for time and repetition. In the simple/task repetition and simple/procedural repetition groups, 7.17 and 14.16 grammatical LREs were identified at Task 2 respectively. Over time, in the simple/task repetition, the number of grammatical LREs increased ($M=11.48$); yet only a marginal decrease in the simple/procedural repetition group was identified ($M=12.00$). Finally, there was no significant interaction between time, task complexity, and task repetition [$F(2, 176) = 2.19, p=.12$].

As discussed earlier, the resolution of LREs was coded based on the following criteria: learner-learner correctly resolved, learner-teacher correctly resolved, incorrectly resolved, and unresolved. Figure 6.2 reveals that, when combining correctly resolved LREs produced by learner-learner and learner-teacher, 85 per cent of LREs produced in the simple/procedural repetition group were correctly resolved with the remainder incorrectly resolved (10 per cent) or unresolved (5 per cent). The simple/task repetition group resolved about 81 per cent LREs,

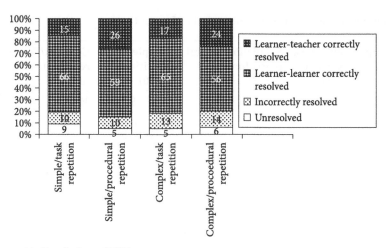

Figure 6.2 Resolution of LREs

leaving 9 per cent unresolved and 10 per cent incorrectly resolved. Similarly, 80 per cent and 82 per cent of LREs were resolved correctly in the complex/ procedural repetition and the complex/task repetition groups. When considering who contributed to the correct resolutions, 59 per cent of the LREs were learner-learner correctly resolved and 26 per cent of the LREs were learner-teacher correctly resolved in the simple/procedural repetition group, whereas, for the simple/task repetition group, 66 per cent of the LREs were learner-learner correctly resolved and 15 per cent of the LREs were learner-teacher correctly resolved. A total of 56 per cent and 65 per cent of LREs were learner-learner correctly resolved by the complex/procedural repetition and the complex/task repetition groups respectively. In sum, while the learners were highly successful with independent resolutions, the learners experienced even more success in the task repetition groups, regardless of complexity.

To summarize, the findings of the current study showed that there were no significant task complexity effects on the occurrence of lexical and grammatical LREs, whereas the characteristics of task repetition significantly impacted the number of lexical and grammatical LREs. Furthermore, when examining the number of lexical LREs produced over time, the results showed that the number of LREs in procedural repetition conditions increased over time regardless of task complexity levels. For the grammatical LREs, similar trends for procedural repetition conditions were observed only between Task 1 and Task 2. With regard to task repetition, the results showed that the number of grammatical LREs tended to decrease only in the complex condition. The analysis of the occurrence of lexical LREs and grammatical LREs over time uncovered an interaction for time and complexity as well as an interaction for time and repetition. Overall, a stronger interaction effect was observed for simple/task repetition and complex/task repetition conditions. In terms of time and task repetition, lexical LREs were much greater at Task 3 for procedural repetition. Patterns of resolution indicated, overall, a high percentage of resolution regardless of task complexity and task repetition. However, under procedural repetition, learners tended to rely more extensively on their teachers to correctly resolve LREs.

Discussion

Building on cognitive and interactionist perspectives of task-oriented SLA research, Robinson's Cognition Hypothesis has been increasingly tested in L2 classroom contexts, particularly during learner-learner interaction (Gilabert, Barón, and Levkina, 2011; Kim, 2009a, 2012; Nuevo, 2006). Previous studies that manipulated the design characteristic [+/− reasoning demands] have generally supported the claim that increased complexity (i.e., + reasoning) promotes interaction-driven learning opportunities during collaborative tasks (e.g., Kim, 2009a, 2012; Révész, 2011). Evidence for increased complexity is not limited to this particular characteristic (see, e.g., García Mayo, 2007; Robinson, 2011b). With the growing body of empirical support for grading task complexity, task sequencing proposals are emerging. Robinson (2010) proposed the SSARC model for task sequencing and is built on the premise that task complexity is the sole determiner of task sequencing. He further proposes that variables along resource-dispersing dimensions should first be increased and be followed by those variables along resource-directing dimensions.

In order to establish optimal task sequencing, we propose other empirical considerations, namely, task repetition. The rationale is that the act of repeating a task or specific components of a task will enable learners to reorganize and consolidate existing information. In task-based language classrooms, teachers often ask learners to repeat tasks and activities (Bygate and Samuda, 2005). In a previous study, Kim (2013) found that learners and teachers attributed benefits to repeating tasks. To date, task repetition research has provided empirical evidence that task repetition draws learners' attention to L2 performance (Bygate, 1996, 2001; Ellis, 2003; Gass, et al., 1999; Lynch and Maclean, 2000; Patanasorn, 2010). Despite the benefits of task repetition, research has not addressed potential interaction effects between repeating certain task characteristics and task complexity and how this would promote attention to form during meaning-oriented tasks over time. The present study was thus guided by the need to determine the interaction between task complexity and aspects of task repetition as a preliminary step for task sequencing decisions.

When examining the role of task complexity on the occurrence of LREs, a complexity effect was not identified. The participants who completed the complex versions of the tasks did not produce more lexical LREs or grammatical LREs than the participants from the simple version. In line with Gilabert et al., (2009), these findings do not support the Cognition Hypothesis: increasing task complexity along resource-directing variables did not have significant impacts on attention to form in this particular context. The analysis also examined whether two specific aspects of task repetition (i.e., procedural repetition and task repetition) promoted attention to form. The findings indicated that learners from the task repetition group produced a significantly smaller amount of grammatical and lexical LREs (i.e., less focus on form) compared to the learners from the procedural repetition group. One possible explanation to account for these findings is that learners disengaged with identical materials and thus ceased to question gaps in their interlanguage. However, the findings may also be attributed to the changes in the cognitive load. According to Levelt (1989), language production entails three primary processes, generating content, formulating, and articulating of the message. As a result of repeating tasks, these processes become more automatic and form–meaning connections may become stronger. Thus, the decrease in the total number of LREs may be a reflection of having activated the grammar and lexis needed to engage in the task, thus facilitating the consolidation of knowledge.

The potential for language development rests largely on the resolution of LREs (Kim and McDonough, 2008; Payant, 2012; Swain and Lapkin, 1998, 2001). The participants from the task repetition groups correctly resolved only a marginally higher percentage of LREs without seeking the help from their teacher. With the teachers' assistance, learners from all task condition correctly resolved a comparable amount of LREs (i.e., between 80–85 per cent). These findings echo Kim (2009a) and Payant (2012) who found that learners were able to successfully resolve LREs during learner-learner interaction. Although neither task repetition nor task complexity mediated the resolution of LREs, these findings provide positive evidence that during learner-learner interaction, learners are afforded opportunities to discuss lexical and grammatical aspects, which has been linked directly to language development in some of the previous LREs studies (Payant, 2012; Swain and Lapkin, 1998, 2001).

Previous task repetition studies that have focused specifically on language performance report task repetition effects. For instance, Bygate (2001) found that task repetition and task type repetition led to significant gains in complexity and fluency; however, accuracy was not impacted. Patanasorn (2010), on the other hand, found that learners from only the procedural repetition and content repetition groups experienced gains in accuracy and fluency. Similar to our findings, task repetition (i.e., repeating both procedure and content) was less influential. Future replication studies are needed to corroborate these findings.

The primary goal of the present study was to examine interaction effects between task complexity and aspects of task repetition on the occurrence of interaction-driven learning opportunities. However, building on the notion that task repetition may lead to the automatization of cognitive processes, a close examination of what transpires during each task implementation also serves to inform task sequencing in task-based instruction. In particular, previous research has not addressed the optimal number of repetitions (i.e., how many times should a task be repeated to maximize task-based language learning?), thus it is important to focus on the changes of the occurrence of LREs over time. When tasks were repeated a first time (Task 2), learners from the complex task groups, regardless of the repetition condition, produced a greater number of lexical LREs. In line with previous findings (e.g., Révész, 2011), LREs initiated by linguistic needs are subject to task complexity, thus providing support, under some conditions, for the Cognition Hypothesis. The manipulation of the resource-directing variable, which required participants to evaluate information and make a decision, appears to have drawn the learners' attention to specific task-relevant constructs (lexis). The increased communicative demands led to more LREs, at least in the short term, given that this trend only persisted for the complex/procedural repetition group. When recycling both content and procedure a second time (Task 3), complexity effects could be attenuated. In other words, students might not experience the same level of complexity while carrying out complex versions of tasks as they repeat tasks. The simple groups, however, showed a different picture. For instance, a continual decrease in the total number of lexical LREs was observed for the simple/task repetition group. These findings suggest that maintaining tasks as simple as possible (i.e., [-reasoning demands]) while recycling content and procedures, may induce fewer language-driven learning opportunities, but that increases in the complexity while repeating content and task procedures may not promote sustained attention to form.

In terms of the occurrence of grammatical LREs, the simple/task repetition group produced a similar, albeit smaller number of grammatical LREs during

Task 2 compared to Task 1; however, the amount of grammatical LREs increased drastically at Task 3. In terms of the easiness of task performance, repeating the exact same simple task (i.e., simple/task repetition) was hypothesized to be the easiest condition out of the four conditions included in the study. Thus, it may follow that automatization of the content was facilitated by repeating the task and content under cognitively less demanding situations, and only then would learners be in a position to notice gaps in their linguistic system, particularly focusing on grammar forms. This could explain why under the complex condition, at Task 3, learners continued to produce fewer grammar-based LREs. A comparison of task repetition effects on lexical and grammatical LREs shows that over time, while task repetition may benefit the development of lexis (less need to discuss vocabulary), having more available resources may induce more discussions about grammar.

The contrasting patterns for lexical and grammatical LREs over time force us to consider the role of task content and its impact on interaction-driven learning opportunities. Although two procedural repetition groups (simple and complex) similarly showed an increasing pattern on the number of lexical LREs between Task 1 and Task 2, there was more noticeable increase in the number of lexical LREs between Task 2 and Task 3. Because lexical LREs might be sensitive to the content of the tasks, carrying out the task on mayoral candidate might induce more discussion on vocabulary use than the task on school event. In terms of grammatical LREs, content can also impact the syntactic structures required to accomplish the task. Despite having familiarity with vocabulary to discuss school events, findings indicate a higher number of grammatical LREs at Task 2 than at Task 3 for both complexity conditions. In order to fully understand how task content or task familiarity plays a role in the relationship between task complexity, task repetition and learning opportunities, future studies which include the content repetition group (i.e., repeating the content only with different procedure) are warranted.

Overall, the present study showed a significant task repetition effect on the occurrence of LREs but did not support the benefits of carrying out cognitively more complex tasks, following Robinson's Cognition Hypothesis (Robinson, 2001b, 2009b, 2011a). These findings provide additional insights into the role of task complexity in learners' attention to form over time. As shown in the current study, the relationship between task complexity and learners' attention to linguistic form could be varied as the learners repeat various aspects of tasks over time. Furthermore, time alone did not seem to impact the occurrence of LREs; however, in the present study, the significant interaction between time and complexity and time and repetition was identified for lexical LREs and grammatical LREs, suggesting a complex interaction between these variables. While there was an interaction between time and complexity for lexical LREs, the findings suggest a stronger interaction for grammatical LREs, especially with the task repetition condition. The interaction between time and repetition appears to be greatest for grammatical LREs, especially under simple conditions. Thus, the present study shows how time and complexity variables may impact how learners focus on the linguistic code with greater attention to form (grammatical LREs), at least under simple conditions.

From this study, theoretical and pedagogical implications can be derived. First, from a theoretical point of view, the findings from the present study do not provide strong support for Robinson's prediction such that complexity alone did not promote greater production of LREs. What appears to be an important determiner is the act of repeating certain characteristics of tasks. Bygate and Samuda (2005) propose that task repetition has two phases: in a first phase, learners organize the cognitive content and during the second, learners build on the schema generated during the first realization of the task. In this respect, task repetition serves planning functions in language production. Therefore, in future task complexity studies, particularly when the studies are carried out in classroom contexts following task-based syllabi, the task repetition factors need to be taken into consideration. The current study did not directly test Robinson's (2010) SSARC model; however, we believe that task sequencing models may also benefit from considering task implementation factors such as task repetition. The findings of the study suggest that the repetition of tasks may equip learners with prior knowledge, gained from completing the initial task.

From a pedagogical perspective, task repetition can positively impact procedural demands and increase automatization. Thus when designing task-based syllabi, it is important to promote procedural knowledge which can be facilitated through a certain degree of repetition (i.e., practice) (DeKeyser, 2007). Another benefit of repeating different characteristics of tasks relates directly to output production. Engaging in familiar tasks with unique content enables learners to produce pushed output, which helps learners notice incomplete knowledge and engage in discussions about the language (Swain, 2005). In the present context, while all learners repeated the procedures, two groups also repeated the same content which could bring up the issue of ecological validity. Yet, by diversifying the make-up of the student dyads on each occasion, learners were exposed to novel constructions. To echo Lynch and Maclean (2000), repeating content does not entail duplication but rather provides opportunities for producing and hearing novel constructions. Research drawing on the Cognition Hypothesis often indicates the value of developing complex tasks in focusing learners' attention to the language; yet few studies have examined how task repetition mediates complexity. Although the benefits of task repetition were more salient than those attributed to task complexity, the present classroom-based research identified some value in developing simple tasks that recycle both content and procedure. As learners repeat a simpler version of a task, cognitive resources are freed up and learners are better positioned to identify gaps in their interlanguage. Finally, it is important to highlight the importance of teacher-mediated resolutions. During learner-learner interaction, learners encounter gaps and rely on their teachers for guidance. This type of interaction can serve to inform teachers of their individual students' interlanguage and tailor their instruction to their specific needs.

When sequencing tasks following Robinson's SSARC model (2010), teachers need to explore to what extent different characteristics of tasks need to be repeated to promote language developing in task-based instruction. For instance, before raising task complexity along with resource-directing dimensions, the question of how many times tasks with different complexity based on resource-dispersing dimensions need to be repeated should be considered. In addition to task features, given the large variation in learner success in terms of L2 development, SLA theories should account for individual differences. Two well-documented variables shown to impact SLA processes are aptitude and motivation (Robinson, 2001a). However, in language classrooms, variation in learner motivation and aptitude, while expected, cannot be manipulated *a priori*. Therefore, while theories of SLA need to consider individual differences, identifying optimal task sequencing based on these variables is difficult to achieve, and at this stage of theorizing, task features that can be manipulated are of greater immediate relevance.

In the present study, we explored learners' resolution of LREs. The results indicated that learners who repeated the same task experienced greater autonomy in correctly resolving LREs, thus placing more responsibility on the learners for their L2 development. This suggests that repeating some aspects of task could be useful to encourage learners to solve their linguistic questions during task-based interaction.

Despite the contributions of the present study, there are several limitations that need to be acknowledged. First, it is important to note that producing LREs is not the same as language learning. In fact, fewer LREs might indicate that learners faced fewer difficulties during task performance. Therefore, future studies should include measures which determine language learning based on LREs (e.g., tailor-made post-tests). Additionally, the study was not carried out in classes where task-based syllabi were followed. In order to increase validity of task-based research, it is important to conduct studies in a context where task-based syllabi are implemented. Finally, when the different contents were selected, we focused on the real events that happened at the students' school or in the city where the school was located. However, learners' familiarity with task content was not explicitly measured or addressed in the current study. Learners' pre-existing familiarity with task contents and procedure could have been controlled more when designing the materials. Needless to say, future studies are warranted to investigate individual differences focusing on learner anxiety, motivation and proficiency to fully understand how task repetition and task complexity interact within various L2 contexts.

Conclusion

The impetus for the development of sound, task-based taxonomies has drawn increasing attention over the last 20 years. Research on the Cognition Hypothesis has shown complex interactions between various task features on language-driven learning opportunities as well as on L2 performance. Yet, in light of the finding that complexity alone does not account for more focus on form opportunities during interaction, we believe that the development of taxonomies should consider task complexity variables as well as the relationship between task complexity and aspects of task repetition. Task repetition, a key feature of a number of communicative language tasks, appears to be an important, yet overlooked, dimension of task-based research. With this study, further empirical evidence supports the idea that repeating tasks benefits form–meaning connections and creates learner autonomy in the resolution of linguistic gaps. We believe that the interaction between task repetition and task complexity is valuable information for task-syllabi sequencing proposals but, more importantly, the findings provide further evidence that the development of taxonomies needs to move away from the study of isolated, fragmented task features and examine how various design characteristics interact.

References

Bygate, M. (1996). Effects of task repetition: Appraising the developing language of learners. In J. Willis and D. Willis (eds), *Challenge and Change in Language Teaching* (pp. 136–46). London: Heinemann.

—— (1999). Quality of language and purpose of task: Patterns of learners' language on two oral communication tasks. *Language Teaching Research*, 3 (3), 185–214. doi: 10.1177/136216889900300302

—— (2001). Effects of task repetition on the structure and control of language. In M. Bygate, P. Skehan and M. Swain (eds), *Task-based Learning: Language Teaching, Learning, and Assessment* (pp. 23–48). London: Longman.

—— (2009). Effects of task repetition on the structure and control of oral language. In K. Van den Branden, M. Bygate and J. M. Norris (eds), *Task-Based Language Teaching: A Reader* (pp. 249–74). Amsterdam/Philadelphia: John Benjamins Publishing Company.

Bygate, M. and Samuda, V. (2005). Integrative planning through the use of task repetition. In R. Ellis (ed.), *Planning and Task Performance in a Second Language* (pp. 37–76). Amsterdam/New York: Benjamins.

DeKeyser, R. M. (2007). *Practice in a Second Language: Perspectives from Applied Linguistics and Cognitive Psychology.* Cambridge: Cambridge University Press.

Ellis, R. (2003). *Task-Based Language Learning and Teaching.* Oxford: Oxford University Press.

—— (2012). *Language Teaching Research and Language Pedagogy.* Malden: MA: Wiley-Blackwell.

García Mayo, M. d. P. (ed.). (2007). *Investigating Tasks in Formal Language Learning.* Clevedon: Multilingual Matters.

Gass, S. M. and Mackey, A. (2007). Input, interaction and output in second language acquisition. In J. Williams and B. VanPatten (eds), *Theories in Second Language Acquisition* (pp. 175–99). Mahwah, NJ: Lawrence Erlbaum.

Gass, S. M., Mackey, A., Alvarez-Torres, M. J. and Fernández-García, M. (1999). The effects of task repetition on linguistic output. *Language Learning*, 49 (4), 549–81. doi: 10.1111/0023-8333.00102

Gilabert, R. (2007). The simultaneous manipulation of task complexity along planning time and (+/– here-and-now): Effects on L2 oral production. In M. d. P. García Mayo (ed.), *Investigating Tasks in Formal Language Learning* (pp. 44–68). Clevedon: Multilingual Matters.

Gilabert, R., Barón, J. and Levkina, M. (2011). Manipulating task complexity across task types and modes. In P. Robinson (ed.), *Second Language Task Complexity: Researching the Cognition Hypothesis of Language Learning and Performance* (pp. 105–38). Amsterdam: John Benjamins Publishing Company.

Gilabert, R., Barón, J. and Llanes, À. (2009). Manipulating cognitive complexity across task types and its impact on learners' interaction during oral performance. *International Review of Applied Linguistics in Language Teaching*, 47 (3/4), 367–95. doi: http://dx.doi.org/10.1515/iral.2009.016

Kim, Y. (2009a). The effects of task complexity on learner-learner interaction. *System*, 37 (2), 254–68. doi: http://dx.doi.org/10.1016/j.system.2009.02.003

—— (2009b). *The Role of Task Complexity and Pair Grouping on the Occurrence of Learning Opportunities and L2 Development*. Unpublished doctoral dissertation. Northern Arizona University.

—— (2012). Task complexity, learning opportunities and Korean EFL learners' question development. *Studies in Second Language Acquisition*, 34, 627–58. doi: 10.1017/S0272263112000368

—— (2013). Promoting attention to form through task repetition in a Korean EFL context. In K. McDonough and A. Mackey (eds), *Second Language Interaction in Diverse Educational Settings*. Philadelphia, PA: John Benjamins.

Kim, Y., and McDonough, K. (2008). The effect of interlocutor proficiency on the collaborative dialogue between Korean as a second language learners. *Language Teaching Research*, 12 (2), 211–34. doi: 10.1177/1362168807086288

Kim, Y. and Payant, C. (forthcoming). Impacts of task complexity on the development of L2 oral performance over time. *International Review of Applied Linguistics*.

Kuiken, F., Mos, M. and Vedder, I. (2005). Cognitive task complexity and second language writing performance. *EUROSLA Yearbook*, 5, 195–222.

Levelt, W. J. M. (1989). *Speaking: From Intention to Articulation*. Cambridge, MA: MIT Press.

Long, M. H. (1991). Focus on form: A design feature in language teaching methodology. In K. De Bot, R. Ginsberg and C. Kramsch (eds), *Foreign Language Research in Cross-cultural Perspective* (pp. 39–52). Amsterdam: John Benjamins.

—— (2005). *Second Language Needs Analysis*. Cambridge: Cambridge University Press.

Long, M. H. and Crookes, G. (1992). Three approaches to task-based syllabus design. *TESOL Quarterly*, 26 (1), 27–56. doi: 10.2307/3587368

Long, M. H. and Robinson, P. (1998). Focus on form: Theory, research and practice. In C. Doughty and J. Williams (eds), *Focus on Form in Classroom Second Language Acquisition* (pp. 15–41). Cambridge: Cambridge University Press.

Lynch, T. and Maclean, J. (2000). Exploring the benefits of task repetition and recycling for classroom language learning. *Language Teaching Research*, 4 (3), 221–50. doi: 10.1177/136216880000400303

Niwa, Y. (2000). *Reasoning Demands of L2 Tasks and L2 Narrative Production: Effects of Individual Differences in Working Memory, Intelligence, and Aptitude*. M.A. dissertation, Aoyama Gakuin University, Tokyo.

Nuevo, A. (2006). *Task Complexity and Interaction: L2 Learning Opportunities and Development*. Unpublished doctoral dissertation. Georgetown University. Washington, DC.

Patanasorn, C. (2010). *Effects of Procedural Content and Task Repetition on Accuracy and*

Fluency in an EFL Context. Unpublished doctoral dissertation. Northern Arizona University.

Payant, C. (2012). *Learner-learner Interaction: An Exploration of the Mediating Functions of Multilingual Learners' Languages in an L3 Foreign Language Classroom.* Unpublished dissertation. Georgia State University.

Révész, A. (2009). Task complexity, focus on form, and second language development. *Studies in Second Language Acquisition,* 31 (3), 437–70. doi: http://dx.doi. org/10.1017/S0272263109090366

—— (2011). Task complexity, focus on L2 constructions, and individual differences: A classroom-based study. *The Modern Language Journal,* 95 (4). doi: 10.1111/j.1540-4781.2011.01241.x

Robinson, P. (1995). Task complexity and second language narrative discourse. *Language Learning,* 45 (1), 99.

—— (2000). *Task Complexity and Reasoning Demands: Effects on Dyadic NNS-NNS Interaction, Fluency, Accuracy, Complexity, and Incorporation of Input.* Unpublished data, Aoyama Gakuin University, Tokyo.

—— (2001a). Individual differences, cognitive abilities, aptitude complexes and learning conditions in second language acquisition. *Second Language Research,* 17 (4), 368–92.

—— (2001b). Task complexity, cognitive resources, and syllabus design: A triadic framework for examining task influences on SLA. In P. Robinson (ed.), *Cognition and Second Language Instruction* (pp. 287–318). New York: Cambridge University Press.

—— (2001c). Task complexity, task difficulty, and task production: Exploring interactions in a componential framework. *Applied Linguistics,* 22 (1), 27–57. doi: 10.1093/applin/22.1.27

—— (2007a). Criteria for classifying and sequencing pedagogic tasks. In M. Del Pilar García Mayo (ed.), *Investigating Tasks in Formal Language Learning* (pp. 7–26). Clevedon, England: Multilingual Matters.

—— (2007b). Task complexity, theory of mind, and intentional reasoning: Effects on L2 speech production, interaction, uptake and perceptions of task difficulty. *International Review of Applied Linguistics in Language Teaching,* 45 (3), 193–213. doi: 10.1515/iral.2007.009

—— (2009a). Syllabus design. In M. H. Long and C. J. Doughty (eds), *Handbook of Language Teaching* (pp. 294–310). Oxford: Blackwell.

—— (2009b). Task complexity, cognitive resources, and syllabus design: A triadic framework for examining task influences on SLA. In K. Van den Branden, M. Bygate and J. M. Norris (eds), *Task-based Language Teaching: A Reader* (pp. 193–226). Amsterdam: John Benjamins Publishing Co.

—— (2010). Situating and distributing cognition across task demands: The SSARC model of pedagogic task sequencing. In M. Putz and L. Sicola (eds), *Cognitive Processing in Second Language Acquisition: Inside the Learner's Mind* (pp. 243–68). Amsterdam/Philadelphia PA: John Benjamins.

—— (2011a). Second language task complexity, the cognition hypothesis, language learning, and performance. In P. Robinson (ed.), *Second Language Task Complexity: Researching the Cognition Hypothesis of Language Learning and Performance* (pp. 3–38). Amsterdam: John Benjamins Publishing.

—— (2011b). *Second Language Task Complexity: Researching the Cognition Hypothesis of Language Learning and Performance.* Amsterdam: John Benjamins Publishing.

Samuda, V. and Bygate, M. (2008). *Tasks in Second Language Learning.* New York: Palgrave Macmillan.

Schmidt, R. (2001). Attention. In P. Robinson (ed.), *Cognition and Second Language Instruction* (pp. 1–32). Cambridge: Cambridge University Press.

Skehan, P. (2003). Task-based instruction. *Language Teaching,* 36 (1), 1–14. doi: http://dx.doi.org/10.1017/S026144480200188X

Skehan, P. and Foster, P. (2001). Cognition and tasks. In P. Robinson (ed.), *Cognition and Second Language Instruction* (pp. 183–205). New York: Cambridge University Press.

Swain, M. (2005). The output hypothesis: Theory and research. In E. Hinkel (ed.), *Handbook on Research in Second Language Teaching and Learning* (pp. 471–84). Mahwah, NJ: Lawrence Erlbaum.

Swain, M. and Lapkin, S. (1995). Problems in output and the cognitive processes they generate: A step towards second language learning. *Applied Linguistics,* 16 (3), 371–91. doi: doi: 10.1093/applin/16.3.371

—— (1998). Interaction and second language learning: Two adolescent French immersion students working together. *The Modern Language Journal,* 82 (3), 320. doi: 10.1111/j.1540–4781.1998.tb01209.x

—— (2001). Focus on form through collaborative dialogue: Exploring task effects. In M. Bygate, P. Skehan and M. Swain (eds), *Researching Pedagogic Tasks: Second Language Learning, Teaching and Testing.* Harlow, Essex: Longman.

Van den Branden, K. (2006). Introduction: Task-based language teaching in a nutshell. In K. Van den Branden (ed.), *Task-based Language Education: From Theory to Practice* (pp. 1–16). Cambridge: University of Cambridge.

7

Teachers' Application of the Cognition Hypothesis when Lesson Planning: A Case Study

Melissa Baralt
Florida International University

Simone Harmath-de Lemos
Cornell University

Sawsan Werfelli
University of Tripoli

Introduction

Very few studies have examined how teachers conceptualize, plan for and sequence tasks of increased cognitive complexity in their lessons. One reason for this is the fact that there is no generally agreed-upon model for how to sequence tasks according to their complexity level. Another reason may be a lack of a connection between second language acquisition (SLA) research on tasks and what teachers actually do with tasks in practice. As argued by Van den Branden (2006), teachers will not implement new methods if they do not have an understanding of them or believe in them. Any method must be 'integrated into the system of teacher cognition that drives teacher actions' in order for it to be adopted by practicing teachers (Van den Branden, 2006, p. 234). A task's level of cognitive complexity, during both lesson planning and in classroom implementation, may be mediated by the teacher's beliefs, views on language learning, goals for his or her students, past experiences, student (perceived) ability, and even subjective intuition. These factors could also be a reason for teachers not to use cognitively complex tasks at all. For example, Van den Branden (2006) reported on two studies where task complexity was one of the main problems that teachers experienced after training on task-based language teaching. In the first study, teachers were uncomfortable using tasks that they perceived as 'too difficult' for the students (Linsen 1994, cited in Van den Branden,

2006, p. 228). In the second study, teachers had similar reactions to a new task-based course: it was difficult for them to accept the idea of giving their students complex tasks, because the students had cognitive and linguistic problems during their task performance. The teachers thus opted not to give them complex tasks; this was due to their belief that students must acquire isolated linguistic elements first (Luyten and Houben, 2004, cited in Van den Branden, 2006, p. 229).

Starting students out with simple tasks, and facilitating their successful performance of more complex tasks where they encounter – and overcome – cognitive and linguistic challenges, is a fundamental tenet of task-based language teaching. Research repeatedly shows that tasks are the most effective means to engage the complex processes involved in using language. Students' mastery of tasks that gradually increase in cognitive complexity will set them up for real-world task performance and facilitate their achievement of communicative competence. A model of how to sequence tasks according to their cognitive complexity level is therefore needed to drive task-based research and inform pedagogy. Any model's validity, however, will in part be determined by the extent to which teachers understand it and incorporate it into their practice. In Chapter 1 (see Baralt, Gilabert and Robinson, this volume), a historic review of past models for task sequencing was provided. To date, the Cognition Hypothesis is one model that has provided specific and detailed suggestions for how to sequence tasks according to their complexity level. There has been an extensive amount of psycholinguistic, laboratory-based research on the Cognition Hypothesis (see Baralt, 2013, for a review) as well as research on independent measures of the construct of complexity to confirm task designers' intentions (e.g., Révész and Gilabert, 2013; Gilabert and Révész, 2013). There has not been hardly any research on teachers' understanding of task complexity.

With this chapter, we aim to contribute to this need by detailing a case study of two teachers' actions during an in-service training workshop. The topic of the workshop was sequencing tasks based on their complexity level in task-based teaching. The data reported on come from a larger-scale study that explored the interactive synergies between: (1) teacher cognition, beliefs, and experience, (2) their planning of task complexity sequences during the workshop, and (3) their implementation of the designed lesson plan after the workshop. For the present study, we discuss the first and second of these components.

Why sequencing cognitive complexity is important

In the most basic sense, cognitive complexity is what makes a task easy or hard to do. This refers to the facility with which students draw upon both cognitive operations and linguistic functions during meaningful use of language to achieve a real-world goal. A task has arguably been mastered if it is no longer a struggle to tap the cognitive and linguistic resources needed in order for that task to be completed. As described by Long and Crookes (1992), a main premise of task-based language teaching is to start out with a needs analysis, determine target tasks, then task types, and from these create pedagogic tasks that teachers and students work on together in the classroom. These pedagogic tasks should be sequenced, increasing in complexity at each stage, so that they approximate the target tasks. A student is ready for a more cognitively complex task when access to the resources needed to complete it is automatized and proceduralized. Sequencing therefore entails increasingly complex approximations to the target task (Long and Crookes, 1992, p. 44), and is critical to consider when creating a syllabus: syllabus design inherently implies sequencing tasks so that they facilitate maximum learning (Ellis, 2003, p. 220). In order for a student's developmental level to increase, the tasks he or she performs also need to increase in complexity. Tasks therefore are supposed to be challenging for learners. They are supposed to be above students' current developmental level. Tasks should result in difficulties, should place attentional and memory demands on learners, and should encourage learners to extend or stretch their linguistic resources. Sequencing tasks from simple to complex will encourage the process of interlanguage stretching and restructuring, and this sequencing is what best results in language learning.

Task complexity sequencing is therefore important, but, arguably, it is even more important to study how teachers design and sequence tasks according to their complexity level. Teachers are task implementers. And as argued by Samuda (2001), an understanding of how tasks work naturally implies understanding how they will be implemented by teachers in the classroom. The wealth of recent task-based research on the types of language processes that support language learning is positive, but it is an omission not to consider teachers in this picture. While task-based research identifies which processes foster learning, it is crucial that we remember that it is the teacher who guides learners to these processes (Samuda, 2001).

The Cognition Hypothesis

The model chosen as the theoretical framework for sequencing tasks in the present project was the Cognition Hypothesis. Briefly, we will review the claims of that hypothesis here. The Cognition Hypothesis (e.g., Robinson, 2001a, 2001b, 2007, 2010, 2011) is essentially made up of three 'prongs': (1) its theoretical claims, (2) the Triadic Componential Framework, and (3) the SSARC model for sequencing tasks. The main theoretical claim of the Cognition Hypothesis, relevant for this study, is that tasks should be sequenced according to their level of cognitive complexity. Robinson gives specific details of what design features do so (Robinson, 2001a, 2001b, 2007; Robinson and Gilabert, 2007). Increasing a task's complexity level can beneficially affect students' language production, features of interaction and learning outcomes (Robinson, 2001b). The second prong, the Triadic Componential Framework, details the task features from which teachers can choose in order to design a task sequence from simple to complex. This framework is provided below in Figure 7.1.

The Triadic Componential Framework lists specific design features that can be implemented into a task. The left-hand column lists those design features that determine a task's level of cognitive complexity. For example, a simple task version would give learners planning time (+planning time), and the next sequenced order, a more complex task, would not (−planning time). The other columns list implementation features, as well as cognitive and affective features that can mediate task performance. The third prong of the Cognition Hypothesis, the SSARC model, explains how to work with these features in order to sequence tasks. It essentially says to first start students out with tasks that are simple on all features. Then, one should increase the complexity of a resource-*dispersing* feature of the task (i.e., take away planning time). The next step is to increase the task's level of complexity by implementing a resource-*directing* feature (i.e., require reasoning). Features for both variable types are provided in the Framework. This suggested sequencing (simple on all accounts first, → increase resource-dispersing complexity level → increase resource-directing complexity level) is theorized to set learners up to for maximum task performance at each sequenced stage. This sequence will facilitate automatization of access to resources needed to perform the task (both cognitive and linguistic), and then interlanguage stretching. The end-goal is to get the learner closer to target task performance so that she or he can perform that task in the second language, in the most target-like way, in the real world.

Task Design Features for Sequencing	Task Design Features for Interaction Set-up and Outcome of the Task	Learner Cognitive and Affective Individual Differences that Affect Task Performance
Task Complexity (Cognitive factors)	**Task Condition** (Interactive factors)	**Task Difficulty** (Learner factors)
(Classification criteria: cognitive demands)	(Classification criteria: interactional demands)	(Classification criteria: ability requirements)
(Classification procedure: information-theoretic analyses)	(Classification procedure: behaviour-descriptive analyses)	(Classification procedure: ability assessment analyses)
a) Resource-directing variables making cognitive/conceptual demands	**a) Participation variables** making interactional demands	**a) Ability variables** and task-relevant resource differentials
+/– here and now	+/– open solution	h/l working memory
+/– few elements	+/– one-way flow	h/l reasoning
–/+ spatial reasoning	+/– convergent solution	h/l task-switching
–/+ causal reasoning	+/– few participants	h/l aptitude
–/+ intentional reasoning	+/– few contributions needed	h/l field independence
–/+ perspective-taking	+/– negotiation not needed	h/l mind/intention-reading
b) Resource-dispersing variables making performative/procedural demands	**b) Participant variables** making interactant demands	**b) Affective variables** and task-relevant state-trait differentials
+/– planning time	+/– same proficiency	h/l openness to experience
+/– single task	+/– same gender	h/l control of emotion
+/– task structure	+/– familiar	h/l task motivation
+/– few steps	+/– shared content knowledge	h/l processing anxiety
+/– independency of steps	+/– equal status and role	h/l willingness to communicate
+/– prior knowledge	+/– shared cultural knowledge	h/l self-efficacy

Figure 7.1 Triadic Componential Framework (adapted from Robinson and Gilabert, 2007, p. 164)

Research on teachers' view of sequencing cognitive complexity

The Cognition Hypothesis has often been described in terms of the support it can ultimately offer teachers in making principled pedagogical decisions. Of course, the impact of the Cognition Hypothesis and SSARC model is dependent on its usability and credibility from the teacher's perspective. So far, there is almost zero literature on how teachers conceptualize, plan for or implement tasks that increase in complexity for their students. The two above-mentioned studies, reviewed by Van den Branden (2006), showed that teachers were not comfortable in utilizing tasks that they perceived to be too complex for their students. They preferred traditional exercises of present-practice-produce where students could master linguistic forms in an isolated fashion. Gurzynski-Weiss (2013) is the only study we know of so far that examined teachers' interpretation of specifically the Cognition Hypothesis for task sequencing. In her study, eight student teachers completed a unit on task complexity and task sequencing as part of their foreign language teaching methodology course. In the unit, they studied the Triadic Componential Framework (Robinson, 2001a, 2001b, 2010), had a guest visitor lecture on task complexity, and designed a two-part task sequence of increased complexity for their class. The outcome of this task sequence was to actually use it in a Spanish foreign language lesson. Gurzynski-Weiss video-taped each student teacher implementing their tasks in their classrooms. Afterwards, she used questionnaires and conducted interviews with the teachers to inquire how they interpreted task complexity sequencing and the overall outcome of the tasks. Gurzynski-Weiss found that teachers' interpretation of Robinson's Triadic Framework was highly varied. Based on their video observations, half effectively implemented sequences of increased task complexity in their classrooms, and half did not. Factors that mediated teachers' interpretations of the outcomes of the tasks in class, as well as their own decisions to put or not put these ideas into practice, centered around institutional pressures, teachers' beliefs, and teachers' perceptions of their students' abilities, much in line with Van den Branden (2006).

Factors that mediate teacher actions

The studies detailed by both Van den Branden (2006) and Gurzynski-Weiss (2013) reveal a complex, interactive and essential relationship between teachers' cognition and teachers' actions, to include actions at both the planning and the implementation stages. *Teacher cognition* is a multifaceted construct that has been shown to be a powerful determinant of what teachers do. Internally, teacher cognition can be moulded by teachers' beliefs, assumptions, education, knowledge, expertise, and even experiences in learning and teaching (e.g., Andon and Eckerth, 2009; Bartels, 2005; Borg, 2006; Freeman and Johnson, 1998; Kalaja and Ferreira Barcelos, 2003; Kalaja, 2008; Woods, 1996). Borg defines teacher beliefs as propositions [that teachers] consider to be true, and which are often tacit, have a strong evaluative and affective component, provide a basis for action, and are resistant to change (Borg, 2011, p. 371). Expertise (Tsui, 2003; Johnson, 2005) and years of teaching experience (Gurzynski-Weiss,

2010) can make a further difference on teachers' actions in planning and in classroom implementation.

Besides these internal factors, there are also external factors that mediate teachers' actions, such as institutional support or constraints, syllabuses, and even the students that teachers teach. For example, Gurzynski-Weiss (2013) reported that student teachers who successfully implemented task sequences that increased in cognitive complexity cited their institution's required methodology class as a reason for trying the new method. Those who did not successfully apply the theory felt that they did not have time to try a new approach in their classroom, citing having to meet syllabus requirements and their students' needs. These factors did not go out of hand with teachers' cognition and beliefs. Specifically, Gurzynski-Weiss showed that while some student teachers reported understanding and believing in TBLT theory, others demonstrated a lack of understanding about TBLT and task complexity, and reported not feeling supported in taking teaching risks or in trying something new. While surveying all internal and external factors that affect teacher actions is beyond the scope of this chapter, our aim is to underscore the critical need to reflect on these factors in order to understand what teachers do or do not do in their practice (e.g., Phipps and Borg, 2009).

Research on how teachers design tasks

Examining internal and external factors that mediate teachers' actions is also important to understand how they design tasks and lesson plans (the planning stage), which was the goal of the present study. To date, one of the most detailed studies on designing language teaching tasks is that by Johnson (2003). Johnson investigated what experts versus novice teachers do when they design tasks. Sixteen subjects were asked to design a task and to verbalize their thought processes aloud during the design process. He transcribed the proceedings and then coded and analyzed them. Johnson's analysis showed that the following factors mediate the way in which teachers design tasks: their views of language teaching, beliefs about classroom management, beliefs about student-teacher roles, task evaluation criteria and post-task design experience. For the design stage, he found that most of the designers relied on existing repertoire (e.g., tasks they have used before, textbooks, pre-existing materials), which he showed is an important source of inspiration for teachers. The experts spent more time analyzing at a microstage level and displayed more metacognition behavior than the novices. Johnson also found that while most of the designers suggested that task design should begin with 'taskification', i.e., 'thinking of real world situations and converting it into a task fit for class use', most of them did not actually do this in practice (Johnson, 2003, p. 82). His detailed study underscores the need to examine teachers' cognition and practices at the design and planning stage, as well as classroom implementation.

The current study

Motivated by the above-reviewed literature, this study sought to examine how teachers apply the Cognition Hypothesis in the design of a simple to complex task sequence, and the way in which they situate that sequence in a lesson plan. We therefore address the planning stage, before teachers implemented their lessons in their actual classrooms. The research questions guiding our study were:

1. In what ways do teachers integrate the task complexity principles of the Cognition Hypothesis, covered in an in-service training workshop, into the design of a task sequence?
2. What factors do they cite when doing so?
3. How do the task-based principles covered in the workshop integrate with teachers' current pedagogical principles?

Method: The participants

Our case study reports on two foreign language teacher participants. Both were practicing teachers in a languages department at a large, public university in the United States. One taught Italian as a foreign language and one taught Spanish as a foreign language. Both were native speakers from Italy and from Spain, respectively, and both were women. The teachers had varying levels of pedagogy training and of experience. The teacher from Spain had completed a certificate in language teaching pedagogy, with a focus on English as a foreign language, in her home country. She had also taken a methodology course in the United States. The teacher from Italy had participated in a few training workshops in the United States. Table 7.1 below provides a visual examination of their demographic information, education and years of experience.

Table 7.1 Teachers' profiles

Teacher	Native language	Education and/or training	Years of teaching experience	Populations taught
Teacher 1	Italian	Some workshops on language teaching, to include College Board© workshops on teaching AP Italian	Nine years	University-level Italian; high school Italian
Teacher 2	Spanish	EFL language pedagogy certificate in native country; methodology course and participation in semester-long practicum in the U.S.	Four years	University-level Spanish

Method: Data collection procedure

The teachers were recruited from a larger group of teachers who chose to participate in individual in-service training workshops as opportunities for continued professional development. Their participation was volunteer-based in nature; the workshops were an opportunity to learn about and apply task-based language teaching principles. The workshop of focus was one of various workshops throughout the year on language teaching. The teachers knew that this workshop would be specific to the Cognition Hypothesis for task design and task sequencing. Both had heard of the model but had not studied it or done training on the topic before. The teachers were informed that the researcher giving the workshop was doing a project on teachers and task-based language teaching, and on how teachers put theory into practice. They expressed enthusiasm and willingness for being interviewed and recorded during the workshop.

Data collection for the present study was completed in the following order:

1. An initial, semi-structured interview to gather background data on the teacher's experience, beliefs and stated practices
2. A recording of an in-service training workshop, done in two sessions, during which the teachers interacted with the researcher-trainer, and during which they were asked to think aloud as they designed their tasks and lesson plan
3. A post-training questionnaire inquiring about the teachers' perceptions of the workshop

Copies of the tasks and lesson plans that the teachers created during the workshop were also collected and included in our analysis.

The in-service training workshops were conducted one-on-one with the teachers, and were done by the same researcher. This was to ensure consistency in the way in which the material was delivered and also to accommodate the teachers' schedules. The workshop was divided into two sessions: Day 1 (theory) and Day 2 (application). On Day 1, the researcher and teacher reviewed task-based language teaching and task-based methodology. They discussed the theoretical and practical relevance of the pre-task, during-task and post-task phases framed around communicative tasks using the Ellis (2003) methodology model, and reviewed examples. This first half of the workshop was interactive in nature, and several instances were taken to stop and reflect on the teacher's own practices in relationship to the task-based principles discussed. Next, the construct of cognitive complexity was defined and examples were given. The researcher and teacher reviewed, reflected on and discussed together the Triadic Componential Framework for Task Classification and Sequencing (Robinson and Gilabert, 2007, p. 164). They went over how to sequence cognitively simple tasks to cognitively complex ones, starting with resource-dispersing features, and then, with resource-directing variables. Next, the researcher went over the following specific examples to illustrate these: (1) having planning time first, to not having planning time; and (2) having prior knowledge of the task content, versus not. The examples to illustrate resource-directing variables included: (1) telling a story in the here-and-now (simple) and then telling the same story in the there-and-then (complex); and (2) not having to take a perspective (simple) and then having to do perspective-taking (complex). For each example, the teachers shared where these features seem to be realized in their own English language learning experience in the United States. After this, the teachers were invited to brainstorm their own examples of how to sequence a simple task and then a complex class following the SSARC guidelines.

Day 2 of the workshop was the application component. Both teachers met with the researcher again to apply the principles covered in the first half of the workshop and to design their tasks and a lesson plan. The teachers were instructed to design a task sequence that increased in complexity level and to situate the sequence into a lesson, as based on their own understanding of the Cognition Hypothesis. Copies of both the Ellis (2003) task phases implementation model (i.e., pre-task, task and post-task phases), as well as of the Triadic Componential Framework (Robinson and Gilabert, 2007), were provided again for teachers to look at while designing. In addition, the teachers were encouraged to design tasks and a lesson plan for an actual upcoming day on their syllabus. This was for the purpose of accomplishing what Johnson (2003) refers to as *task proclivity*, or the 'freedom to design tasks that reflect teachers' own views of language teaching and their own design style' (p. 28), while making the workshop outcome authentic to their real teaching needs. The teachers were told to think aloud while designing their tasks and were recorded while doing so. Some parts of the design and planning component of the Workshop Day 2 were interactive as opposed to thinking aloud individually; for example, the teachers sometimes stopped to share anecdotes about their students or classrooms.

Analysis

Reflecting the qualitative nature of this study, data analysis was iterative in nature and involved the researchers' moving back and forth between the different data sources (interviews, comments during the theoretical and application parts of the workshop, questionnaires and materials designed during the workshop). Employing a case study method allowed us to focus on each teacher individually in order to provide insight into the complexities of what we were examining; iterative, qualitative analysis among the triangulated data sources complemented our holistic analysis of both teachers' workshop and design experiences.

Findings

Initial interview

It is first essential to report on some factors that came out of the initial semi-structured interview, to allow for a reflection on the extent to which the principles covered in the workshop converged with or challenged teachers' existing practices. First, both of the teachers stated that they believe in communicative language teaching (Brandl, 2008) and that they teach in this way in their classrooms. To illustrate this, the teachers shared that they did a lot of group work in the classrooms by putting students in pairs or in small groups. They were not very familiar with task-based language teaching. They had heard about it as a reference point mentioned in training workshops; its presentation to them, however, had always been theoretical.

Interestingly, their reflection on teaching in a communicative way was followed up by a reflection on teaching grammar. Both reported that they taught grammar explicitly and said they always do so before students carry out a task.

The Spanish teacher, whom we will call Ines, stated that it would be impossible for students to carry out a task without having had the grammar explained to them beforehand. The Italian teacher, whom we will call Magdalena, shared that she 'loved' grammar, and that her students did as well. Ines and Magdalena also mentioned the importance of error correction, and the role of the teacher in doing this. For example, Magdalena stated:

> *The teacher is leading them and has to give them feedback so as not to make the same mistakes and I think it is very useful to make a list of most common mistakes made during those interactions, once in a while, so that another day those errors can be corrected with the whole class. Students are very perceptive and they like the challenge of correcting errors.*

Ines and Magdalena also shared frustrations with institutional pressures that were out of their control. For example, both taught with a grammar-based syllabus that was issued to them by their department; they did not have any involvement in the syllabus's design. From this forms-focused syllabus, their role (as stated to them by their department) was to teach in a communicative way. The Italian teacher, Magdalena, shared that she did not really like the textbook she had to use, and the Spanish teacher, Ines, felt that one of her main roles was to prepare students for the exams, which were also designed by their department.

Teacher 1, Magdalena Magdalena, the Italian teacher participant, began the workshop by highlighting how excited she was to learn more about task-based teaching. She shared that knowing how to design and sequence tasks is hard for her at the planning stage, and so learning about the Cognition Hypothesis would hopefully help her to think more consciously about sequencing tasks according to their complexity level. At the theoretical level, she demonstrated an understanding of the theory and of the features of the Triadic Componential Framework. Illustrative of this were the ways in which she brainstormed her own English acquisition experience:

> *So much of this theory and the [Triadic Componential Framework] makes me think about how I learned English! It is true, when you have the time to prepare, the planning time?, it makes a difference, but then when you can do something spontaneously, right on the spot, that shows you've learned. I can think of so many examples where I needed to plan [my English] first . . . this one, the +/– here-and-now . . . it is true, [-here-and-now] is much more complex for the mind, when I was learning English, telling stories or I guess things that happened to me in the past were the hardest part . . .*

As this quote demonstrates, Madgalena thought of real-life circumstances that the Cognition Hypothesis targeted. When it came to Day 2 of the workshop, however, this real-life application and reflection of theory switched in focus to the linguistic form that she had to teach:

> *I love the implications of what this theory says about how to make tasks more complex, how to order them for my students. How to know what order I should give them the tasks in class is one of the greatest challenges for me. But so, now, how can I apply it to teach the Italian* passato prossimo? *I have to teach it on this day, see? This is a very difficult form for my students because it is slightly different than English. For example, you have to choose between two auxiliary verbs:* essere *and* avere. *Then, in combining the auxiliary verb with the past participle form, there can be a gender and number agreement on the participle, but not always. So the trick is knowing when. So let's see ...*

Magdalena's change from reflecting on real-life tasks to an isolated linguistic form was obviously mediated by the institutional syllabus. In addition, her beliefs about how language learning happens were demonstrated in this change of focus:

> *... this is such a hard form for them to learn, they have to know the difference here [*essere *versus* avere*] before they can use it ...*

Thus, Magdalena's approach to design and planning was prefaced by considering a form-focused syllabus requirement as well as her own view that students need to learn isolated forms first before doing anything communicative.

Magdalena then went on to think about what task she would make with which to teach the *passato prossimo* (present perfect) form. She shared that she had the perfect task: a PowerPoint with pictures she had created once, that elicited her students' use of the present perfect via their descriptions of pictures. This was a task she had used in the past and she reported that it worked very well. Magdalena explained that the PowerPoint had pictures on the slides of kids doing funny things (kids like *Denny la minaccia*, or Dennis the Menace). Alongside the pictures in the PowerPoint, she had given prompts in the infinitive verb form, such as *rubare le uova di Pasqua* (to steal the Easter eggs). To complete the task, students had to describe the pictures and change the infinitive verb forms to the present perfect. Magdalena therefore brought pre-existing repertoire to the applied component of the workshop. This repertoire was for her a positive source of task inspiration, because of its success in the past:

> *It really did work well; they were all using the* passato prossimo.

It was then that Magdalena moved to apply the newly learned theory. In looking at the Triadic Componential Framework, Magdalena selected the resource-directing variable +/− perspective-taking. She continued thinking aloud about how to apply the Cognition Hypothesis to this pre-existing task. For the simple task (-perspective-taking), students would work in pairs to describe what one of the children in the pictures has done, thereby describing the picture and its accompanying prompts in the PowerPoint.

> *So it's kind of like the example we saw yesterday [Day 1 of the workshop], this could be not-perspective taking, because the students they do not have to take a perspective on the actions of each child in the photo. Because I already give them that information in the presentation. They simply describe the pictures. And then . . . well then I can make it more complex by taking away the prompts.*

For the next task in the sequence (+perspective-taking), Magdalena used another slide in her PowerPoint, which showed a picture of another 'menace', *Jacopo il terribile* (Jacob the terrible). She took away the prompts and decided to use the pictures only as the task input:

> *Now students will have to describe it on their own. This is like how I teach vocabulary. To make them speak, I recur to visual thinking strategies: I show a photo or artwork and ask them three questions 'What's going on?' 'What does it make you to say so?' 'Is there something else you want to add?' . . . So in having to explain themselves what Jacopo has done, it is their own perspective.*

For the more complex sequence then, there were no prompts; students had to look at the picture and come up with all of the menacing things the child had done (i.e., *Jacopo* **has painted** *his little brother*). Magdalena's conceptualization of how to make a task more cognitively complex was therefore a transition of students transforming infinitive verb forms to having to come up with the verb forms themselves. Magdalena's task complexity sequence is provided in Figure 7.2.

Before beginning the application of this task into a lesson plan, Magdalena shared that she had a 50-minute class session during which she could do this task. She directly applied the pre-task, during-task and post-task phases covered in the first half of the workshop when writing out the lesson plan on paper, and juxtaposed these task-phase methodological recommendations with the SSARC recommendations. Specifically, resource-dispersing complexity increases were

Simple task

> *Che cosa ha combinato Denny la minaccia?* (What has Dennis the Menace done?)
> **A.** Vedrete ora una foto di Melissa, una bambina veramente birichina! Seguite le istruzioni e raccontate quello che ha fatto. Dovete descrivere sei azioni, usando i verbi indicati.
> *Translation: You will see a photo of Melissa, a very naughty girl! Follow the instructions and say what it is that she has done. You must describe six actions, using the indicated verbs.*
> [Picture in PowerPoint of a young girl stealing her younger brother's goodies from his Easter basket.]
> prompts:
>
> | | |
> |---|---|
> | 1.(rubare le uova di Pasqua) | *to steal the Easter eggs* |
> | 2.(prendere i giocattoli del suo fratellino) | *to take her brother's toys* |
> | 3.(mangiare tutte le caramelle, anche quelle di suo fratello) | *to eat all of the candy, even her brother's* |
> | 4.(prendere il trenino) | *to take the train* |
> | 5.(parlare tanto) | *to talk a lot* |
> | 6.(essere egoista!) | *to be selfish* |

Complex task

> Ora vedrete la foto di un bambino terribile, che più terribile non si può: Jacopo!
> Che cosa ha fatto? Con il vostro compagno, descrivete almeno SEI cose che ha combinato in soggiorno. Potete chiedere aiuto alla professoressa. Siate creativi e, se volete, fate ricorso alla fantasia.
> *Translation: Now you will see a picture of a terrible child, who couldn't be more terrible: Jacob! What has he done? With your partner, describe at least SIX things that he has done in the living room. You can ask the teacher for help. Be creative, and use your imagination if you'd like!*
> [Picture in PowerPoint of a young boy who has painted the entire living room: the sofa, floor, television set, furniture items, and even his baby brother. The mother has clearly caught him in action.]

Figure 7.2 Summary of Teacher 1's task complexity sequence

done in the pre-task phases. For this, she chose +/− planning time. Resource-directing complexity increases were sequenced across two different tasks. Below we summarize the task-phase portions of Magdalena's lesson plan. Where illustrative, we provide her think-aloud comments made during and/or after writing out what she would do in each phase:

Magdalena's simple task

Pre-task Ask students if they know who *Denny la minaccia* is (open the task by drawing a comparison to the cultural equivalent of the Dennis the Menace character). Tell students they will now do a task where they see some menace kids. Their task is to describe what each 'menace' has done. Provide a model with the PowerPoint. [The first six slides of the teacher's PowerPoint showed pictures of 'menaces': children doing something silly or crazy. Each slide contained prompts and vocabulary words to help students.] Divide the class into pairs and explain that they will now do the same thing to describe another menace in the PowerPoint, Melissa. Tell students they are to work together and write what she has done.

So you see here I will give them the planning time.

Task In pairs, students view the picture of Melissa and use the prompts to write all of the things she has done. Go around and monitor their production, providing feedback where necessary.

This is the -perspective-taking, this is the simple version, they don't have to come up with their own perspective of what each child [shown in the PowerPoint picture] has done . . .

Post-task Ask three volunteer groups to share their answers in front of the whole class. Provide explicit feedback on the *passato prossimo* where necessary.

Well Ellis says we need a task outcome, so I can have them share their answers.

Here is how Magdalena planned for the complex task version.

Magdalena's complex task

Pre-task Tell students they will now do a similar task, but it is little more difficult in that they have to describe what Jacopo has done on their own (with no prompts). Provide a model (using same picture on Instructions slide). Students are to work in the same pairs as the first task.

Actually for this I'll just guide the discussion. I hope I have time for this . . . I wonder does this count as a planning time too?

Task Students are shown the picture of Jacopo and the paint job he has done to his parents' living room and little brother. They brainstorm and write down six things that he has done. Go around the room, monitor, and provide feedback where needed.

Here it is more complex because now I don't give them the verbs. They have to think of it themselves. Oh my goodness this picture is so funny. They will have lots to say about what Jacopo has done!

Post-task Ask three volunteer groups to share with the class what they came up with. Invite others to share their creative answers too if they wish. Do a brief grammar focus with the class on the *passato prossimo* form, using students' creative answers as examples.

Well I will have to explain to them the grammar again . . .

Madgalena's task design and planning began with looking at her syllabus requirements. Next, her beliefs and past experience (both with repertoire and with students) informed her decision-making and thought processes. For example, her view that she must teach students grammar explicitly first appeared to inform the way in which she approached the design of her lesson. Instead of coming up with a new task, i.e., using theory to design a task, Magdalena thought of a past, successful task, and applied the task to the theory. Upon concluding the workshop, Magdalena reported feeling excited about her lesson plan, and said that she was eager to implement it into her actual class.

Teacher 2, Ines Ines, the Spanish as a foreign language teacher, was our second teacher participant. Like Magdalena, Ines began the application part of the workshop by highlighting how glad she was to have such an in-service training opportunity. She shared that researchers and practitioners should work together more, and emphasized on more than one occasion that she would like more practice opportunities:

> *I think the researchers can work together with the teachers to apply more communicative tasks on the target language. Those activities could use current news, people or things that are closer to the students and their ages. I think we need more of this and more examples . . . I just don't have enough examples.*

In addition, Ines shared about a few of her own principles as well as external restraints that mediate her actions:

> *I really think that group work is beneficial because students talk to each other and exchange views. Besides, they also give each other corrective feedback. At least my students do! . . . I definitely try to do as much group work as possible, but I sometimes do have time constraints. I have to prepare them for the exams.*

Thus, Ines's acknowledgement of a lack of concrete examples by which to go by, as well as the constraints she dealt with (time, having to prepare students for assessments), were themes with which she started out the applied component of the workshop; these themes were of great importance and relevance to her. After receiving the instructions on thinking aloud for the task design and lesson plan, Ines commented on her understanding of the Cognition Hypothesis:

I like this theory very much ... looking at the [Triadic Componential Framework], it makes me realize I already do a lot of these in my class with my students. I definitely agree that these [resource-directing variables] make a task harder ...

Next, and just like Magdalena had done, Ines referred to her syllabus and pointed out the fact that she had to teach a specific form on the day for which she was designing the task:

The thing is that for this day, I have to cover the present perfect ... Guaranteed it will be on their exam. I really like what [Robinson] says about how sequencing tasks from simple to more complex will best help the students to learn. So now I need to make it apply [to the present perfect form].

Ines therefore changed her focus from thinking about theory to thinking about syllabus requirements and how to accommodate those requirements with the theory.

She then shared about past exercises that she had done with her students that worked well to elicit this form:

For the present perfect ... hmmm ... I remember I did a task where I brought in some pictures from the Hola *Magazine, a magazine from Spain, and I asked my students to say what some famous celebrities in Spain have or have not done. I think I [looking at the copy of the Triadic Componential Framework] can apply this ... what do you think, maybe a simple version is where I tell them about the celebrity, and then the complex version is where they have to try and guess? Think aloud, that's right [laughter]. Ok, I will try the ... I will do the +/− perspective taking. That was one of the examples from yesterday.*

This quote reveals that Ines, too, relied on existing repertoire, which, for her and for her classroom needs, had been successful in the past. In applying the resource-directing variable +/− perspective taking, Ines adapted her previously used task to make it 'fit' the Cognition Hypothesis and the SSARC model for sequencing. She did this by explaining that her students would move from transforming verb forms from prompts given to them in the task input, to having to describe pictures on their own; this was her conceptualization of +/− perspective-taking. It was almost identical to the designing and planning demonstrated by the Italian teacher, Magdalena. The way Ines planned to do this was to use pictures of famous Spaniards from the magazine *Hola* and give pictures to groups of two in her class:

> *So on the back of each picture, I'll write three sentences in Spanish, each*
> *in the simple past about that famous person. Ok let's see, so for this person*
> *I can write ... 'She married the king of Spain. She created numerous*
> *non-profit organizations.' And then for the simple task version [-perspective*
> *taking] the students use this to describe what the famous person has done.*
> *So they'll have to describe it using the present perfect ... 'She HAS MARRIED*
> *the king of Spain', 'She HAS CREATED many non-profit organizations.'*
> *Ah they probably won't know how to say non-profit, I will have to explain*
> *that ...*

To make the task more complex, Ines went on to explain that she would then have her students, in pairs, brainstorm their own reasons for which the person in their picture might be famous:

> *A ver, a ver, this can be +perspective-taking, because the students will have to*
> *share their own perspective. They have to say why the person is a celebrity or*
> *what the person has done in her life. So that's how I make the task more*
> *complex with this model.*

As with the simple task version, Ines said that she would have the student groups think up three things that the pictured person has done in his or her life. Ines's task complexity sequence is provided below in Figure 7.3.

Next, after adjusting the task so that it reflected the Cognition Hypothesis (in terms of sequencing and in use of one of the resource-directing variables from the Triadic Componential Framework), Ines went on to design her implementation plan with the task sequence by using the task-based methodological principles, also covered in the first half of the workshop. For both the simple and the complex task, she planned what she would do in the pre-, during-, and post-task phases. Just like Magdalena had done, Ines incorporated the resource-dispersing variable of +/−planning time in the pre-task phase. We summarize Ines's planned task sequence implementation below; her think-aloud comments for each of her planned phases are provided, where illustrative:

Ines's simple task

Pre-task Give students instructions and model the task with my own picture. Explain to students that each of their pictures of famous Spaniards has three factual sentences on the back, which explains why they are famous. They use this information to say what the celebrity *has done*. I use my own picture, with

Simple task

Sample sentences provided on back of photo taken from magazine
(reina de España)

La reina española:
1. Ella se casó con el rey de España.
2. Creó varias organizaciones sin ánimo de lucro (*non-profit*).
3. No murió.

Translation: The queen of Spain:
   1. She married the King of Spain.
   2. She created various non-profit organizations.
   3. She did not die.

¿Qué **ha hecho** la reina de España?

¿Qué **ha hecho** la reina de España? Utilizad la descripción que tenéis detrás de la foto para explicárselo a la clase usando el presente perfecto.

1.
2.
3.

Complex task

Ahora, haced uso de vuestra imaginación para inventar razones por las cuáles la reina de España es famosa y conocida. ¿Qué más ha hecho? ¡Sed creativos! Tenéis que pensar e inventar por lo menos tres cosas que ha hecho ella (usando el presente perfecto). (Por supuesto podéis usar vuestro libro).

1.
2.
3.

Translation:
A. What has the queen of Spain done? Use the description that you have on the back of the photo to describe to the rest of the class what she has done, using the present perfect.

B. Now, use your imagination to invent reasons for which the Queen of Spain is famous and well-known. What else has she done? Be creative! You must think of at least three things that she has done in her life (using the present perfect). (Of course, you may use your book).

Figure 7.3 Summary of Teacher 2's task complexity sequence

three descriptions, to give them a model (emphasize the present perfect form with my voice). Students are then paired into groups of two and get two minutes of planning time. Tell them they will have to share their descriptions with the class.

> *The planning time is here ... and see, this is one of the ways we make the task more complex, or well, make it be simple to begin with.*

Task Students work in pairs to say what their pictured person has done. I go around the class, monitor their production, give feedback where necessary.

This is the simple version [the -perspective-taking], because they are having to use the descriptions I provide for them. They really like this when I bring in pictures from Spanish magazines or newspapers . . .

Post-task Choose five groups, randomly, to report to the class. Each group pair is to stand up, tell us about their famous person, and explain what she/he has done in their life to be considered famous. Give feedback where necessary.

I'll have them do a report for the post-task phase.

Ines's complex task

Pre-task Explain to students that they now have to think of their own reasons for which the pictured person is famous. Give instructions, encourage creativity, and model the task for students (use my own picture again). Tell students that they will have to share their inventions.

I won't give them planning time here, but it is really essential that I give them a model. Otherwise they won't be able to do it.

Task In the same group of two, students work together to think of three other things or events that their pictured person has done. Go around the class, monitor, and provide feedback.

So I will change it a little bit to make it more complex, so [Robinson] says +perspective-taking makes it more challenging, so here . . . now they will have to give their own perspective and think of other reasons for which the celebrity is famous. This will definitely be more difficult for them. And they will use the present perfect.

Post-task Ask five groups to share with the class the things that their celebrity has done to be famous. Provide feedback where necessary; draw students' attention to the present perfect again on the board.

After writing out her plan, Ines made a comment about reviewing the grammatical form explicitly before versus after the simple task:

I may have to teach it to them beforehand though, because otherwise I just really do not think they will be able to do it.

The extent to which Ines would actually implement her plan, where a focus on form was done in the post-task phases – a method covered in the workshop – is unknown. She applied this task-based principle in her planning, but this quote demonstrates that it may not conform to her beliefs about how students learn.

Like Magdalena, Ines relied on repertoire to which she applied the new, task-based principles on cognitive complexity sequencing. She understood clearly the phases associated with task-based methodology, and planned for these around her two adapted tasks. The features she chose to 'make the theory fit' to her task were some that were used as concrete examples in the first half of the workshop; in fact, she chose precisely the same variables (both resource-dispersing and resource-directing) as Magdalena, perhaps because these were examples given in the workshop. Ines explicitly referenced the importance of examples, saying how having examples is, to her, essential for her to understand:

I really learn best by examples. I'd like to have more in future workshops.

Ines's workshop experience, as well as her think-aloud comments said during her design and lesson planning, reveal a possible divergence between her beliefs and the new task-based principles covered. This was specific to the way and chronological timing of explicit grammar review around the task. Also notable was the precedence that institutional requirements (her syllabus) took in mediating her approach to the planning. She, like Magdalena, referred to her repertoire of past-used tasks that had been successful in eliciting her students' production of grammatical form. Even though the pre-existing task was more of a controlled practice exercise, her 'designing' happened by making the Cognition Hypothesis 'fit' to a pre-existing task.

Discussion

Even though this case study reports on the actions of just two teachers, it is notable that they both integrated the task complexity principles of the Cognition Hypothesis into the design of a task and lesson plan in the same fashion. Both of the teachers followed the same steps and sequence:

1. Consider what must be taught on the day for which they were planning, as mandated by the syllabus;
2. Consider institutional and classroom management issues, such as upcoming exams or time constraints;
3. Reflect on repertoire (Johnson, 2003) to use, i.e., tasks have they used in the past that worked well and met institutional, management and student needs;

4. Adapt the pre-existing task so that it 'fits' to the new Cognition Hypothesis principles covered;

5. Sequence the adjusted task into a lesson plan.

It was also striking that Magdalena and Ines opted to apply the exact same variables to their pre-existing tasks: +/– planning time and +/– perspective taking. Both of the teachers 'operationalized' a resource-dispersing complexity increase as taking away the opportunity for planning time in the second pre-task phase. To implement an increase in complexity along resource-directing variables, they both made their tasks adjust to the concept of +/– perspective taking. Perspective taking was realized, in their conceptualizations and planning, as a move from simple transformation of sentences to having to come up with new sentences. The teachers did this by planning to have the students start out with a transforming of sentences; in Madgalena's plan, students would conjugate infinitive verb forms into the *passato prossimo*, and in Ines's plan, students would transform simple past tense forms into the present perfect. This was their rendition of a task being cognitively simple.

To make the task more cognitively complex, the teachers planned on taking away the sentence prompts, providing the students with pictures only (either in a PowerPoint presentation or with magazine picture input). Requiring 'perspective taking', therefore, meant asking students to come up with descriptions of the photos themselves. For both Magdalena and Ines, this was an application of making a task more cognitively complex.

This finding underscores the importance of practical training opportunities, with clear examples for teachers. For example, whether or not Magdalena and Ines chose these specific design variables due to a thorough understanding, versus selecting them because they were examples provided in the first half of the workshop (before the design component), is not clear. In fact, both of their post-workshop questionnaires highlight that it may be for the latter reason. Ines, for example, reiterated that she learns by having concrete examples and that teacher training is often too theoretical. It seems to be the case then that they 'operationalized' the same cognitive complexity variables from the Triadic Componential Framework because these variables were most clear to them as demonstrated via concrete examples provided during training.

The similar ways in which both Magdalena and Ines applied the Cognition Hypothesis to their task design and lesson planning highlight another important finding: namely, institutional pressures and classroom management issues as more relevant to what the teachers do in planning than new theoretical ideas.

For both teachers, a workshop in which they applied theory to their practice started out by considering what they had to teach, according to their syllabus. In addition, consideration of timing limitations, as well as successful teaching activities in the past (where students correctly used the targeted linguistic forms and which best prepared them for upcoming exams, in the teachers' view) mediated how they would approach the design of a task. These factors were fundamental and guided their actions during the workshop.

There were several factors that the teachers cited when designing and lesson planning. In addition to syllabus requirements, Magdalena and Ines often referred to their beliefs about language learning and teaching. One belief that was referred to multiple times by both was the necessity of explicit teaching of isolated grammatical forms first, before students could use these forms in more spontaneous speech. Both mentioned that students are not able to perform communicative tasks without having learned the forms necessary to do such tasks.

Interestingly, Magdalena and Ines's lesson plans did not explicitly reflect this belief. Following the Ellis (2003) model covered in the workshop, they both planned for a focus-on-form in the post-task phases. This deviated a bit from their stated beliefs, where grammar should be taught before students perform the task. It is not known whether the teachers would deviate from this 'task-based' plan in its classroom implementation. In fact, Ines's post-lesson-plan comment, that she may have to teach the present perfect form first, indicated that she probably would end up changing her lesson plan to better reflect her belief system. Indeed, some studies have shown that what teachers actually do in the classroom is not consistent with their stated beliefs (e.g., Fang, 1996; Basturkmen, Loewen and Ellis, 2004). This disconnect may also exist between planning in a task-based way, and then actually implementing that plan.

Another finding of note was Magdalena and Ines's difficulty with the concept of task as a learning vehicle in task-based language teaching, i.e., where learning could happen as a result of performing the task (as opposed to being taught grammar explicitly before the task). This pattern echoes findings reported on by other researchers. For example, Andon and Eckerth's (2009) case study showed that the teachers found perceiving tasks as 'knowledge-creating devices' very hard to accept. They used tasks in conjunction with form-focused activities. At the same time, it is worth mentioning here that teaching in a task-based way does not nor should not denigrate the use of form-focused activities. Perhaps, in accordance with the institutional requirements they deal with, as well as their belief system on language teaching, Magdalena and Ines would find it more acceptable to teach in a task-supported way as opposed to task-based (e.g., Ellis, 2003). This is what the teachers in Andon and Eckerth's (2009) study did when implementing new, task-based principles into their actions, and it worked for them. Similarly, studies reviewed by Van den Branden (2006) showed that allowing teachers to incorporate new task-based teaching methods, while at the same time sticking to what they normally do, resulted in successful implementation of task-based teaching. These studies support a gradualist approach in introducing task-based principles to practicing teachers, and perhaps future teacher training could accommodate such an approach.

In reflecting on whether or not the task-based principles covered in the workshop integrated with the teachers' current pedagogical principles in this study, we admit the answer may be no. Based on the two cases of Magdalena and Ines, it seems that the teachers only made cosmetic changes to what they typically plan for in practice. Borg (2011) has shown that teacher education and training can make teachers more aware of their beliefs, and can also serve to create new beliefs and even change teachers' beliefs. Based on the findings reported on here, we are not so sure that the one-time workshop succeeded in doing so. Changes in teacher actions will by requisite imply a change in their teacher cognition. And admittedly, one workshop is not enough to cause such a change. In fact, the teachers themselves pointed this out. In their post-workshop questionnaires, Magdalena and Ines reiterated their desire for and need of more concrete examples. Thus, one limitation of our study could be the design of the workshop itself. It may have been too theoretical and too short in scope. Teachers need much more exposure to, and practice with, any teaching principles that are not in line with their current practices. There were a couple of instances during the workshop where both Magdalena and Ines wanted a confirmation that their task design was a 'correct' operationalization of the Cognition Hypothesis. It may have been more effective to do an interactive and practical workshop, where teachers receive feedback and can share and collaborate first, before collecting data on how they are designing and applying new theory.

This leads to the important consideration of what in-service training should look like in order to be successful. Van den Branden (2006) poignantly stated the common 'paradox' of what in-service trainers do: 'in-service trainers [typically adopt] a theoretical approach in order to tell the participating teachers not to use a theoretical approach in their language classrooms' (Van den Branden, 2006, p. 223). Thus, a fruitful and necessary area of research in task-based language teaching should also investigate trainers and the types of training needed that resonate the most with teachers. This should include the design and planning stages, as was the focus of this study, as well as classroom implementation.

Conclusion

We conclude by reiterating: tasks should be sequenced so that they optimize the processes shown to lead to language learning, and, so far, the Cognition Hypothesis is the most detailed and investigated model in the field with which to do so. But, and as pointed out by one reviewer, teachers are not empty vessels waiting to receive the Cognition Hypothesis. It is a limitation to test the claims of the Cognition Hypothesis in only laboratory-based settings, without taking into account how teachers understand and implement (or not) its components. This fundamentally requires an examination of the external and internal factors, such as syllabus requirements, management issues, teachers' beliefs and even views on what teachers think tasks should do. It also requires an important reflection on the researcher–practitioner relationship. For example, what does it mean to show successful 'uptake' of task-based principles? How do these complement all of the other factors that teachers must consider when they teach? Tasks, and task sequencing effects (whether at the level of syllabus or lesson plan), cannot be studied in isolation without considering the teacher. And as rightfully pointed out by Samuda, 'the role of the teacher as a mediating factor in task-based language development remains virtually unexamined' in task-based research (Samuda, 2001, p. 119). Components of teacher cognition and teacher actions are arguably just as important to examine when it comes to understanding how tasks should be designed and sequenced according to their level of complexity. This study was a first step in trying to contribute to this need, but arguably more studies that are longitudinal in scope and that involve more teachers are needed. We hope future researchers follow suit.

References

Andon, N. and Eckerth, J. (2009). Chacun à son gout? Task-based L2 pedagogy from the teacher's point of view. *International Journal of Applied Linguistics*, 19, 286–310.

Baralt, M. (2013). The impact of cognitive complexity on feedback efficacy during online versus face-to-face interactive tasks. *Studies in Second Language Acquisition*, 35, 689–725.

Bartels, N. (2005). *Applied Linguistics and Language Teacher Education*. New York: Springer.

Basturkmen, H., Loewen, S. and Ellis, R. (2004). Teachers' stated beliefs about incidental focus on form and their classroom practices. *Applied Linguistics*, 25, 243–72.

Borg, S. (2006). *Teacher Cognition and Language Education: Research and Practice*. London: Continuum.

Carless, D. (2004). Issues in teachers' reinterpretation of a task-based innovation in primary schools. *TESOL Quarterly*, 38, 639–62.

Ellis, R. (2003). *Task-based Language Teaching and Learning*. Oxford: Oxford University Press.

—— (2009). Task-based language teaching: Sorting out the misunderstandings. *International Journal of Applied Linguistics*, 19, 221–46.

Fang, Z. (1996). A review of research on teacher beliefs and practices. *Educational Research*, 38, 47–64.

Freeman, D. and Johnson, K. (1998). Reconceptualising the knowledge base of language teacher education. *TESOL Quarterly*, 32, 397–417.

Gilabert, R. and Révész, A. (2013). *Cognitive Aspects of Task-based Language Teaching*. Invited colloquium at the 5th International Conference on Task-based Language Teaching, Banff, Canada, October.

Gurzynski-Weiss, L. (2010). *Factors Influencing Oral Corrective Feedback Provision in the Spanish Foreign Language Classroom: Investigating Instructor Native/Nonnative Speaker Status, Second Language Acquisition Education, and Teaching Experience* (unpublished doctoral dissertation). Georgetown University, Washington, DC.

—— (2013). *Spanish Instructors' Operationalization of Task Complexity and Sequencing in Non-experimental Foreign Language Lessons*. Paper presented at the 5th International Conference on Task-based Language Teaching, Banff, Canada, October.

Johnson, K. (2003). *Designing Language Teaching Tasks*. Basingstoke: Palgrave.

—— (2005). *Expertise in Second Language Learning and Teaching*. Basingstoke: Palgrave.

Kalaja, P. (2008) *Narratives of Learning and Teaching EFL*. Basingstoke: Palgrave.

Kalaja, P. and Ferreira Barcelos, A. M. (2003). *Beliefs about SLA*. Berlin: Springer.

Linsen, B. (1994). Met vallen en opstaan: de introductie van taakgericht taalonderwijs. Een praktijkbeschrijving uit het basisonderwijs in Vlaanderen. In S. Kroon and T. Vallen (eds), *Nederlands als Tweede Taal in het Onderwijs. Praktijkbeschrijvingen uit Nederland en Vlaanderen* (pp. 131–59). 's-Gravenhage: Nederlandse Taaluine Voorzetten 46.

Long, M. H. and Crookes, G. (1992). Three approaches to task-based syllabus design. *TESOL Quarterly*, 26, 27–56.

Luyten, L. and Houben, L. (2002). *Bonte Was: Verslag Pilootfase*. Leuven: Centrum voor Taal en Migratie. Internal report.

McDonough, K. and Chaikitmongkol, W. (2007). Teachers' and learners' reactions to a task-based EFL course in Thailand. *TESOL Quarterly*, 41, 107–32.

Révész, A. and Gilabert, R. (2013). *Methodological Advances in TBLT Research: Measurement of Task Demands and Processes.* Colloquium conducted at the meeting of the American Association of Applied Linguistics, Dallas, Texas. March.

Robinson, P. (2001a). Task complexity, cognitive resources, and syllabus design: A triadic framework for examining task influences on SLA. In P. Robinson (ed.), *Cognition and Second Language Instruction* (pp. 287–318). Cambridge: Cambridge University Press.

—— (2001b). Task complexity, task difficulty, and task production: Exploring interactions in a componential framework. *Applied Linguistics*, 22, 27–57.

—— (2007). Criteria for classifying and sequencing pedagogic tasks. In María del Pilar García-Mayo (ed.), *Investigating Tasks in Formal Language Learning* (pp. 7–27). Clevedon: Multilingual Matters, Ltd.

—— (2010). Situating and distributing cognition across task demands: The SSARC model of pedagogic task sequencing. In M. Putz and L. Sicola (eds), *Inside the Learner Mind: Cognitive Processing in Second Language Acquisition* (pp. 239–64). Philadelphia, PA: John Benjamins.

—— (2011). Task-based language learning: A review of issues. *Language Learning*, 61, 1–36.

Robinson, P. and Gilabert, R. (2007). Task complexity, the Cognition Hypothesis and second language learning and performance. *International Review of Applied Linguistics in Language Teaching*, 45, 3, 161–76.

Samuda, V. (2001). Guiding relationships between form and meaning during task performance: The role of the teacher. In Bygate, M., Skehan, P. and Swain, M. (eds), *Researching Pedagogic Tasks: Second Language Learning, Teaching, and Testing* (pp. 119–40). Harlow: Longman.

Schart, M. (2008). What matters in TBLT – task, teacher, or team? An action research perspective from a beginning German language classroom. In J. Eckerth and S. Siekmann (eds), *Task-based Language Learning and Teaching: Theoretical, Methodological, and Pedagogical Perspectives* (pp. 47–66). New York: Lang.

Tsui, A. B. M. (2003). *Understanding Expertise in Teaching: Case Studies of Second Language Teachers.* Cambridge: Cambridge University Press.

Van den Branden, K. (2006). *Task-based Language Education: From Theory to Practice.* Cambridge: Cambridge University Press.

Woods, D. (1996). *Teacher Cognition in Language Teaching.* Cambridge: Cambridge University Press.

8

Learning to Perform Narrative Tasks: A Semester-long Classroom Study of L2 Task Sequencing Effects

Craig Lambert
Kitakyushu University

Peter Robinson
Aoyama Gakuin University

Introduction: Task-based syllabus design

In an often cited article entitled 'Towards task-based language learning' Candlin (1987) argued that tasks might provide a basis for classroom action, and a 'means for realizing certain characteristic principles of communicative language teaching and learning, as well as serving as a testing-ground for hypotheses in pragmatics and SLA'. Furthermore, Candlin claimed that 'task-based language learning is not only a means to enhancing classroom communication and acquisition but also the means to the development of classroom syllabuses' (1987, p. 5).

In addition to arguing for 'tasks' as the 'units' of syllabus design, rather than linguistic units such as grammatical structures, functional phrases or vocabulary lists, Candlin was also suggesting that classroom tasks could serve as constructs for examining theoretically motivated hypotheses about SLA processes, and for gathering empirical evidence on whether these processes were prompted or inhibited by performing one pedagogic task in contrast to another when these tasks differed along dimensions in their design or in their implementation. This issue is still at the heart of task-based language learning research, in both experimental settings, and in various educational settings, across various periods of time (as the chapters in this book testify). Candlin (1987) then went on to say:

Tasks must . . . be defined and their means of operationalisation explained. It will be necessary to offer ideas for their classification and their targeting.

Above all their centrality to the syllabus cannot be taken for granted without evaluating how they can be selected and sequenced in a principled fashion.

(Candlin, 1987, p. 5)

This issue raised by Candlin, of selecting tasks, and component features of holistic real world tasks, to be performed *in sequences* is also at the heart of much current SLA research (see Robinson, 2007a, 2010, 2011; Robinson and Gilabert, 2007), as it is in other educational domains (e.g., Reigeluth, 1999; Merrill, 2007; van Merrinboer and Kirschner, 2007) and involves consideration, not only of how differently designed *tasks* might affect opportunities for learning in different ways, but also of how sequences of tasks – in the *different combinations* that sequencing decisions afford, and across the *different timescales* performing them requires – impact upon these learning opportunities. In what follows we describe the claims of the Cognition Hypothesis (Robinson, 2001, 2003, 2005) concerning task sequencing and second language development, and relate them to the SSARC model (Robinson, 2010) of how the component dimensions of task demands can be manipulated so as to progressively increase complexity.

The Cognition Hypothesis

The fundamental pedagogic claim of the Cognition Hypothesis is that *pedagogic tasks* should be designed and sequenced to increasingly approximate the complex cognitive demands of real world *target tasks*. For example, one target task may be to give directions using an authentic street map to another person while driving quickly through an unknown city. If so, then cognitively simple tasks are designed and performed first in the L2, in which learners have planning time, and use a small map of an already known area. Subsequently, incrementally more complex versions are performed, by first taking away planning time, then by making the map a larger one, and finally by using an authentic map of an unknown area, etc. The idea is basically the same as the procedures guiding educational decision-making and training in many areas of instruction (see the extended discussion in the first chapter of this book), such as pilot training, or mathematics education, where simple tasks and simulations are performed before more complex ones.

The Triadic Componential Framework (Robinson, 2007a) describes a taxonomy of task characteristics that can be used to examine the implications of the Cognition Hypothesis for classroom practice and syllabus design. This taxonomy distinguishes between the cognitive demands of tasks, which determine their intrinsic *complexity* (e.g., the need for causal or intentional reasoning), and the abilities (e.g., working memory capacity) and affective responses (e.g., performance anxiety) that learners bring to tasks, which determine the perceived *difficulty* for these learners. Furthermore, Robinson distinguishes these factors of task *complexity* and task *difficulty* from those of task *conditions*, which relate to the interactive demands of tasks (e.g., one-way versus two-way information flow), and the grouping of participants (e.g., same gender versus different genders). This Triadic Componential Framework (TCF) provides a means of analysing the complex classroom learning situation as a basis for designing and sequencing pedagogic tasks in language programs. Underpinning the pedagogic claim of the Cognition Hypothesis are *five ancillary theoretical claims* which we summarize below (see Robinson, 2011 for more extended discussion):

1. *Output* The first of these is that increasing the cognitive demands of tasks contributing to their relative complexity along certain dimensions described in the TCF will push learners to greater accuracy and complexity of L2 production in order to meet the consequently greater functional/ communicative demands they place on the learner. That is, greater effort at conceptualization will lead learners to develop the L2 linguistic resources they have for expressing such conceptualizations.
2. *Uptake and interaction* The second claim is that cognitively complex tasks not only promote greater amounts of interaction (between two or more participants) but also heightened attention to and memory for input (whether provided on monologic or non-monologic tasks), so increasing learning from the input, and incorporation of forms made salient in the input. So, for example, there should be more uptake of oral recasts on complex, compared to simpler interactive, tasks, or more use of written input provided to help learners perform either monologic or interactive tasks.
3. *Memory* Related to this, the third claim is that on complex tasks there will be longer-term retention of input provided (written prompts, oral feedback, etc.) than on simpler tasks.
4. *Automaticity* Fourthly, the inherent repetition involved in performing simple to complex sequences will also lead to automaticity and efficient scheduling of the components of complex L2 task performance.
5. *Aptitudes* Fifthly, and importantly, individual differences in affective and cognitive abilities contributing to perceptions of task difficulty will

increasingly differentiate learning and performance as tasks increase in complexity. That is, we know that individual differences in, say, aptitude for mathematics aren't reflected in performance on doing very simple addition problems (e.g., adding 2 and 6). However, they are reflected in success at doing complex maths problems, like calculus, or quadratic equations. Similarly, aptitudes for task performance will matter most on complex L2 task performance.

The SSARC model of task sequencing

The claim that we examine in the study reported in this chapter is that task sequencing is most effective if learners perform versions simple on relevant dimensions of complexity first, and then subsequently perform versions that are more demanding along these dimensions. We operationalize sequencing decisions so as to progressively increase the complexity of task versions following the two instructional-design *principles* for task sequencing in the three-step SSARC (Simplify, Stabilize–Automatize–Restructure, Complexify) model described below.

SSARC model: Task sequencing principle 1

Only the cognitive demands of tasks contributing to their intrinsic conceptual and cognitive processing complexity are sequenced. Following this principle, for example, tasks that do not require intentional reasoning are performed before those that require it. In contrast, the interactive demands of tasks (such as whether they require one-way or two-way information exchange) are not used in sequencing, but replicated each time pedagogic task versions are performed so as to help ensure deep semantic processing (Craik and Lockhart, 1972), rehearsal in memory (Robinson, 2003), and elaboration and successful transfer of the particular 'schema' for interactive or monologic task performance to real-world contexts of use (Robinson, 1996; Schank, 1999; Schank and Abelson, 1977).

SSARC model: Task sequencing principle 2

Increase resource-dispersing dimensions of complexity first (e.g., from + to – *planning time), and then increase resource-directing dimensions (e.g., from – to +*

Table 8.1 The SSARC model for increasing task complexity

Step 1	SS (stabilize, simplify) = i × e [('s'rdisp) + ('s'rdir)]^n
Step 2	A (automatize) = i × e [('c'rdisp) + ('s'rdir)]^n
Step 3	RC (restructure, complexify) = i × e [('c'rdisp) + ('c'rdir)]^n

where i = current interlanguage state; e = mental effort; 's' = simple task demands; 'c' = complex task demands; rdisp = resource-dispersing dimensions of tasks; rdir = resource-directing dimensions of tasks; and n = potential number of practice opportunities on tasks, which are determined in situ by teachers observing pedagogic task performance

intentional reasoning). This principle requires task designers to incrementally increase the demands of tasks in three steps. First, tasks simple on all dimensions are performed (e.g. + planning, – intentional reasoning). Task performance thus draws on the simple, stable (SS) *'attractor state'* of current interlanguage (cf. Larsen-Freeman and Cameron, 2007; van Geert, 2008). Next, complexity on resource-dispersing dimensions is increased (e.g., – planning, – intentional reasoning). This promotes speedier access to, and so automatization (A) of, the current interlanguage system. Finally complexity on both resource-dispersing and resource-directing dimensions is increased (e.g., – planning, + intentional reasoning). This promotes restructuring (R) of the current interlanguage system, and the development of new form-function/concept mappings along resource-directing dimensions of task demands (cf. Andersen, 1984; Andersen and Shirai, 1996; Doughty, 2001; Ellis and Robinson, 2008; Li and Shirai, 2000; Meisel, 1987; Robinson, Cadierno and Shirai, 2009; Robinson and Ellis, 2008; von Stutterheim and Carroll, 2013; von Stutterheim and Klein, 1987) and introduces maximum complexity (C) – in line with the demands of the target task – thereby destabilizing the current interlanguage system (cf. Long, 2003). These steps are summarized in notational form in Table 8.1, and constitute the SSARC model for increasing L2 pedagogic task complexity, providing a heuristic to guide task design and sequencing decisions.

Research questions

The study sought to determine whether performance outcomes on a story summarization task would vary between two intact groups of English majors at a public university in Japan. One group received instruction in which tasks were sequenced from simple to complex according to the SSARC model (Robinson, 2010), and the other received content-based instruction in which they completed full versions of the task and were left to their own devices in improving their performance. The specific research questions asked whether learners' performance in the respective groups would differ significantly with respect to three aspects of L2 use: syntactic complexity, markers of explicit intentional reasoning, and grammatical accuracy. In addition, the study explored whether proficiency and working memory capacity would have significant moderating effects on these three dependent measures. Finally, expert ratings of successful task performance and learner ratings of the respective courses were compared to help triangulate the findings on these three dependent variables.

Method

Design

The study employed a quasi-experimental research design referred to by Campbell and Stanley (1963) as a *non-equivalent control group design*. An experimental group and a control group were both given a pre-test and a post-test. However, the groups did not have pre-experimental sampling equivalence, and constituted naturally assembled collectives (intact groups) that were as similar as availability permitted. In other words, participants were not assigned to groups randomly from a common population. Although careful pre-testing on a range of relevant variables can reduce the threat to internal validity introduced by non-equivalent groups, it cannot replace randomization. In spite of this drawback, however, Campbell and Stanley (1963) stress the value of this particular intact groups design for researchers. It provides a means of bringing experimental thinking into field research in contexts where randomization is impossible.

Educational context

The study was conducted with two groups of second-year English majors enrolled in a required basic studies course at a public university in southern Japan. Approximately 120 English majors enter the English Department each year and are placed into four groups based on the order in which their names occur in the Japanese syllabic system. These groups are assigned to instructors without foreknowledge of the individual learners, their needs or their interests. The two sections of the course observed were taught by the researcher who arbitrarily determined which was to be experimental and which was to be control. As the learners in both groups were still completing their required basic studies courses in the department, the other courses that they were concurrently enrolled in were very similar.

The course met for one 90-minute session each week over a 15-week term. English was the language of instruction, and a content-based approach to instruction was typically used. Learners read authentic plays or short stories in English as homework and completed activities which helped them to organize their ideas on topics related to the text for in-class discussions. Tests typically required them to write short essays in which they summarized the pieces they had read and supported an opinion on an aspect of each that appealed to them. In short, all aspects of the course were meaning-focused, and learners were left to their own devices regarding the language that they used and learned. If teachers corrected mistakes, it was usually on an individual basis within the context of naturally occurring communication.

Materials

The goal of both sections of the course was to develop learners' ability to summarize short stories in a way that required them to attribute intentions and mental states to others and reason from this to a conclusion about why others performed certain actions (Robinson, 2010, p. 253). The initially simplified versions of the story task used with the experimental group were based on picture stories from the children's book *Mr. I* (Trondheim, 2007). In these 60 picture-frame wordless narratives, the protagonist Mr. I becomes interested in some clear objective (e.g., obtaining a piece of pie), creates a series of strategies and engages in a series of corresponding sub-plots in his frustrated attempts to achieve it.

Resource-Directing Manipulations The module used with the experimental group moved through three levels of resource-directing task demand (Robinson, 2003, 2007a, 2010) which are summarized in Table 8.2. Each level required two 90-minute class sessions to complete. The module as a whole thus consisted of six weekly class sessions or nine hours of instruction.

In the first level, simplified versions of each 60-frame story were created by choosing a subset of 24 pictures which illustrated only the main events

Table 8.2 Resource-directing task factors manipulated

	Level 1	Level 2	Level 3
# of Elements	Observable Events	+ Mental States	+ Extraneous Events
Reasoning Demands	None	Intentional	Intentional

of each narrative. Each picture represented one concrete, observable event. The meaning of each story was thus relatively transparent and the need for a relevancy search (e.g., Hidi and Anderson, 1986) was greatly reduced, if not eliminated completely. In the second level, the stories were expanded with additional picture frames which showed the character(s) in various states of planning, deliberation or frustration before and after each concrete action or event. Learners had to incorporate these additional elements into their narratives. This required them to interpret each of these picture frames or groups of frames and say what non-observable behaviours (or mental states) might be going on in them. Finally, the third level consisted of full versions of the task. Learners were faced with the full range of elements in an authentic short story and had to select and narrate the events for their summaries, attribute mental states and reason to a conclusion.

Resource-dispersing manipulations Resource-dispersing task demands (Robinson, 2003, 2007a, 2010) were also manipulated to initially ease the performance demands of the tasks at each level and then increase them in line with the natural demands of the pedagogic task (see Table 8.3).

At all three levels, learners were initially provided with time to plan (i.e., rehearse the tasks three times with one set of partners before changing groups to perform them with others). However, this planning time was minimized on subsequent story tasks to the standard one-minute preview that is typically

Table 8.3 Resource-dispersing task factors manipulated

	Level 1	Level 2	Level 3
Planning Time	+ → −	+ → −	+ → −
Prior Knowledge	+ → −	+ → −	+ → −
Number of Steps	8 to 24 Pictures	60 Pictures	Authentic Stories
Multi-Tasking	Single	Dual	Dual

provided before picture-based L2 narration tasks. Furthermore, learners were provided with prior knowledge of the initial stories at each level through listening activities based on audio recordings of native-speaker peers completing the task. These recordings were created by asking British exchange students studying at the university to complete the respective tasks. While listening to these recordings, learners sequenced pictures or completed cloze activities. Again, this form of prior knowledge was not provided for the subsequent stories at each level.

In addition to the manipulation of planning time and prior knowledge at each level, the number of steps and the number of simultaneous tasks that learners had to perform were manipulated across the module. Level 1 began with tasks in which the simplified 24-picture narratives were initially divided into three sub-narratives of eight frames each to ease performance demands before being combined in subsequent performances. These same narratives were then expanded into the full 60-frame versions in the second level of the module. Finally, in the third level, full-length authentic narratives were used. Learners were thus only required to complete tasks of a few steps at the beginning, but progressively longer narratives as the module progressed to culminate in full-length short stories. Furthermore, regarding the number of simultaneous tasks, Level 1 began with the single task of narrating key events. In Levels 2 and 3, however, the learners were required to simultaneously perform the two separate tasks of narrating key events and motivating them with the mental states of the characters involved.

Procedures

As mentioned above, the goal of the two sections of the course was to develop learners' ability to summarize short stories in a way that required them to attribute intentions and mental states to others and reason from this to a conclusion about why others performed certain actions (Robinson, 2010, p. 253). Both groups received the same instruction for the first half of the semester. During this time, pre-test data were collected both to assess the ability of learners to complete the target task before the respective treatments as well as to establish the equivalence of the groups on key variables related to L2 performance. This initial period also allowed the instructor to acquaint both groups with basic concepts in analysing short stories (i.e., plot, character, setting, mood and tone) and to further establish the comparability of the groups by developing similar classroom dynamics, procedures and expectations.

During the first half of the course, both groups read the same set of stories in conjunction with graphic organizers which helped them think about the stories and organize their ideas and opinions about them. They provided no specific language. Learners' most recent institutional TOEIC scores were also collected as a general measure of proficiency, and they all completed the reverse digit span test as a measure of their working memory capacity (Blackburn and Benton, 1957). In administering and scoring this test, four items for each digit span were given regardless of learners' performance, and the total number of correct items was tallied. They also completed a questionnaire on their motivational orientation based on Kormos, Kiddle and Csizer (2011). Finally, immediately before the respective treatments began, learners in both groups took a written pre-test of their ability to complete the story summarization task. They were told that they would summarize three stories they had read, but not which ones. The two pre-test task performances collected from the groups during the first half of the semester were thus used to pilot the target task and confirmed that it was at an appropriate level for the participants in the study. However, the various simplified versions of the task used in the SSARC treatments (see *Materials*) could not be piloted with the groups prior to the respective treatments because this may have produced an equalizing effect on the treatments.

During the second half of the semester, the groups were given distinct treatments. The learners in the control group continued to complete full versions of the task and were left to their own devices as to how they might improve their performance on it (see *Educational context* above). The learners in the experimental group, on the other hand, were given tasks sequenced from simple to complex based on the SSARC model of L2 task sequencing (see the *Materials* section above). Both groups received approximately equal amounts of class time to practise the target task during this period. Following the respective treatments, both groups completed a written post-test. As on the pre-test, they were told that they would have to summarize three stories that they had read, but they were not told which ones. This allowed the same story to be included on both tests for comparability between and within groups.

Finally, official course evaluations were conducted at the end of the term by the Office of Academic Affairs. The L1 questionnaire asked learners to rate key aspects of the course that they had completed, and their own performance in it, on a scale of 1 to 5. Learners completed the questionnaires while the instructor was out of the classroom and submitted them directly to the Office of Academic Affairs at the university where the study was conducted.

Analyses

The task performances were analysed for syntactic complexity, explicit intentional reasoning and grammatical accuracy. They were then rated for successful task performance. The procedures used for each of these analyses are discussed in turn below.

Syntactic complexity Multiple measures were used to capture the complexity of learners' written L2 production. Coordination was measured by the number of coordinated verbs per 100 words, and subordination was measured by the number of subordinated verbs per 100 words. In addition, Coh-Metrix (McNamara, Louwerse, Cai and Graesser, 2005a) was used to extract the mean number of modifiers per noun phrase as an index of nominalization (see also Biber, Gray and Poonpoon, 2011; and Norris and Ortega, 2009, for discussion of other indices of noun phrase complexity). Coh-Metrix is a tool that analyses texts on multiple levels of language, discourse, cohesion and world knowledge on the basis of extant computational linguistic modules (Graesser, McNamara, Louwerse and Cai, 2004). Although the primary purpose of Coh-Metrix is to estimate the difficulty of texts in terms of explicit markers of cohesion in the language and coherence in the concepts that they express, the information that Coh-Metrix extracts from texts can also be organized to provide insights into aspects of language production that are relevant to current theories of task-based L2 performance.

Explicit reasoning Following Lee and Rescorla (2008: cf. Robinson, 2007b), four classes of mental state words (MSW) were identified in the story summaries relating to: (1) emotion (e.g., *happy, excited*), (2) desire (e.g., *want, need*), (3) cognition without propositional complement (e.g., *considered carefully, planned his strategy, pretended to be a customer*), and (4) cognition with propositional complement (e.g., *thought they would not come back, decided that it was okay*). The number of each was calculated per 100 words of text.

In addition, Coh-Metrix was used to estimate the amount of explicit intentional reasoning in each text. In narrative texts, the situational or mental model that the text is describing includes characters, objects, spatial setting, actions and events as well as the plans, thoughts and emotions of the characters (Zwann and Radvansky, 1998). Choosing words and particles (such as prepositions and conjunctions) which explicitly clarify and connect actions, goals, events and states thus facilitates the communicative effectiveness of such texts. Four dimensions of the situational model for narrative texts for which Coh-Metrix provides indices are: (1) causation, (2) intentionality, (3) time, and

(4) space (Graesser, McNamara, Louwerse and Cai 2004). Different sets of particles are associated with each, although some may be applicable to more than one dimension (McNamara, Louwerse, Cai, and Graesser, 2005b). When texts refer to protagonists who perform actions in pursuit of goals, explicit intentional relationships become an important element in effective communication. One Coh-Metrix estimate of intentional reasoning in texts is the incidence of intentional actions, events and particles per 1000 words of text. Actions and events are main verbs that are classified as intentional in WordNet (Miller, Beckwith, Fellbaum, Gross and Miller, 1990) and that are performed by animate subject nouns, whereas intentional particles (e.g., *for the purpose of, by means of*) connect clauses containing such content. The higher the incidence of intentional elements in a text, the more the text can be assumed to convey goal-driven content (McNamara, Louwerse, Cai, and Graesser, 2005b).

Grammatical accuracy Accuracy was calculated as the number of errors on familiar forms per 100 words of text. Rather than calculating all errors, only errors for which systematic variation at the group level could be expected were examined. A list of common errors occurring in the data was drawn up by a highly proficient and experienced Japanese teacher of English. From this list, errors relating to forms which all Japanese learners are taught and tested on explicitly in the national secondary school curriculum were selected. The motivation behind this approach to measuring grammatical accuracy was that if increased attention to L2 production which resulted from task demands increased learners' attention to form, and thus resulted in more accurate production, these effects might be manifest most clearly in forms that learners had been made aware of and practised. Errors on forms which were beyond their control would be less likely to vary as a result of task demands. Examples of some specific forms included and excluded in the analysis are provided in Table 8.4.

Following an initial training session, 10 per cent of the database was independently coded by the researcher and a hired assistant for each of the seven variables (i.e., coordinated verbs, subordinated verbs, emotion mental state words, desire mental state words, cognitive mental state verbs with and without propositional complements, and grammatical errors). After establishing inter-rater agreement on each of these measures to be 90 per cent or higher, the research assistant coded the remainder of the data.

Expert ratings Finally, ratings on criteria of successful task performance were collected. The rater was an experienced Japanese teacher of English who had no knowledge of the SSARC model or the design of the study. Each written summary was rated on five criteria: (1) relevance of the events,

Table 8.4 Forms used in calculating grammatical accuracy

Errors included	Errors excluded
Mixed tenses	Articles
Subject–verb agreement	Prepositions
Number agreement	Spelling
Wrong part of speech	Punctuation
Possessives	Clausal connectors

(2) intentional reasoning, (3) motivated conclusion, (4) appropriate connectors, and (5) overall quality. Each criterion was rated on a scale of 1 to 5. The main analysis consisted of a two-by-two MANCOVA using SPSS19 for Windows to compare gains in the scores within and between the two groups following the instructional treatments as well as possible mediating effects of proficiency and working memory capacity. The first factor in the analysis was test at two levels (pre-test and post-test), and the second factor was group at two levels (SSARC and Control).

Results

The results for (1) initial comparisons to establish the equivalence of the groups on key variables, (2) the comparisons of gains within-groups and between-groups connected with the treatments, (3) the moderating effects of proficiency and working memory capacity, and (4) the results of learners' evaluations of the respective courses are discussed in turn below.

Group comparability

Initial comparisons were made between groups on individual differences relevant to L2 performance (i.e., proficiency, working memory capacity, motivational orientation and educational background). Following Campbell and Stanley (1963), it was hoped that such comparisons would help to reduce the threats to internal validity introduced by non-equivalent groups.

Proficiency and Working Memory A comparison of means for the institutional TOEIC and reverse digit span scores of the learners in each group is provided in Table 8.5. Two-way independent-sample t-tests showed no significant differences between the groups on either proficiency or working memory capacity.

Motivational Orientation Ranked group means for the ordinal-scale questionnaire items on L2 motivation are provided in Table 8.6. The factors targeted in the questionnaire ranked in an almost identical order for the two groups. The learners were studying English because they enjoyed it and wanted to be able to communicate with people outside Japan in the future. Contrary to common opinion, peer pressure rather than anxiety played a key role in their L2 behaviour. While getting jobs, passing tests and parental encouragement also played a role in their motivation, these latter factors played a less important role in their motivation than the former ones. Furthermore, they did not particularly identify with native speakers of the language or have a strong belief in their ability to succeed in it. Nor did they feel that they were able to regulate their own

Table 8.5 Proficiency and Working Memory capacity of the groups

	Group	Mean	SD	t	Sig.
Proficiency	Control	614	127		
	SSARC	644	113	.789	.435
Working Memory	Control	13.06	5.87		
	SSARC	13.67	3.74	.412	.683

Table 8.6 Motivational profile of the groups

	SSARC	Control
International Orientation	4.43	4.54
Intrinsic Motivation	4.32	4.45
Peer Pressure	4.13	4.32
Resourcefulness	3.74	3.90
Instrumental Motivation	3.69	3.79
Parental Encouragement	3.60	3.80
Integrative Motivation	3.59	3.53
Anxiety	3.50	3.27
Self-Regulation	3.47	3.43
Self-Efficacy	3.42	3.44
Motivational Intensity	3.19	3.06
Satiation Control	2.76	2.66
Technological Resources	1.97	1.99

Table 8.7 Educational background

			Primary	Secondary	Tertiary
Study Abroad	Control	23%			
	SSARC	24%			
Started English	Control		71%	29%	
	SSARC		71%	29%	
Mother's Education	Control			39%	61%
	SSARC			58%	42%
Father's Education	Control			43%	57%
	SSARC			67%	33%

studies, overcome boredom, or make the effort required to do their best. They also made little use of computer-based technology in learning English.

Educational background The data on learners' educational background and experience are summarized in Table 8.7. Essentially the same proportion of learners in each group had studied abroad (24 per cent experiment, 23 per cent control). The same proportion had also started studying English privately in primary school (71 per cent experiment, 71 per cent control) as opposed to beginning in secondary school when it was required in the national curriculum. Although a slightly larger proportion of the SSARC group's parents had completed tertiary-level education than the control group's parents, the educational background of the learners in the two groups was very similar. The high level of similarity between groups in proficiency, working memory capacity, motivation and educational background thus reduces to some extent the threats to internal validity introduced by non-equivalent groups (Campbell and Stanley, 1963, pp. 47–8).

Gains between tests

Using Pillai's trace, within-subjects results for MANCOVA showed a significant effect for test on learners' L2 production, $V=0.712$, $F(10,28)=6.935$, $p<.001$, partial eta square$=.712$). In other words, the learners' performances improved significantly between the pre-test and the post-test. Post-hoc tests isolated the specific sources of this effect with respect to the variables connected with each aspect of performance.

Syntactic complexity Means for the measures of syntactic complexity are provided in Table 8.8. Although separate univariate analyses revealed no significant effect for these tests on the three measures syntactic complexity, pairwise comparisons after Bonferroni adjustment revealed significant differences between individual means for both coordination (MD=3.225, p<.000, 95% CI=2.257-4.193) and subordination (MD=2.854, p<.008, 95% CI=.792-4.916). In other words, learners coordinated and subordinated significantly more verbs on the post-test than they had on the pre-test. The amount of NP modification showed a slight trend in the opposite direction, but this difference was not significant.

Explicit reasoning Means for the measures of explicit reasoning are provided in Table 8.9. Separate univariate analyses revealed significant differences

Table 8.8 Means for syntactic complexity within and between groups

		Pre-test	Post-test
Coordination	Control	3.61	6.78*
	SSARC	3.96	7.22*
Subordination	Control	8.00	10.67*
	SSARC	6.57	9.61*
Nominalization	Control	0.82	0.77
	SSARC	0.77	0.75

* Statistically significant differences

Table 8.9 Means for explicit reasoning within and between groups

		Pre-test	Post-test
Emotion	Control	1.72	3.78*
	SSARC	1.74	4.06*
Desire	Control	1.33	1.56
	SSARC	1.22	1.52
Cognition (−)	Control	0.78	0.89
	SSARC	0.87	1.22
Cognition (+)	Control	1.61	2.06
	SSARC	1.48	2.09
Intentionality	Control	28.21	24.93
	SSARC	27.92	31.21

* Statistically significant differences

Table 8.10 Means for grammatical accuracy within and between groups

		Pre-test	Post-test
Errors/100 Words	Control	5.06	6.11
	SSARC	4.17	4.00

for test on learners' use of emotion MSWs (F=5.387, p<.26, partial eta squared =.127). Pairwise comparisons also revealed the use of more MSWs relating to emotion on the post-test than the pre-test (MD=2.193, p<.000, 95% CI 1.429-2.958).

Grammatical accuracy Means for grammatical accuracy are provided in Table 8.10. There was no significant difference in the accuracy of learners' performance between the two tests.

Differences between groups

Complexity, reasoning and accuracy Using Pillai's trace, between-subjects results for MANCOVA showed no significant main effect for the group factor (V=0.255, F (10, 28) = 0.958, p<.499). Furthermore, post-hoc comparisons revealed no significant pairwise differences between the learners' performances in the two groups related to complexity, reasoning or accuracy (see Tables 8.8–10).

Successful task performance Means for the ordinal-scale expert ratings on criteria of successful task performance are summarized in Table 8.11. Although the SSARC group's performance on all criteria was initially rated lower than that of the control group, their performance had equalled or surpassed that of the control group on the post-test. Although both groups showed considerable gains on all of the criteria, the rate of gain for the SSARC group was considerably higher than that of the control group (14 per cent control; 38 per cent SSARC). Thus, in spite of their initial disadvantage, the SSARC group *outperformed* the control group on each of the individual criteria with the exception of the use of appropriate connector words. With respect to this variable, both groups' performance was approximately equal on both of the tests. These findings, derived from expert rating of successful task performance, point to the possibility that some important aspects of performance on tasks may not have been captured by the quantitative measures used in the study.

Table 8.11 Means for expert ratings within and between groups

		Pre-test	Post-test
Events	Control	3.28	4.17
	SSARC	3.29	4.50
Motivations	Control	3.70	3.70
	SSARC	2.10	3.80
Conclusions	Control	2.67	3.22
	SSARC	2.38	3.29
Connectors	Control	2.72	3.00
	SSARC	2.71	3.00
Quality	Control	3.33	3.78
	SSARC	3.00	4.00
Average	Control	**3.14**	**3.57**
	SSARC	**2.70**	**3.72**

Moderating effects of proficiency and working memory

In terms of the analysis of covariance, MANCOVA showed that proficiency had a significant moderating effect on the amount of subordination in learners' L2 production (SS=233.547, $F(1)$=5.330, p<.027, partial eta squared=.126). Learners with higher scores on the institutional TOEIC test produced more subordinated verbs per hundred words of text than those with lower scores.

Working memory capacity, on the other hand, had a significant moderating effect on the use of cognitive MSW without propositional complement (SS=8.044, $F(1)$=9.957, p<.003, partial eta squared=.212) as well as on grammatical accuracy (SS=118.953, $F(1)$=7.982, p<.008, partial eta squared=.177). However, the direction of these results was the in the opposite direction to the results for the effects of proficiency. Learners with higher working memory scores used fewer cognitive MSW and made more grammatical errors than learners with lower scores.

Learner evaluations of the courses

The results of the course evaluation are summarized in Table 8.12. Learners in the SSARC group evaluated their own performance more highly on all factors

Table 8.12 Learner evaluation of the courses

		SSARC		Control
Self	Attendance	3.92	❯	3.74
	Attitude	3.50	❯	3.15
	Preview-Review	3.79	❯	3.41
	Previous Interest	3.17		3.19
Course	Knowledge Gained	2.96		3.22
	Interest Generated	2.79		3.18
	Level	3.33	❯	2.85
	Pace	3.33		3.48
	Materials	3.30		3.41
	Overall Satisfaction	2.83		3.15

than the learners in the control group. The learners in the SSARC group felt that they put more effort into attendance, attitude, preparation and review than those in the control group in spite of the fact that the initial interest of the two groups in the course was very similar. It might also be mentioned that six out of the original 31 learners in the control group (19 per cent) dropped out of the course before the final examination, whereas only three of the original 29 learners in the SSARC group (10 per cent) dropped out. In spite of these apparent advantages of the SSARC instruction, however, the learners in the SSARC group felt the course to be less to their liking than those in the control group. In addition to being less satisfied with the course overall, they felt that they learned less and gained less ongoing interest in the field. It is difficult to know why learners responded in this way. On the other hand, the only aspect of the SSARC instruction that learners rated more highly than those in the control group was the difficulty level. The learners in the SSARC groups felt the course to be better suited to their level of ability than those in the control group, and this is a major goal of effective syllabus design and curricular planning.

Discussion

Learners in both groups were told that they needed to learn how to summarize the key events of stories, attribute intentions and mental states to the characters, and reason from this to a conclusion about why they acted the way they did.

One of the groups was given structured practice in performing this task following the SSARC model while the other was simply given time to practise and left to their own devices. The learners in both groups used significantly more syntactically complex language in terms of coordinated and subordinated verbs and more emotional MSWs following the respective treatments than they had before them. However, both approaches had similar effects on the measures of complexity, reasoning and accuracy observed. There were no significant differences in the performance of the SSARC group and the control group on any of these measures. However, expert ratings on criteria of successful task performance suggested that the SSARC treatment may have resulted in a higher rate of gain than the control treatment. Further research on such criteria and how they might be operationalized is needed to determine whether this is the case.

One explanation for the lack of difference between the two groups may be the English learning experience of the two groups. While piloting of the target task in the form of pre-testing before the respective treatments combined with the significant gains in performance on the task made by both groups as a result of study confirm that the task was at an appropriate level for students, it must be remembered these learners were very successful English learners within the larger population of Japanese students. They had studied English for several years and passed the entrance examinations to major in English at university. Once they were told what they needed to be able to do, their experience in learning English may have enabled them to reach the performance goals of the task more independently than learners with less experience. The effect of the structured help in mastering the tasks that SSARC instruction provides thus might not have been as evident with these learners as it would have been with learners more representative of the general population of Japanese learners such as intact groups of learners in a public secondary school.

The role of individual differences might also not have been as apparent with these learners as the groups were relatively homogenous with respect to all of the variables measured. Nevertheless, proficiency and working memory capacity still had significant moderating effects on some aspects of their performance. Learners in the higher proficiency range subordinated more verbs overall than learners in the lower proficiency range. Furthermore, learners with higher working memory capacity made more grammatical mistakes and used fewer cognitive mental state words (MSWs) without propositional complements than learners with lower working memory capacity. It is difficult to know why this was the case, but these findings demonstrate that individual differences cannot always be assumed to affect learners' performance on tasks in intuitive ways and highlight the need for future empirical work to consider these variables and their interactions carefully in interpreting L2 task performance data.

Finally, the course evaluations showed that although the learners in the SSARC group felt they had invested more effort into the course, they were less satisfied with it overall. These results must be interpreted in light of the motivational orientation of these learners. These learners were studying English for enjoyment rather than for the achievement of specific goals, and they were not disposed to put forth the effort required to do their best. The higher rate of satisfaction with the control course may thus have been connected with the fact that the learners in the SSARC course had to work harder than those in the control course. Had the two courses been implemented with learners who had a high level of motivational intensity and self-regulation in their studies, their satisfaction with the more focused SSARC instruction might have been considerably higher.

Overall, the study demonstrates the feasibility of SSARC for educational planning and provides a heuristic for operationalizing a representative range of resource-directing and resource-dispersing variables in narrative task design and sequencing. In addition, the study highlights the importance of using multiple measures of each performance construct and triangulating data from multiple sources. Some aspects of successful performance on tasks may not have been captured by the quantitative measures used in the study. The study also shows that individual difference variables are likely to moderate performance on task, but that these effects may not always affect performance in ways that might seem intuitively obvious. It is thus hoped that the study will provide a basis for further research on the SSARC model for L2 instructional design, and the role that such individual difference variables may play in performance.

References

Andersen, R. (1984). The one-to-one principle of interlanguage construction. *Language Learning, 34*, 77–95.

Andersen, R. and Y. Shirai (1996). The primacy of aspect in first and second language acquisition–The pidgin-creole connection. In W. Ritchie and T. Bhatia (eds), *Handbook of Second Language Acquisition* (pp. 527–70). San Diego, CA: Academic Press.

Biber, D., Gray, B. and Poonpon, K. (2011). Should we use characteristics of conversation to measure grammatical complexity in writing? *TESOL Quarterly, 45*, 5–35.

Blackburn, H. and Benton, A. (1957). Revised administration and scoring of the digit span test. *Journal of Consulting Psychology*, 21 (2), 139–43.

Campbell, D. and Stanley, J. (1963). *Experimental and Quasi-experimental Designs for Research*. Boston: Houghton Mifflin.

Candlin, C. (1987). Towards task-based language learning. In C. Candlin and D. Murphy (eds), *Language Learning Tasks* (pp. 5–22). London: Prentice Hall.

Craik, F. and R. Lockhart (1972). Levels of processing: A framework for memory research. *Journal of Verbal Learning and Verbal Behavior*, 11, 671–84.

Doughty, C. (2001). Cognitive underpinnings of focus on form. In P. Robinson (ed.), *Cognition and Second Language Instruction* (pp. 206–57). Cambridge: Cambridge University Press.

Ellis, N. C. and Robinson, P. (2008). An introduction to Cognitive Linguistics, second language acquisition and language instruction. In P. Robinson and N. C. Ellis (eds), *Handbook of Cognitive Linguistics and Second Language Acquisition* (pp. 3–24). New York: Routledge.

Graesser, A., McNamara, D., Louwerse, M. and Cai, Z. (2004). Coh-metrix: Analysis of text on cohesion and language. *Behavior Research Methods, Instruments, and Computers*, 36 (2), 193–202.

Hidi, S. and Anderson, V. (1986). Producing written summaries: Task demands, cognitive operations, and implication for instruction. *Review of Educational Research*, 56 (4), 473–93.

Kormos, J., Kiddle, T. and Csizer, K. (2011). Systems of goals, attitudes, and self-related beliefs in second-language-learning motivation. *Applied Linguistics*, 32(5), 495–516.

Larsen-Freeman, D. and Cameron, L. (2007). *Complex Systems and Applied Linguistics*. Oxford: Oxford University Press.

Lee, E. and Rescorla, L. (2008). The use of psychological state words by late talkers at ages 3, 4, and 5 years. *Applied Psycholinguistics*, 29, 21–39.

Li, P. and Y. Shirai (2000). *The Acquisition of Lexical and Grammatical Aspect*. Berlin: Mouton de Gruyter.

Long, M. H. (2003). Stabilization and fossilization in interlanguage. In C. Doughty and M. Long (eds), *Handbook of Second Language Acquisition* (pp. 487–536). Oxford: Blackwell.

McNamara, D., Louwerse, M., Cai, Z. and Graesser, A. (2005a). *Coh-Metrix Version 1.4.* Retrieved [November 2011], from http//:cohmetrix.memphis.edu

—— (2005b). *Coh-Metrix Version 2.0 Indices.* Retrieved [December 2011], from http//:cohmetrix.memphis.edu

Meisel, J. (1987). Reference to past events and actions in the development of natural second language acquisition. In C. Pfaff (ed.), *First and Second Language Acquisition Processes* (pp. 206–24). Cambridge, MA: Newbury House.

Merrill, M. D. (2007). Hypothesized performance on complex tasks as a function of scaled instructional strategies. In J. Elen and R. Clark (eds), *Handling Complexity in Learning Environments* (pp. 265–82). Amsterdam: Elsevier.

Miller, G., Beckwith, R., Fellbaum, C., Gross, D. and Miller, C. (1990). Introduction to
WordNet: an online lexical database. *International Journal of Lexicography*, 3 (4),
235–44.

Norris, J. and Ortega, L. (2009). Towards an organic approach to investigating CAF in
SLA: The case of complexity. *Applied Linguistics*, 27, 590–616.

Reigeluth, C. (1999). The Elaboration Theory: Guidance for scope and sequence
decisions. In C. M. Reigeluth (eds), *Instructional Design Theories and Models*, Vol. II
(pp. 457–82). Mahwah, NJ: Lawrence Erlbaum.

Robinson, P. (1996). Task-based testing, performance-referencing and program
development. In P. Robinson (ed.), *Task Complexity and Second Language Syllabus
Design: Data-based Studies and Speculations* [Special Issue], University of
Queensland Working Papers in Language and Linguistics, 1 (1), 95–116. Brisbane:
CLTR.

—— (2001). Task complexity, cognitive resources, and syllabus design: A triadic
framework for investigating task influences on SLA. In P. Robinson (ed.), *Cognition
and Second Language Instruction* (pp. 287–318). Cambridge: Cambridge University
Press.

—— (2003). The Cognition Hypothesis, task design and adult task-based language
learning. *Second Language Studies*, 21 (2), 45–107. <http://www.hawaii.edu/sls/
uhwpesl/ 21 (2)/ Robinson.pdf>

—— (2005). Cognitive complexity and task sequencing: Studies in a componential
framework for second language task design. *International Review of Applied
Linguistics in Language Teaching*, 43, 1–32.

—— (2007a). Criteria for classifying and sequencing pedagogic tasks. In M. P. Garcia
Mayo (ed.), *Investigating Tasks in Formal Language Learning* (pp. 7–27). Clevedon,
UK: Multilingual Matters.

—— (2007b). Task complexity, theory of mind, and intentional reasoning: Effects on L2
speech production, interaction, uptake and perceptions of task difficulty.
International Review of Applied Linguistics, 45, 193–214.

—— (2010). Situating and distributing cognition across task demands: The SSARC
model of pedagogic task sequencing. In M. Putz and L. Sicola (eds), *Cognitive
Processing in Second Language Acquisition: Inside the Learner's Mind* (pp. 243–68).
Amsterdam: John Benjamins.

—— (2011). Second language task complexity, the Cognition Hypothesis, language
learning, and performance. In P. Robinson (ed.), *Second Language Task Complexity:
Researching the Cognition Hypothesis of Language Learning and Performance*
(pp. 3–37). Amsterdam: John Benjamins.

Robinson, P., Cadierno, T. and Shirai, Y. (2009). Time and motion: Measuring the effects
of the conceptual demands of tasks on second language speech production. *Applied
Linguistics*, 30, 533–54.

Robinson, P. and Ellis, N. C. (2008). Conclusion: Cognitive Linguistics, second language
acquisition and L2 instruction – Issues for research. In P. Robinson and N. C. Ellis

(eds), *Handbook of Cognitive Linguistics and Second Language Acquisition* (pp. 489–545). New York: Routledge.

Robinson, P. and Gilabert, R. (eds) (2007). *Task Complexity, the Cognition Hypothesis and Second Language Instruction.* Special issue of *International Review of Applied Linguistics,* 45 (3).

Schank, R. (1999). *Dynamic Memory Revisited.* New York: Cambridge University Press.

Schank, R. and Abelson, R. (1977). *Scripts, Plans, Goals and Understanding.* Hillsdale, NJ: Erlbaum.

Trondheim, L. (2007). *Mr. I.* New York: Nantier, Beall and Minoustchine.

Van Geert, P. (2008). The Dynamic Systems approach in the study of L1 and L2 acquisition: An introduction. *Modern Language Journal,* 92, 179–99.

van Merrinboer, J. and Kirschner, P. (2007). *Ten Steps to Complex Learning.* London: Routledge.

von Stutterheim, C. and Carroll, M. (2013). Concept-oriented approach to Second Language Acquisition (CoA). In P. Robinson (ed.), *The Routledge Encyclopedia of Second Language Acquisition* (pp. 110–13). New York: Routledge.

von Stutterheim, C. and Klein, W. (1987). A concept-oriented approach to second language studies. In C. Pfaff (ed.), *First and Second Language Acquisition Processes* (191–205). Rowley, MA: Newbury House.

Zwann, R. and Radvansky, G. (1998). Situation models in language comprehension and memory. *Psychological Bulletin,* 123 (2), 162–85.

Index

The abbreviation TS represents the phrase 'Task Sequencing'
Locators shown in *italics* refer to tables and figures.

Lightning Source UK Ltd.
Milton Keynes UK
UKOW06f2311190116

266713UK00006B/121/P